330.1
W129t
B

D1196895

FONDREN LIBRARY CENTER

ECONOMIC RHYTHM

ECONOMIC RHYTHM

A THEORY OF BUSINESS CYCLES

BY

ERNST WAGEMANN

Professor in the University of Berlin, President of the Statistical Office of the German Reich, Director of the German Institute for Business Cycle Research, Honorary Fellow of the Royal Statistical Society, Honorary Member of the International Institute of Statistics

TRANSLATED BY

D. H. BLELLOCH

International Labor Office at Geneva

WITH A PREFATORY NOTE BY

WESLEY C. MITCHELL

FIRST EDITION

LIBRARY OF
Southern Methodist University
DALLAS, TEXAS

McGRAW-HILL BOOK COMPANY, INC.
NEW YORK: 370 SEVENTH AVENUE
LONDON: 6 & 8 BOUVERIE ST., E. C. 4
1930

30 - 19591

Copyright, 1930, by the
McGraw-Hill Book Company, Inc.

Printed in the United States of America

*All rights reserved. This book, or
parts thereof, may not be reproduced
in any form without permission of
the publishers.*

THE MAPLE PRESS COMPANY, YORK, PA.

PREFACE TO THE ENGLISH EDITION

The publishers, on the advice of eminent economists in the United States, decided to undertake the publication of an English edition of this book. Personally, the author was inclined to fear that, in making such a decision, they might run the risk of "carrying coals to Newcastle." America is justly regarded as the country where the methods of economic forecasting were originated and where they have been carried to a high degree of perfection, thanks to the labors of such distinguished scholars as Mitchell, Bullock, Persons, Snyder, Hardy, Ayres and others. This important branch of economic science has, however, been transplanted to Europe in the meantime, where its cultivation has yielded new and interesting fruit. This is due not merely to the special development of European science, but also to the quite different economic organization of the Old World, which is certainly more diversified and more complicated and perhaps also more liable to variation than that of America which reveals a tendency towards rapid progress in a straight line. This European peculiarity would appear to render a more comprehensive and complex system of economic observation necessary. Experience teaches the European that economic rhythm can only be studied by the use of a multiplicity of methods and instruments, just as medicine can never succeed in curing all maladies by adopting one single line of attack.

The author wishes that he could venture to regard the present work as a small contribution towards the repayment of the debt which Europe owes to America in the field of research into economic dynamics.

He takes this opportunity of expressing his hearty thanks to Mr. D. H. Blelloch for substantial labor on the translation, as well as his deep sense of gratitude to his

v

62246

friend, Dr. Constantine E. McGuire, for his most valuable help and advice in many directions of this undertaking.

ERNST WAGEMANN.

BERLIN, GERMANY,
   April, 1930.

American students of business cycles will welcome the opportunity afforded by this translation to become better acquainted with Dr. Ernst Wagemann's *Konjunkturlehre*. This treatise, published two years ago in Berlin, has a character all its own derived from the author's varied experience. Growing up in Chile, Dr. Wagemann has been able to look at European conditions with the partial detatchment that sharpens insight. Rising to the presidency of the Imperial Statistical Office, he has become thoroughly familiar with one of the most efficient statistical organizations in the world. A university professor, he has had the stimulus to scientific inquiry which comes from association with scholars. As director of the Institut für Konjunkturforschung, he has dealt practically with the fascinating but difficult problem of forecasting future business developments from analysis of current conditions. Perhaps no other investigator has enjoyed such a combination of advantages for studying business cycles.

The outcome is what one might expect. In all his work, Dr. Wagemann makes use whenever possible of statistical data and statistical technique. But his interest is the scientific interest of a university professor. The data and technique are means to a larger end. Most American forecasters have held rigidly aloof from "theorizing" about business cycles. The wisdom of this attitude is doubtful; for theorizing, properly understood, means an effort to comprehend a subject in general terms. Dr. Wagemann feels an urge to understand and to explain how cyclical fluctuations come about, quite as strong as his urge to develop a successful technique of forecasting. Indeed, each effort promotes the other. His work should contribute not a little toward closing the unfortunate gap which has developed in the United States between business-cycle "statisticians" and business-cycle "theorists."

The forecasting technique which Wagemann uses has been deeply influenced by a critical study of the methods developed by Warren M. Persons and his colleagues in the Harvard group.

But Wagemann thinks that the "great plural-curve barometers" have "failed"—that of the Harvard service among others. The next step, as he sees matters, is to use a more comprehensive system of indicators. Production, employment, movements of goods into storage and out of storage, foreign trade in its bearing on the domestic market, the volume of business transactions, credit conditions, commodity prices, and the interrelations among the prices of commodities, securities and loans are all represented independently in his present scheme. Conclusions are based upon an analytic study of the changes in these variables, regard being had not merely to the figures, but also to what we know at large concerning the way in which one business factor influences other factors.

How this plan will work in the long run remains to be seen. So far, Dr. Wagemann feels pleased with his results. But experience will suggest improvements, as in all scientific work. Perhaps American students will attempt to better Wagemann's technique of analysis, as he has attempted to better the practice of earlier American workers. That is the type of international competition which enriches all parties.

WESLEY C. MITCHELL.

CONTENTS

ix

LIST OF DIAGRAMS

BOOK I

GENERAL CONSIDERATIONS ON THE BUSINESS CYCLE

ECONOMIC RHYTHM

INTRODUCTION

ORIGIN AND DEVELOPMENT OF MODERN
BUSINESS-CYCLE THEORY

The study of business cycles is the most recently established branch of economic science. Its subject matter is the interplay of economic forces, the fluctuations of employment and business activity, of quantities and values, as viewed more particularly from the standpoint of business management. Its course of development has thus been that of a kind of connecting link between political economy and business administration. It seeks to substitute scientific method and universality of economic outlook for the instinctive judgments and appreciations of the business community, formed within the narrow compass of individual experience and routine, of ideas based on tradition or on a specialized technical viewpoint. At the same time, it aims to render economic theories fruitful by forcing them to take account of practical business experience.

Earlier Theories of Business Cycles.

It has long been realized that those processes the study of which forms the subject matter of economics are conditioned by numerous frictions and disturbances, checks and stimuli, and that the idea of a harmonious interplay among the various economic forces is a pure fiction. Economists have, nevertheless, in the vast majority of cases, in dealing with economic phenomena, presupposed such a fictitious equilibrium. They have dealt with the problem of disturbances in the economic process only incidentally, regarding it as something outside the scope

3

of their studies or as a side issue or, at best (as in the case of Böhm-Bawerk), as one of the finishing touches to be put to a system of political economy. The various theories of economic crises have thus developed in a kind of backwater of economic research; they deal not with the general interplay of economic forces as a whole but rather with an obvious but minor aspect of the whole subject, namely, economic crises; and they attach more importance to the discovery of the causes of crises than to the crises themselves and their thorough analysis.

A business crisis is a grave economic convulsion, consisting in a sudden collapse of economic prosperity and manifesting itself in extensive liquidation, a drop in prices, and the failure of large numbers of undertakings. According to the traditional theories, the immediate cause of such crises is to be found either in a disturbance in the equilibrium between production and consumption in general (overproduction or underconsumption theories) or in a modification of the normal relationship among the individual branches of production (disproportionality theories). The various authors differ very widely in regard to the actual precipitating cause of such dislocations. Some identify it in an excessive accumulation of capital in relation to income (Malthus), others in a faulty distribution of income (Owen, Sismondi, Rodbertus). Marx attributes crises to a defective relationship among the various factors of production inherent in the capitalist system and, particularly, to an undue increase in fixed capital; others, again, attribute them to unsound currency emission (currency school) and to vicissitudes in the production of the precious metals. Many authors (for example, Jevons) ascribe them also to harvest fluctuations. As a last resort, the blame is laid on the psychology of the business man or even on the anarchical character of capitalistic methods of production. Characteristic of all these theories, even when considered in their most fundamental aspects, is the fact that they are purely hypothetical. Even where the argument possesses many qualities of individual brilliance and acuteness, it is usually either quite insufficiently supported by facts or totally lacking in such support. The theories in question are usually based on deductions, more or less regardless of empirical data. They have, consequently, tended to lose their way in sociological profundities and even in the depths of metaphysics. It has never occurred to their authors to furnish any basis whatever for the practical facts of business management and business policy.

The Foundations of the Modern Doctrine of Business Cycles.

The modern study of business cycles has developed, to some extent, in the theoretical atmosphere described above but, still more, in opposition to it. Its real beginnings are to be found in inquiries concerning the rhythms of economic life. Perhaps the first of such inquiries was initiated by the French economist Clement Juglar, who utilized bank balances and other statistics in order to account for cyclical movements. As his researches were based on a comparatively broad basis of fact, he succeeded in establishing a more exact classification of economic variations and more accurate observations on their periodicity than his predecessors. Important progress on the lines laid down by Juglar was made in the work of the Russian economist Tugan-Baranowski, published in 1900, on the theory and history of business crises in England. Tugan-Baranowski's empirical investigation of economic fluctuations was a milestone of special importance in the early stages of the movement toward a scientific study of the question. In the same group may be classified the studies of Bouniatian and of the French investigators Lescure and Aftalion, as the work of these authors, while based on a deductive system, took considerable account of the material facts. As far as Germany is concerned, special mention may be made in this connection of the work of the historical school—in the first place of Schmoller's "Grundriss," secondly of the series of studies issued by the Verein für Sozialpolitik on *Störungen im deutschen Wirtschaftsleben während der Jahre* 1900 *ff.* (Disturbances in the Economic Life of Germany in 1900 and the Following Years), vols. 105 to 113, and, lastly, of the works of Sombart, Pohle, Oldenberg, Tönnies, Spiethoff, Eulenburg, Esslen, Feiler, and others.

Research on business cycles has been carried on by statisticians, to some extent, independently of the investigations of the political economists. Their object has been not so much to inquire into economic causation as to establish statistical means of representing economic fluctuations. Work in this field has been carried out, in particular, by Neumann-Spallart (1887), de Foville (1888), Beveridge (1909), Julin (1911), Sorer, and Mortara (1913). The subject of these studies is partly the compilation of a general index of cyclical fluctuations (Julin, Mortara), partly the dissection of the economic complex by distinguishing between general development and progress, on the one hand, and cyclical fluctuations, on the other (Neumann-Spallart, Julin, Mortara).

Beginnings of the Modern Business-cycle Service.

The two lines of investigation—that of the realistic economists and that of the mathematical statisticians—were carried on for some time side by side, without any intimate collaboration. The approach to the question was, in both cases, essentially theoretical in character and was as far removed from any sympathetic considerations of the needs of business practice and business policy as in the case of the earlier cyclical theories. Their utility, for practical business, dates from the moment at which they established contact with each other. A synthesis of this kind has been brought about in the course of the last decade in the United States of America. It is noteworthy that the first steps were taken not by the scholars themselves but by business men and practical economists, who placed the equipment supplied by the investigations of the statisticians and historical economists at the service of the business community. They were not afraid to utilize the work of the scientists for the purpose of business forecasting and supplying advice and suggestions of a very special character to their commercial clientèle. Two of the earliest services of this kind to be organized were the *Brookmire Economic Service* and the *Babson Statistical Organization*. The specifically American and commercial character of these institutions caused them to be treated with scepticism or entirely ignored by the scientific world. They were received favorably, however, in business circles.[1] In order to form a proper estimate of the scientific importance of these institutions, abstraction must be made of excrescences arising out of their profit-making character. If their work be examined in this spirit, there can be no doubt that their contribution to knowledge and to the improvement of methods of investigation has been most useful and valuable.

The effect of these practical experiments has, in any case, been to force the scientific economists gradually to abandon their attitude of reserve and, finally, to take up the study of business diagnosis and forecasting, notwithstanding the risk involved in dealing with subjects so closely connected with the battles of daily life. On the Continent of Europe, however, and particularly in Germany, the men of science shrank from treading on such dangerous ground—especially as the historical school of investigators, who might have been expected to display the greatest interest in business research, remained loyal to the principle which they have always most emphatically maintained, that the infinite complexities of business life cannot be forced into the straightjacket of exact theories and formulæ. The life of society goes on its way, as they

[1] A number of other similar institutions were founded in the course of time. Some of these, notwithstanding their markedly profit-making character, did excellent scientific work. Among others may be mentioned: Standard Statistics Company, Moody's Investors' Service, Poor's Publishing Company, Franklin Statistical Service, Karsten's Statistical Laboratory, Bureau of Business Conditions, Alexander Hamilton Institute, Silberling Business Service.

saw it, regardless of the strict decrees of the laws of nature, and it was, therefore, impossible to forecast its future course. Business phenomena, notwithstanding the efforts made to distinguish typical cases, were regarded rather as isolated historical facts than as regularly recurring events, comparable, in many respects, with technical or natural processes.

It was, therefore, left to the American, Wesley C. Mitchell, in his great work on "Business Cycles" (1913), to complete for the first time the synthesis between the work of the theoretical-historical school of economics and that of the mathematical statisticians in the investigation of business cycles. In this work, he analyzes economic fluctuations on the basis of a comprehensive mass of material and investigates the periodicity and course of the various series of cyclical movements. Mitchell's work was supplemented by Warren M. Persons, who carried out a further series of investigations, of which a paper published in the *American Economic Review* (1916) on The Construction of a Business Barometer may be mentioned as the most important.

These were the foundations on which the Harvard University Committee of Economic Research—the first research institution on business cycles to win recognition from the scientific world—was set up in 1917 under the direction of Warren M. Persons and Charles J. Bullock. In this institution, the association of current observation of economic phenomena with methodical studies, of experience with theory, of a "business service" with economic research, was effected with very valuable results.

Essentially similar objects were pursued by the National Bureau of Economic Research, directed by Mitchell. The Institute of Economics at Washington, now a part of the Brookings Institution, is also concerned with aspects of these problems. A number of business research institutes on the model of the Harvard committee were also founded in Europe—at Stockholm at the end of 1922, at London in 1923, at Paris in the same year, and at Rome in 1926.

The *American* type of business service is characterized—in so far as it is permissible to generalize about institutions the activities and objects of which vary so widely—by the fact that it treats economic life as essentially a mechanism, a powerful piece of machinery the course of which can be represented and foretold with the aid of mathematical methods of calculation, in such a manner that, in the last resort, it can be expressed within the limits of a simple formula. The search for such a formula, for a general index or barometer, is, therefore, specially typical of American methods of investigation, disturbing factors being eliminated or sidetracked.[1]

The *Russian* business investigation service and the research work carried on in connection with it afford, to some extent, a contrast to the above. The service was founded in 1920 and is even externally and organizationally distinguishable from the American model owing to its extremely intimate association with the state control of public economy. It is an important element in the work of "Gosplan," the state department of economic planning, which lays down annually the lines on which the government's fiscal and economic policy is to be directed. The most noteworthy feature of the aims pursued by the Russian investigators consists in the special attention which they devote to the main questions of general economic development. Thus, while the Americans, for instance, eliminate "trend," the Russians endeavor to take it into account in their calculations.

A feature common to the American and Russian methods consists in their mathematical and arithmetical treatment of the subject. The Russians have, indeed, done a great deal of very important independent work in the field of mathematical economic statistics.[2]

---

[1] A conscious tendency has recently become evident to abandon such monistic methods of interpretation.

[2] See, especially, the work of Chuprov, Chetverikov, Yastremski, Kondratiev, Ignatiev, Slutzki, Romanovski, Bobrov, Oparin, Weinstein.

The *German* Business Research Institute (Institut für Konjunkturforschung) was founded in the middle of 1925[1] as an independent scientific research institute, officially supported by the most important central economic organizations and associated with the Federal Statistical Office by personal ties. The latter institution itself also enjoys rights for carrying on independent research work similar to those possessed by analogous bodies (the Kaiser-Wilhelm Society, the Kiel Institute, etc.).

The German institute, like those of America and Russia, has adopted as one of the most important principles for the organization of its work the application of mathematical methods. At the same time, however, the process of investigation in Germany has developed an orientation which essentially distinguishes it from those of other countries. This difference may perhaps be best expressed by saying that while the American methods are those of engineering, and the Russian those of astronomy, the German institute represents the medical, or, better, the organic-biological point of view. It regards the national economic system as an organism the course of whose inner life can never be adequately interpreted by concentrating attention on a single point of its external surface. The institute is, therefore, not in the habit of diagnosing economic symptoms with the help of a single economic barometer. Indeed, it does not always form its diagnoses by a mere study of barometers, which it uses for the purpose of estimating business prospects in much the same way as a doctor uses the numerous methods of diagnosis known to medicine as a basis for the formation of his opinion of a case; in both cases, that is to say, the diagnosis is based on a complete study of individual signs and

---

[1] The *Frankfurter Zeitung's* economic curve (prepared in collaboration with E. Kahn) may be mentioned as a parallel activity. It may also be noted that early in 1926 the "western" section of the Business Research Institute was founded in Essen, under the direction of Dr. Däbritz. In this connection, reference may also be made to the similar attempt begun in the prewar period by Calwer, Pohle, and Plenge but subsequently abandoned.

symptoms, and it serves, in turn, as a basis for forecasting the future course of the malady.

The Organic-biological Principle.

The research work of the institute, like its observation of cyclical phenomena, is built up on the organic-biological principle—on the basic assumption that the economic system is a living organism, which has in common with the living organisms in the zoological and botanical worlds not merely the intimate interconnection of all its separate parts, arising out of the internal interdependence of its various functions.[1] It also shares with them a peculiarity which may be defined as consisting in the power to regulate its own movement. This power has its immediate expression in an interplay of forces which is anything but mechanical, and which has in common with mechanical movement

---

[1] See MENGER, "Untersuchungen über die Methode der Sozialwissenschaften," pp. 139 *ff.*, Leipzig, 1883: "We observe in natural organisms an almost impenetrable complexity of detail and, particularly, a great multiplicity of parts (or individual organs). All this multiplicity serves, however, for the preservation, development, and propagation of the organism as *a whole.* Each part has its own function to fulfil toward this single end, and any disturbance in its fulfilment of that function causes, in proportion to the intensity of the disturbance or the importance of the organ concerned, a more or less intense disturbance in the fulfilment by the remaining parts or by the organism as a whole of their respective functions; and, conversely, a disturbance in the interrelation between the parts and the whole reacts similarly on the state and conduct of the separate organs. The normal functioning and development of an organism as a whole is thus conditioned by that of its parts, that of the parts is conditioned by their union in a whole superior to them, and that of each individual organ by that of the remaining organs . . . It is obvious that a certain analogy thus exists between the nature and functioning of natural organisms and those of social structures.

"This applies, in particular, to the question of the origin of any series of social phenomena. In the case of natural organisms, accurate observation will reveal, in practically every case, a really marvelous adaptation of all parts in relation to the whole; but this adaptation is an effect not of human calculation but of natural constitution. Similarly, in many social institutions we may also observe an obvious adaptation in relation to Society as a whole, and closer observation will show that such institutions do not result from any deliberate striving after a higher object or, in other words, from any agreement between the members of Society or any positive legislation. They, too, represent rather (in a sense) 'natural' products, the non-deliberate effects of historical development . . . "

only the mere fact of movement association,[1] the nature of the association being quite different. The starting, the direction, the duration, and the intensity of an organic series of movements thus possess the character of a more or less free rhythm, in contrast to the strictly regular beat of a machine. The independent organic character of economic fluctuations is, however, particularly noticeable in the manner in which they receive outside influences; they stand up to such influences and transform them, so that the latter's effect is merely that of stimuli. It is, therefore, not surprising that a political event, a war, or a natural catastrophe—however greatly the effects of such interferences from outside may vary, both qualitatively and quantitatively—communicates motion to the economic system in a manner which, perhaps, never varies, much as the heart reacts in an identical manner to quite dissimilar shocks, whether chemical or physical in character. On a mechanistic interpretation of economics, one would be tempted simply to estimate the strength and nature of external influences and to express their economic influence by means of an equation. The organic theory, on the contrary, refuses to proceed on such lines, as it regards all economic movement as fundamentally autonomous and, in that sense, as endogenous and, therefore, rejects any possibility of a calculable equivalence between external influences and internal development. This does not mean that the theory denies the possibility that the final impulse, the final causation of economic fluctuations comes from outside—is, in other words, exogenous; on

---

[1] This fact makes it permissible occasionally to speak of the mechanism or even the automatism of economic movement. The fact that I casually used such an expression in a lecture delivered at Vienna has led one of the younger representatives of the historical school (Walter Heinrich, in his "Grundlage einer universalistischen Krisenlehre"—a painstaking and notable book, though in many respects somewhat immature) to the conclusion that I was doing homage to "the view that economic life proceeds on mechanistic lines." On the same occasion, I referred to business cycles as "the content of the phenomena of reaction," so that the author ought to have reflected that phenomena of reaction are primarily indicative of an organic process.

the contrary, it insists that such a possibility must be recognized.

In order to avoid misunderstanding, let me repeat that the organic-biological principle, by which my work is guided, involves the following theses or, rather, hypotheses:

1. All parts of the economic system are interconnected in an intimate functional union; the system thus formed is closed and compact and is subject to its own laws.

2. Influences from outside, whether they proceed from non-economic spheres or from foreign economic organisms, affect the system simply as stimuli, which cause to be set in operation the forces inherent in the economic organism under observation.

This, and nothing else, is what I mean when I say that the theory of business cycles which I represent is based on the organic-biological principle. It may be true that the validity of the principle can be demonstrated only in the sense that it has proved itself very useful for practical purposes. There is no telling whether at a later stage of investigation it will be necessary to abandon it or whether it will be possible to extend its scope to the required extent. There can be no question, so long as such a basic principle is maintained, of relapsing into the old-fashioned game of inventing metaphors. My adoption of it amounts simply to this, that I propose until further notice to apply, in part, the system of reasoning proper to organic subjects to the study of business cycles.[1]

There is, however, another sense in which the modern study of business cycles proceeds on similar lines to biology or natural history; at the present stage of its investigations, it relies more on inductive than on deductive methods.

Theoretical and Empirical Methods.

A consideration of the way in which the problem of business cycles is usually handled by the political econo-

---

[1] See DRIESCH, HANS, "Philosophie des Organischen," 2d ed., Leipzig, 1921; "Ordnungslehre," Jena, 1923.

mists of Germany and Austria—particularly by a number of professors and their pupils—will show a considerable resemblance to the study of medicine in the Middle Ages, which, as is well known, was entirely dominated by theoretical concepts and methods of work. Anyone who makes the comparison will be vividly reminded of the pathology of the thirteenth and fourteenth centuries, with its fantastic system of "humors," as described by modern scientific historians.[1]

It was not until the sixteenth century that empirical methods of medical study were able gradually to take the place of "pure theory" and it became possible for Hohenheim to tell his fellow doctors that their guiding principle should no longer be *perscrutamini scripturas* but *perscrutamini naturas rerum*.

Are not the same two tendencies striving for the upper hand in German business-cycle theory today?

The recently published collection of papers on business-cycle investigation and theory,[2] edited by Karl Diehl, the universally respected dean of German economists, for the Verein für Sozialpolitik, is, in this respect, a characteristic document. Diehl begins by raising the characteristic question "how far the practical study of business cycles can serve to illustrate specific economic theories," and the answers supplied to this question are more characteristic still. The "empirical methods" of the business research institutes are contrasted with the "theoretical outlook" of the authors; and the former are to be allowed the honor of assisting in "substantiating" the latter.[3]

In reality, the only point at issue consists in the fact that the business research institutes prefer the inductive method and Diehl and his followers, the deductive. Every-

[1] MEYER-STEINEG and SUDHOFF, "Geschichte der Medizin," 2d ed., p. 223, Jena, 1922.

[2] DIEHL, KARL (ed.), "Wissenschaftliche Gutachten über, Konjunkturforschung und Konjunkturtheorie." Munich, 1928.

[3] One hopeful representative of the "theoretical school" feels constrained to classify business research institutes as "commercial services," owing to the fact that they issue current reports.

body knows that the two methods, mutually interdependent as they necessarily are, cannot be entirely separated from each other; and yet sonorous terms, borrowed at second or third hand from the great philosophical controversies between nominalism and realism, idealism and materialism, have been imported into the petty dispute as to the relative practical value of the methods of work adopted by two schools of economic investigation. This could hardly have happened had the fundamental question as to the primacy of thinking or being been properly understood; otherwise, "theory" and "empiricism" could not have been, respectively, treated as synonyms for "deduction" and "induction."

The faults described by Adolf Wagner in 1892 in his "Grundlegung"[1] still flourish in our midst. He says:

> The customary controversies between various schools as to the "right" method have been charmingly illustrated recently in German economic writings. In the literary criticisms published by certain intellectually self-conscious authors on the work of other "schools," the ignoring or false estimation of the part played by the factor to which allusion has been made above manifests itself in a most unpleasant series of consequences: arrogant, narrow-minded, pedantic condemnation of all work which differs from that of themselves and their own particular clique, the judging of all literary productions by the standard of the critics' own intellectual tendencies, which are, of course, in such cases set up as a kind of final, solitary, and infallible court of appeal.

The uncomprehending attitude of the "theorists" toward the new methods of investigation, firmly based on experience, is illustrated by the enthusiastic applause aroused among them by such categorical declarations as that of Löwe,[2] to the effect that

> . . . our insight into the theoretical cohesion of economic circulation and its underlying laws has gained practically nothing from all the descriptions of various phases and the calculations of correlation . . . To expect an increased empirical understanding to be of immediate

---

[1] WAGNER, ADOLPH, "Grundlegung der politischen Ökonomie" Vol. I, 1, pp. 32–33.

[2] In his essay entitled Wie ist Konjunkturlehre überhaupt möglich? in *Weltwirtschaftliches Archiv*, vol. 24, Part II, p. 166, 1926.

assistance in the construction of a theoretical system is to misapprehend the logical relationship between theory and realistic investigation.

The same spirit, to quote a further example, inspires the argument of Mises in the second edition of his "Theorie des Geldes und der Umlaufsmittel," to the effect that the theory of money had nothing new to learn during the whole of the inflation period.

Such "theory" is not merely unreal—it is inspired by fanatical hostility to all reality. A science, pronouncedly empirical in character, has arrogated to itself the claims of a purely ideal science; it desires, just as mathematics obeys its own intellectual laws, to exercise absolute sway in the realm of pure thought, to conceive its premises in a complete vacuum, and, as far as possible, to avoid the rude shocks which await it in the world of fact. Such "theory" is a trembling denizen of the professor's study. It shrinks in terror from anything so rude and coarse as mere figures! "How difficult," it says to itself, "the actual facts of economic experience might make the process of substantiation!" Why, economic laws have even been discovered which are absolutely incapable of being substantiated! The theory of marginal utility, for instance, has adopted this brilliant solution; in the concept of subjective value, it has built up a synthesis of supply and demand, between which and the actual facts in regard to prices there is a gulf which can never be bridged. The theory sanctions in advance any and every method of price-fixing; its verity is substantiated *ipso facto*, once and for all.

This fear and avoidance of facts has now, however, produced two disastrous results for German political economy. The economists do, indeed, appear to feel some uneasiness in regard to the first of these, at least— to the fact, that is to say, that their work is developing in marked opposition to its subject, namely economic phenomena. It has thus forfeited, to a considerable extent, the position of honor and influence due it in the national community. Yet they accept, without either regret or self-reproach, the fact that (apart from a very

few famous exceptions) they have played no part in dealing
with the immense economic problems called into existence
by the World War and that in regard to the vast currency
problems of the postwar period they have adopted an
attitude of complete detachment—that in regard, particularly, to the "miracle of the *Rentenmark*" they have
shown a complete lack of comprehension. The second
result, by which I mean the fact that they are in a state
of permanent mutual contradiction, is both more painful
for them and more significant in fact. In regard, particularly, to the theory of crises and business cycles, each of
them is at loggerheads with all the rest over the whole
ground to be covered, from the enunciation of definitions
to the formation of judgments. What is one to think
when a conception so important as that of the alteration
of the basic economic data is treated in the "Wissenschaftliche Gutachten" as quite self-evident and as needing no
further explanation, but the significance attributed to it
differs, even diametrically, from page to page? On page
156, for instance, it is stated that "only known changes
in the basic data of a national economic system, in the
sense of expansion and contraction, are to be termed
'business cycles'"; while on page 257, the changes in
economic data are set up in contrast—with greater truth,
incidentally—to the conjunctural movement.[1]

There is no wonder that economic theory built up on
such shifting foundations of ideas should lead to self-
contradictory conclusions. We are now accustomed to
the fact that practically every "theoretical" economist has
his own theory of crises. We cannot, however, help
feeling uneasy when intelligences in themselves acute,
reach, on the basis of practically identical premises,
conclusions so mutually incompatible as the following:

[1] The quotations on this and the following page are all taken from "Wissenschaftliche Gutachten," mentioned on page 14, which, although it
consists of papers by various authors—of widely varying value, it may be
said in passing—I treat as a single work, as I wish merely to illustrate
a general statement of facts and not to draw attention to the errors of
individuals.

It follows necessarily from the above that only a change in the national economic situation consequent on an increase in the quantity of money in circulation and/or the velocity with which it circulates *can* cause business cycles [p. 158].

The fact that these casual connections are still constantly misunderstood appears to be due to the tendency—a tendency which is extraordinarily hard to eradicate, notwithstanding a century of criticism directed against the quantity theory ("that sloppy but serviceable platitude," as Robertson has called it)—to use the formal statement of the exchange equation as a basis for the explanation of causes [p. 305].

An extension of the volume of credit in a national economic system must, other conditions remaining unchanged, be bound up with a reduction in the rate of interest by the credit-providing banks [p. 189].

The assumption of the monetary theory of crises, according to which the rate of interest determines the volume of credit and this, in turn, determines the price level, ignores the ultimately decisive factors in the economic process [p. 178].

Even though the "theoretical" economists shrink in horror from the more inductive method of investigation, they ought at least to exercise greater care in their own deductions than they frequently do. It will be sufficient, in this connection, to point out the feebleness and inadequacy of the arguments by which they attempt to account for the connection between fluctuations in the rate of interest and productive activity. On page 187 *ff.* of the "Wissenschaftliche Gutachten," for example, the author arrives at the conclusion, without producing any serious evidence, that a low interest rate stimulates production (in which he is following more illustrious examples); but then, on page 191, he turns a complete somersault and declares that an increasing demand must immediately extend to the means of production (see below, Chap. XVIII). Another logical absurdity appears, for instance, on page 162, where it is declared that according to the monetary theory of business cycles all phenomena are "cyclical" which accompany a change in the volume of

inflationary credit.   This view is protected against any
attempt at substantiation by the construction of an ingen-
ious intellectual seesaw—for it is stated that all phenomena
which do not accompany such changes are simply "structural" and not "cyclical."

In order to preserve our own equanimity, let us conclude
this review by quoting the following outburst by Sombart,
written under similar provocation:

> Our friends the "theorists" have, of course, no time for such weari-
> some work.   They prefer to play all sorts of games in a suitable semi-
> obscurity with their venerable ideas, none of which can stand the
> full light of criticism.   One is frequently astonished, casting a glance
> through their "systems," their "textbooks," or even their monographs,
> at the small amount of common sense, logic, and intelligence with
> which one can nowadays become a respected "theorist" in our field.[1]

Bibliography

HISTORY OF THEORIES

BERGMANN, E. VON: "Die Wirtschaftskrisen, Geschichte der national-
ökonomischen Krisentheorien," 1895.

ZIMMERMANN, PAUL: "Das Krisenproblem in der neueren nationalökono-
mischen Teorie," Halberstadt, 1927.

HEINRICH, WALTER: "Grundlagen einer universalistischen Krisenlehre,"
Jena, 1928.

DIEHL, K., and P. MOMBERT: Wirtschaftskrisen, "Ausgewählte Lese-
tücke zum Studium der politischen Ökonomie," vol. 7, Karlsruhe, 1913.

LOWE, A.: Der gegenwärtige Stand der Konjunkturforschung in
Deutschland, "Festgabe für Brentano," 1925.

THE OLDER THEORIES

SAY, J. B.: "Traité de'économie politique," 5th ed., 1826.

MILL, JAMES: "Commerce Defended," London, 1808.

RICARDO, DAVID: "Principles of Political Economy and Taxation,"
London, 1821.

OWEN, ROBERT: "Two Memorials in Behalf of the Working Classes,"
London, 1818.

OVERSTONE, SAMUEL JONES LLOYD, LORD: "Tracts and Other Publications on Metallic and Paper Currency," London, 1858.

MILLS, JOHN: On Credit Cycles and the Origin of Commercial Panics,
Transactions of the Manchester Statistical Society, session of 1867–1868.

---

[1] *Weltwirtschaftliches Archiv*, p. 28, July, 1928.

TORRENS, R.: "The Principles and Practical Operation of Sir Robert Peel's Act of 1844 Explained and Defended," London, 1847.

SISMONDI, SIMONDE DE: "Nouveaux principes d'économie politique," 2 vols., Paris, 1819; "Études sur l'economie politique," vol. 1, Paris, 1837.

MALTHUS, R.: "Principles of Political Economy," London, 1820.

RAU, K. H.: "Malthus und Say über die Ursachen der jetzigen Handels-stockung," Hamburg, 1821.

PROUDHON, J. P.: "Qu'est-ce que la propriété, ou recherches sur le principe du droit et du gouvernement," 1840; "Oeuvres complètes," 33 vols., vols. 1, 6, Paris, 1868–1873.

ENGELS, FREDERICK, and KARL MARX: "Manifest der kommunistischen Partei," 1848.

MARX, KARL: "Das Kapital," vol. 1, 4th ed., 1890; vol. 2, 2d ed., 1893; vol. 3, 1st ed., 1894. English Translation, "Capital," New York, 1929.

RODBERTUS-JAGETZOW, KARL: "Soziale Briefe an von Kirchmann," No. I, Die soziale Bedeutung der Staatswirtschaft, Berlin, 1850; "Die Handelskrisen und die Hypothekennot der Grundbesitzer," Berlin, 1858.

SCHÄFFLE, ALBERT E. F.: Zur Lehre von den Handelskrisen, Zeitschrift für die Staatswissensschaft, Tübingen, 1858, "Bau und Leben des sozialen Körpers," vol. 1, 4, Tübingen, 1875–1878.

LASSALLE, FERD: "Herr Bastiat Schulze von Delitzsch," Berlin, 1864.

THE NEWER ECONOMIC AND PRACTICAL SCHOOL

JUGLAR, CLÉMENT: "Des crises commerciales et de leur retour périodique en France, en Angleterre, et aux États-Unis," Paris, 1860, 2d ed., 1889.

TUGAN-BARANOWSKI, MICHAEL VON: "Studien zur Theorie und Geschichte der Handelskrisen in England," 1894, German ed., Jena, 1901.

BOUNIATIAN, MENTOR: "Studien zur Theorie und Geschichte der Wirtschaftskrisen," 2 vols., Munich, 1908.

LESCURE, JEAN: "Des crises générales et périodiques de surproduction," Paris, 1907, 2d ed., 1910.

AFTALION, ALBERT: "Les crises périodiques de surproduction," 2 vols., Paris, 1913.

SCHMOLLER, GUSTAV: "Grundriss der allgemeinen Volkswirtschaftslehre," vol. 2, pp. 530–562, Munich and Leipzig, 1904, 2d ed., 1919. Schriften des Vereins für Sozialpolitik, vols. 105–113. Die Störungen im deutschen Wirtschaftsleben während der Jahre 1900 ff. Leipzig, 1903, 1904.

SOMBART, WERNER: "Der moderne Kapitalismus," vol. 2, sec. I, pp. 208 ff., Leipzig, 1902, 2d ed., 1917.

SPIETHOFF, ARTHUR: Krisen, "Handwörterbuch der Staatswissenschaften," 4th ed., 1924.

FEILER, ARTHUR: "Die Konjunkturperiode 1907–1913," Jena, 1914.

TÖNNIES: Die Gesetzmäszigkeit in der Bewegung der Bevölkerung, Archiv für Sozialwissenschaft und Sozialpolitik, vol. 39, Nos. 1, 3, July, 1914, July, 1915.

POHLE, LUDWIG: "Bevölkerungsbewegung, Kapitalbildung, und periodische Wirtschaftskrisen," Göttingen, 1902.

HERKNER, HEINRICH: Krisen, "Handwörterbuch der Staatswissenschaften," 3d ed.

SCHUMPETER, JOSEPH: Über das Wesen der Wirtschaftskrisen, *Zeitschrift für Volkswirtschaft, Sozialpolitik, und Verwaltung,* vol. 19, 1910.

SPIETHOFF, ARTHUR: "Beiträge zur Analyse und Theorie der allgemeinen Wirtschaftskrisen," 1905; Die Krisentheorie von M. von Tugan-Baranowski und L. Pohle, *Schmollers Jahrbuch,* vol. 27, 1903.

CASSEL, GUSTAV: "Theoretische Sozialökonomie," 4th ed., Leipzig, 1927.

EULENBURG, FRANZ: "Die Preissteigerung des letzten Jahrzehnts," Leipzig, 1912; Die gegenwärtige Wirtschaftskrise, *Jahrbuch für Nationalökonomie und Statistik,* 3d ser., 1902.

BREZIGAR, EMIL: "Vorboten einer Wirtschaftskrise in Deutschland," Berlin, 1913.

BEVERIDGE, SIR WILLIAM: "Unemployment," 1909.

THE MATHEMATICAL-STATISTICAL SCHOOL

NEUMANN, SPALLART: Sur la meilleure méthode pour apprécier l'état social et économique d'un pays à une époque déterminée, *Bulletin de l'Institut International de Statistique,* vol. 2, 1887.

FOVILLE, DE: Essai de météorologie économique et sociale, *Journal de la Société de Statistique de Paris,* 1888.

JULIN: "Précis du cours de statistique," 3d ed., Paris, 1912.

MORTARA: Numeri indici delle condizioni economiche d'Italia, Institut International de Statistique, 14th sess., *Report 3.*

SORER, RICHARD: Über die Berechnung von Korrelationskoeffizienten zwischen den Symptomen der wirtschaftlichen Entwicklung in Osterreich, *Allgemeines Statistisches Archiv,* p. 193, 1914; Einige Indexzahlen zur wirtschaftlichen Entwicklung Österreichs. Ein Beitrag zur Lehre der ökonomischen Symptome, *Bulletin de l'Institut International de Statistique,* vol. 20, Part 2, Vienna, 1915.

CALWER, RICHARD: *Das Wirtschaftsjahr,* 1902–1913, and the weekly *Die Konjunktur* (discont.).

Economic curve of *Frankfurter Zeitung,* 1921 *ff.,* ed. with collaboration of E. Kahn.

JASTROW, I.: *Der Arbeitsmarkt* (discont.).

POHLE, LUDWIG: *Monatliche Übersichten über die allgemeine Wirtschaftslage,* 1909–1922, vol. 1, suppl. of *Zeitschrift für Sozialwissenschaft* (discont.); Konjunkturschwankungen und Konjunkturberichterstattung, *Zeitschrift für Sozialwissenschaft,* 1910, No. 1.

VOGEL: "Konjunkturkunde," 1913.

MODERN BUSINESS-CYCLE STUDY

MITCHELL, WESLEY C.: "Business Cycles," Berkeley, 1913.

PERSONS, WARREN M.: Construction of a Business Barometer, *American Economic Review,* December, 1916; "The problem of business forecasting," London, 1924.

Harvard Review of Economic Statistics (quart.) and *Weekly Letters,* Harvard Economic Service.

"Die weltwirtschaftliche Lage Ende 1925," Berlin, 1926; *Vierteljahrshefte zur Konjunkturforschung (V.z.K.)*,[1] with supplementary numbers since the beginning of 1926; the *Wochenberichte*, since April, 1928; all published by the Business Cycles Research Institute in Berlin.

Monthly Bulletin, London and Cambridge Economic Service.   "Indices du mouvement général des affaires en France et en divers pays," published by *Revue Politique et Parlementaire*, Paris (quart.).

Economic Bulletin of Business-cycle Institute, Moscow (monthly).

Monthly Report, Austrian Business Research Institute.

[1] On the following pages, the abbreviation *V.z.K.* will be used for *Vierteljahrshefte zur Konjunkturforschung*.

SECTION I

A DESCRIPTION OF ECONOMIC FLUCTUATIONS

CHAPTER I

ECONOMIC DYNAMICS

Statics and Dynamics.

In the study of physics, a distinction is made between statics, by which is meant the study of objects in a state of equilibrium, and dynamics, by which is meant the study of bodies in motion. The same distinction has been imported into political economy, and it has become customary (following Comte, J. S. Mill, and J. B. Clark) to speak of a static economy when referring to the fiction of a constant and smoothly working economic system. Such a system is conceived in abstraction from fluctuations in values and prices, from displacements in production and consumption—in short, as a kind of perfectly efficient and unvarying piece of clockwork.

The Interplay of Forces.

Such a condition has, in fact, never been attained. The economic system is thoroughly dynamic in character. The growth of the population, technical progress, changes of fashion, the conquest or loss of foreign markets, and the like, are sufficient to set up changes in a capitalistic national economic system so extensive as to create an extremely complex and involved interplay of movement. All economic processes succeed each other in an endless series of alternations. Prices, sales, and turnover vary from month to month, from week to week—indeed, they vary every day and every hour. Production and business activity can be regarded as constant only for very brief periods. Economic

23

activities are interconnected in an infinitely varied manner. The exchange of goods, services, landed property, shares, and mortgages, of producers' and consumers' goods, of manual and intellectual work, of stock-in-trade and realty takes place in a quite unstable sequence and with a constantly varying system of connections. The elucidation of the process of "diosmosis" which thus takes place as between the various factors in a business community is rendered the more difficult by the fact that money interposes itself as medium in all acts of natural exchange. Money itself, moreover, changes in appearance, like the chameleon; it assumes the guise of receipts and expenditure, of short- or long-term loans, of investment or deposits, of costs of production, of wages and interest, and, further, it sets up reactions which are, to some extent, entirely independent of the natural processes of exchange. This unrestrained round of economic processes and activities, this vast interplay of forces, is the subject matter of business-cycle theory, which might also be termed the theory of economic motion, or economic dynamics. Its task is to disentangle the Gordian knot formed by the infinitely complex interaction of economic forces. This it can do only by utilizing a number of artifices and relying on hypotheses, which it is, for the present, obliged to establish tentatively; and, to some extent, by using metaphorical notions borrowed from altogether different branches of science, and especially from biology, physics, meteorology, astronomy, and so forth.

The Economic Elements.

The phrase "economic movement" is a metaphorical expression for the mutations of the several economic *elements* and of their mutual relationships. By "economic elements" is meant the economic factors or circumstances which we are obliged on practical or theoretical grounds to postulate as units. It is customary to regard as economic elements both imports in the aggregate and imports of particular commodities, such as raw materials in general, or timber; currency in general and, again, the fiduciary or metallic currency; both industry as a whole and, as an example, the coal-mining industry or even a single pit; both the average of all wholesale prices and the prices of separate classes of commodity, or even the prices of particular commodities. We may, therefore, define economic elements as meaning those economic factors or circumstances which, for the purposes of a particular investigation, do not appear to require any further dissection.

Structural and Cyclical Elements.

The various economic elements undergo, in the course of actual economic development, continual, though by no means uniform, modification. They may be classified, according to the character of the modifications to which they are subject, as "structural" and "cyclical" elements.

By "structural" elements we mean those which are usually defined as "bases," as "known quantities," or, by many modern writers, as "data." In the current literature, the selection of these "data" depends more or less entirely on the individual fancy of the author. They are, however, generally considered as including population and territorial area, natural and geological circumstances, workmanship and management, consumers' tastes, and forms of business organization. Such a distinction, though for the most part arbitrarily drawn, is nevertheless plainly based on one criterion which I propose to regard as decisive. "Structural" elements are to be defined, for the purposes of the present study, as those economic elements which are subject only to a determinate kind of modification. On this basis, we may divide economic elements into two classes, namely, (a) elements which are liable to periodical, rhythmical change—and which we may define as "cyclical elements"[1]—and (b) elements which are either invariable or are liable by their natural character only to isolated variations (or "structural" changes). Thus, structural

---

[1] It is, of course, true that seasonal fluctuations are rhythmical in character; they do not, however, concern us here.

variations may be contrasted with cyclical fluctuations.[1] Structural variations are, as it were, organic, constitutional transformations of the economic system, while cyclical fluctuations, on the other hand, are, so to speak, purely functional phenomena.

The meaning of the above distinction may be illustrated by one or two examples. Thus, the fact that the German nitrogen industry has driven Chilean saltpeter from the German market or that exports to Russia have fallen off considerably represents an alteration in the economic structure; while fluctuations in German imports of raw materials are *cyclical* phenomena. Again, the fact that whereas in Germany before the World War the amount of business done in commodities was roughly identical with that done in securities, at the present day the former is several times as great as the latter is to be defined as an alteration in structure; while the fact that commodity prices follow the course of security prices at a certain interval, and at a rate which is faster now than formerly, is a cyclical phenomenon. These examples, while they illustrate the difference between structural variations and cyclical fluctuations, show, at the same time, that the former influence the latter; for the fact that imports of raw materials have, on the whole, fallen off is a consequence of the widely noticeable modern tendency toward self-sufficiency on the part of the various national economic systems; and the fact that the sequence of security prices and commodity prices is no longer the same as formerly is clearly due to the sharp displacement which has taken place in the proportional amount of business done in the two markets. It is thus immediately evident that the dissection of the course of economic development into these two component parts is an artificial device, which must be employed only with great prudence.

Whether an economic element is to be classified as structural or cyclical in character can be decided only by reference to its dynamic behavior. Thus, prices, which

[1] This distinction has already been drawn by the author in *V.z.K.*

in a free economic system are eminently cyclical elements, become structural elements in a rigid system with fixed prices. The population figure, on the other hand, in an economic unit of territory with a considerable, cyclically conditioned migration movement, is in no sense a "datum," a structural element, but must, in such a case, be regarded as a cyclical element.

Bibliography

AMONN, A.: Die Probleme der wirtschaftlichen Dynamik, *Archiv für Sozialwissenschaft und Sozialpolitik*, vol. 38, Tübingen, 1914.

CLARK, JOHN B.: "Distribution of Wealth," 1899; "Essentials of Economic Theory," 1907; The Field of Economic Dynamics, *Political Science Quarterly*, 1905.

COMTE, A.: "Soziologie," Jena, 1907–1911.

FEILEN, JOSEF F.: "Die Umlaufsgeschwindigkeit des Geldes," Berlin, 1923.

HONEGGER, HANS: "Volkswirtschaftliche Systeme der Gegenwart," 1925.

MARSHALL, A.: "Principles of Economics," vol. 1, 8th ed., London, 1920.

MILL, J. S.: "Principles of Political Economy," ed. by W. J. Ashley, New York, 1920.

PATTEN, SIMON S.: "The Theory of Dynamic Economics," Philadelphia, 1892.

SCHUMPETER, JOSEPH: "Wesen und Hauptinhalt der theoretischen Nationalökonomie," Leipzig, 1908; "Theorie der wirtschaftlichen Entwicklung," 2d ed., Munich and Leipzig, 1926.

OPPENHEIMER, FRANZ: "System der Soziologie," vol. 1, Part 2, Jena, 1923.

STRELLER, RUDOLF: "Statik und Dynamik in die theoretischen Nationalökonomie," Sächs. Forsch.-Institut für Volkswirtschaftslehre, Leipzig, 1926.

ZWIEDINECK-SÜDENHORST, O. VON: Beiträge zur Erklärung der strukturellen Arbeitslosigkeit, *V.z.K.*, vol. 2, suppl. 1.

CHAPTER II

ECONOMIC CIRCULATION (ECONOMIC STATICS)

In attempting to disentangle the complex interplay of economic forces, it appears convenient, as a first approach toward reality, to begin by investigating the notion of economic circulation. Curiously enough, the study of this phenomenon is reckoned, in current economic terminology, as a branch of statics, although the idea of circulation includes that of movement. It would be more logical to understand statics as referring not to space-time relationships but to space relationships only—in other words, not to the physiology but only to the anatomy of economics; just as in physics the problems of bridge building are dealt with by statics, while the movement of the pendulum is a subject for dynamics.

Kinetics.

It might, perhaps, be most convenient to classify the study of economic circulation as a branch of kinetics. Just as kinetics signifies the science of motion in abstraction from mass, so the notion of economic circulation involves abstraction, for example, of the economic agent. We prefer, however, to fall in with the general usage and classify the notion under the head of statics.

The notion of circulation is formed as soon as one attempts to depict (*a*) the flow of money and (*b*) the transmutations of labor power. We speak of the circulation of money, because a single sum of money figures in a continual and well-nigh endless succession of payments, without risking the destruction of its value, in such a way that it tends to return to the hand of the individual by which it was originally paid out; the circuit is also completed in another sense, as we shall see when we come to deal with "equations of exchange." Again, in the study of economics

28

from the side of commodities, we have to adopt the notion of circulation, because producers of goods are simultaneously consumers of labor, since the consumption of the product of labor is the necessary basis for further production.

It may at first sight appear absurd to separate the circulation of money from the turnover of commodities, seeing that "money" and "commodity" are complementary ideas. Goods become "commodities" when they come up against money, while money loses its significance if there is nothing for it to buy—that is, no commodities. The isolation of the two notions, however, reveals the significance of a number of relationships.

It is justified, moreover, by the fact that commodities and money possess essentially different forms of value.

Political economy considers those objects as possessing value which are at the same time useful and rare. But commodities are rare and useful in a quite different sense from money. Commodities procure "real" satisfaction, and money only "circulational" satisfaction (to borrow Knapp's terminology) . . . Commodities are produced, money is created. If the value of goods and services is defined as intrinsic (or labor) value, that of money must be regarded as being an extrinsic (or book) value.[1]

THE CIRCULAR FLOW OF GOODS

The Removal of the Money Veil.

Let us now consider the circulation of labor—the circular flow of goods. In order to do so, we shall need to adopt the device which since the days of the classical economists has been so popular: the "removal of the money veil."

How this can be effected can best be made clear if one supposes oneself in the position of an inhabitant of Mars, looking down at the earth through a powerful telescope. One would then be able to observe how coal is extracted from the bowels of the earth, how iron is produced by the blast furnaces, how the harvest is gathered in the fields. One would note how man transports these and a thousand

[1] See WAGEMANN, "Allgemeine Geldlehre," Theorie des Geldwerts und der Währung, vol. 1, pp. 8 *ff.*, 1923.

THE CIRCULAR FLOW OF GOODS

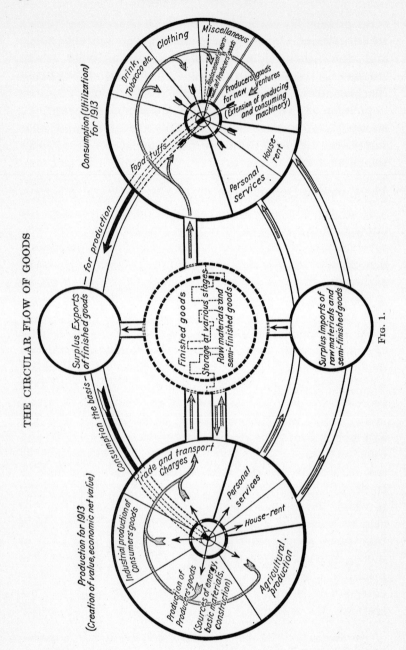

FIG. 1.

other products in carts, ships, and railway trains for further transformation, how he redespatches the finished goods and stores them in warehouses, up to the point where (frequently through many roundabout channels) they reach the consumer. Thus viewed, the earth would give the impression of a vast ant heap, busily engaged in production, transport, storage of supplies, foreign trade, and consumption—the sum total of which processes constitutes the circular flow of goods.

The Common Denominator of the Circular Flow of Goods.

If we try to proceed further in our consideration of the circulation of goods in abstraction from the notion of money, we come up against the great difficulty of finding a common denominator by which to represent the process of natural exchange. Even in the case of isolated categories of goods, it is difficult to devise such a common denominator, which will enable us to relate individual products with each other according to their economic significance. In the case of combustible material, heating power might be taken as a denominator, and in the case of foodstuffs, the calory, which is the unit of food value.[1] For other commodities, however, we have to fall back on a calculation of hours of labor (which, in certain cases, can be reckoned up from the available industrial statistics) or on the use of some unit of monetary value. We are justified in leaving money as such out of account by the same considerations as permit us to draw a sharp distinction between the concrete medium in which payment is made and the unit of value; for it is easy to imagine an economic order in which exchange would take place simply on the basis of price lists, no form of money being interposed in the exchange of goods.[2] The primitive economy of peoples living in a state of nature corresponds, in many respects, to such a pattern; for what else are the customary exchange conditions, on which

[1] See WAGEMANN, Die Lebensmittelteuerung und ihre Gesetzmässigkeiten, *Schmollers Jahrbuch*, 1919.
[2] See WAGEMANN, "Allgemeine Geldlehre,"1923, pp. 69 *ff.*

trade is carried out where money is still unknown, than a kind of price-table system?

Quantitative Proportion.

We are, therefore, logically justified, for the purpose of forming notions of quantitative proportion in respect of the circular flow of goods, in making use of units of value. It suits our purpose to do so, moreover, as we are thus enabled to form a clearer idea of the relations between the commodity aspect and the money aspect.

The National Income.

In order to obtain a picture of the circular flow of goods such as to assist us in comprehending the interconnection of production and consumption, foreign trade, warehousing, and goods transport, we may begin by reckoning up the *national income*. The national income supplies a practically perfect reflection of national economic production; that is to say, so far as the figures established for the national income represent the sum of the incomes of the individual units in the national economic system, they give us an idea of the total value of the services rendered within the framework of the system in exchange for compensation. For our purpose, therefore, they should not include "derivative" income, by which I mean receipts not based on the rendering of any economic service—for example, charitable donations, allowances paid to students, presents. All receipts, however, which are obtained as hire for labor power or capital are primary income and are, therefore, essential elements in our reckoning.[1] The total

---

[1] A different distinction is frequently drawn between primary and derivative income, primary income being, roughly speaking, regarded as income based on commodity prices (wages, profits, interest), while all other forms of income are considered as derivative: for example, officials' salaries, lawyers' fees, lecturers' fees, etc. Such a classification is inadequate, however; for a chemist, for instance, who works in a factory and whose salary is reckoned among the costs of production for the undertaking, cannot conceivably be regarded as in a different position economically from the independent chemist, who charges the same undertaking a fee for his advice (See Wagemann, "Allgemeine Geldlehre," p. 153).

primary income accordingly reflects the total production of the national economic system, provided that the distinction drawn above is maintained. The physiocrats, of course, considered agriculture as the sole branch of production, and agricultural labor as alone productive. By the time of the classical economists, it had become self-evident that industry and trade were also to be counted as branches of production. Nevertheless, the question was for a long time debated, whether or not commercial activities were also to be regarded as productive. The dispute has long been settled in favor of trade. Even at the present day, however, some doubt is still felt as to whether the work of officials, of members of the liberal professions, of artists, of scholars, and even of domestic servants is to be classed as productive; yet productive it is no less than that of the remaining occupational groups.

Production.

Now, if we look at production through the mirror supplied by income figures, we must realize that the image reflected is a mere caricature, as long as a correct measure of the *quantity* of work done, in the form of labor-hour figures, is not supplied simultaneously, for labor is remunerated at very varying rates. Still less, however, do the income figures express the technical, artistic, or scientific quality of the work, for income is measured solely by the value attributed to labor on the markets. This economic value of services rendered is, however, the only kind of value which an economic investigation can take into account. Artistic, technical, scientific, and spiritual evaluations are the concern of quite other spheres of study. It is important that this point should be emphasized, for the layman frequently looks at the production values reflected in statistics from a non-economic point of view or, at best, from a point of view which confuses philosophical or political considerations with those proper to economics— as when he argues that the importance of agriculture is not even remotely reproduced in the statistics of production value.

Under the heading of income based on services rendered, we must reckon the sums which the *entrepreneur* gains from his work (including profits); these can be estimated only by a computation, whereas income by way of wages represents a concrete calculable item. Similarly, we must calculate the income received by property owners by adding together the concretely manifest interest paid to creditors, including dividends, and the surplus amounts received by way of profits on capital employed in the owner's own undertaking.

It should also be noted that this analysis presupposes a view in regard to the significance of house ownership and the rent of dwelling accommodation in the economic scheme of values which differs from that adopted by other observers. We should, however, find ourselves involved in serious difficulties if we failed to understand clearly that the building of dwelling houses is naturally a part of industry and belongs more particularly to the group of industries engaged in producing the means of production. Owners of dwelling houses or the managers of such property, who have taken over the product of the house-building industry (that is, the dwelling house) are in a position similar to that of persons engaged in commerce, who take over movable goods from industry and agriculture, in order to store them and distribute them to the consumer. House owners may be considered as in a sense storing and distributing dwellings; and just as the trader fixes his prices by calculating various basic costs and adding thereto a certain amount for interest and other charges, so rents are fixed (*a*) by calculating the amount necessary to redeem the purchase price, plus interest, and (*b*) by adding thereto the management charges, which correspond, roughly speaking, to the additional charges exacted by the retail trader. The question which the theorists are fond of raising, as to whether the dwelling-house trade (house owners and managers together with their subordinate assistants, that is, doorkeepers, and the like) is to be reckoned among the productive branches is thus—on the view explained above—decided without difficulty in the latter's favor.

THE GERMAN NATIONAL INCOME, 1913[1]

(Billions of marks)

	Species of income				Total
	Labor's		Property's		
	Wages	Business income	Business income	Rent	
Constructive branches of industrial activity:					
Agriculture..................	4.4	2.0	1.0	1.6	9.0
Industry....................	14.0	3.0	1.0	2.0	20.0
Activities abroad.............	....	0.3	0.5	0.5	1.3
Total....................	18.4	5.3	2.5	4.1	30.3
Distributive branches:					
Transport..................	2.3	0.2	1.3	0.2	4.0
Trade......................	2.3	2.2	0.5	0.5	5.5
Dwelling-accommodation trade.	0.1	0.4	1.0	2.5	4.0
Total....................	4.7	2.8	2.8	3.2	13.5
Ancillary branches:					
Domestic service.............	0.5	...	...	...	0.5
Military service.............	1.0	...	...	...	1.0
Public services, liberal professions.....................	3.5	...	...	...	3.5
Total....................	5.0	...	...	...	5.0
Grand total..............	28.1	8.1	5.3	7.3	48.8

[1] This estimate is based on an unpublished investigation by the author. As we are here concerned only with the essential subdivision and not with the figures for the various items, the figures are reproduced without any further explanation as to the manner of arriving at them.

From the total of 49,000,000,000 we need only deduct income received by Germany from abroad, in order to form a reflected picture of Germany's national economic production; we thus arrive, for the year 1913, at a figure of about 48,000,000,000 marks.

A summary estimate for the various main productive branches in 1925 gives the following figures for the values created:

	Billions of marks
Agriculture	10
Industry and handicrafts	25
Commerce and housing	12
Services	6
Total	53

The following estimate of the values created by the main groups of industries may be tentatively offered:

	Billions of marks		Per cent	
1. Sources of power		1.9		7.5
2. Basic materials		4.3		17.1
3. Construction		7.3		29.5
a. Building	2.9		11.6	
b. Engineering, etc	4.4		17.9	
Total for all industries producing producers' goods		13.5		54.1
4. Food, drink, tobacco, and the like		2.8		11.3
5. Clothing		4.9		19.6
6. Dwelling accommodation, luxuries, cultural utilities		3.8		15.0
Total for all industries producing consumers' goods		11.5		45.9
Grand total		25.0		100.0

Industry Dissected.

It is possible for us to examine the composition of national economic production still more closely, as is shown by the following dissection of German industry, based on the industrial census for 1925.

NUMBERS EMPLOYED IN GAINFUL ACTIVITIES, AS SHOWN BY THE OCCU-
PATIONAL AND INDUSTRIAL CENSUS, 1925[1]

(Thousands of persons)

I. Agriculture and forestry.................................. 9,762

II. Industry:

  A. Industries producing producers' goods:

    Sources of power (coal, electricity)..........   827

    Basic materials (iron, chemicals, paper, build-

    ing materials, etc.)...................... 1,936

    Construction (building, engineering, etc.).... 3,914

      Total for all industries producing pro-

      ducers' goods........................... 6,677

  B. Industries producing consumers' goods:

    Food, drink, tobacco, etc.................. 1,356

    Clothing............................... 2,590

    Dwelling accomodation, luxuries, cultural

    utilities............................... 1,975

      Total for all industries producing con-

      sumers' goods.......................... 5,921 12,598

III. Commerce, transport, and communications:

  Trade................................... 2,903

  Banking.................................   213

  Insurance...............................   97

    Total for trade, banking, insurance............3,213

  State railways...........................   756

  Post office..............................   356

  Other branches of transport and communi-

  cations................................   343

    Total for transport and communications....... 1,455

  Hotels, restaurants, etc......................   716   5,384

IV. Services:

  A. Administration...........................   648

    Education..............................   363

    Army and navy.........................   142

    Church................................   90

    Health................................   472

    Law and justice........................   109

    Entertainment.........................   151

      Total................................. 1,975

  B. Domestic service........................... 1,394   3,369

    Total for all gainful occupations..............   31,113

[1] The table is not based directly on the occupational and industrial census figures but
was compiled by the author from the standpoint of the relations between production and
income and published for the first time in *V.z.K.*, vol. 2, No. 4. For this purpose, it was
necessary, to some extent, to combine the occupational census figures ("inhabitants classified
according to their main occupation") with those of the industrial census, as the analysis of
industries into groups producing producers' and consumers' goods, respectively, was possible
only on the basis of the detailed classified indications of the industrial census. The ideas
underlying the group titles "inhabitants classified according to their main occupation"

In the foregoing table, the group "industries producing consumers' goods" includes all industries the products of which are bought with that part of the income which is expended on consumption. I have, therefore, included in it the food, drink, tobacco, and clothing industries, together with all industries producing household effects, etc., (furniture, glass, china, etc.) and branches the product of which satisfies requirements of a cultural or luxury character (musical instruments, pharmaceutical products, toys, a certain proportion of rubber goods, and the like). This group of industries also includes those which prepare the raw materials and half-finished products intended solely for the use of the industries in the consumers'-goods group (for example, the clothing group includes spinning and weaving). As an exception to this principle, however, agriculture is not attached to the food-drink-and-tobacco group, for reasons which concern the productive aspect.

The group "industries producing producers' goods" includes only those industries which stand in no direct and immediate relationship to consumption expenditure. The product of these industries is bought partly out of the funds which political economy defines as industrial capital (such expenditure being included in the price of consumers' goods as part of the cost of production), but partly, also, out of the portion of income devoted to accumulation. Just as we have included the whole of the textile industry in the consumers'-goods group, although its products serve, to some extent, as means of production, so we have included in the producers'-goods group a number of branches which, to some extent, prepare products for immediate consumption (for example, the coal industry, which incidentally produces coal for domestic use). The same applies, for instance, to the paper industry, which— contrary to the usual practice—must be considered as

---

and "occupied persons" do not always coincide, as the industrial census figures, to some extent, also cover persons engaged in accessory occupations. As, moreover, the industrial census figures do not include persons unemployed owing to sickness or lack of work, their total of 31,113,000 gainfully occupied persons does not exactly correspond to the figure of 32,000,000 shown by the occupational census. For the detailed analysis, see Appendix, p. 270.

predominantly engaged in producing means of production; for, in the last resort, even the newspaper industry, notwithstanding the cultural requirements which it satisfies, is primarily financed by advertisement revenue and only at second hand out of income from sales, as a rule.

While we have grouped the various branches of the consumers'-goods-producing industries according to their consumptional object, those in the producers'-goods group are listed in a certain order of precedence—(1) sources of power (coal, etc.), (2) basic materials (iron, wood, building materials, etc.), and (3) construction (building and engineering). The criterion of proximity to consumption (that is, of the degree of relationship to income) on which this order of precedence is based is, in practice, of course, only partly utilizable for purposes of classification.

The inclusion of the building industry as a whole (including the building of dwelling houses) in the producers'-goods group is quite deliberate; for the product of the house-building industry—namely, dwelling accommodation—stands in a quite different relationship to consumers' expenditure from, for example, textile raw materials. In the economic sense of the word "consumption," it is not the house, but the use of the house, which is placed at the disposal of the consumer. As we have seen, it is the occupational group constituted by the owners and managers of house property, which represents the parallel to the textile industry, and not the building industry, the relationship of which to the "consumption" (use) of dwelling houses is analogous to that of textile-machinery construction to clothing.

The Disposal of the Fruits of Production.

We have now to consider the disposal of the fruits of production. Personal services enter immediately into consumption, and the same is true of dwelling accommodation. The goods produced are, generally speaking, first taken to the warehouse and, thereafter, in so far as they do not remain there, either enter into immediate consumption or are employed as means of production. In this connection, a distinction has to be drawn among:

1. Goods which are only the first elements toward consumption (raw materials, sources of energy).
2. Goods which are intended to replace worn-out means of production (*e.g.*, an old locomotive is replaced by a new one).
3. Goods which serve to extend:
   a. The productive system (*e.g.*, new factories).
   b. The consumptive system (*e.g.*, new housing accommodation).

The respective quantities involved can be only indirectly estimated, by examining the manner in which income is expended. This gives us the following figures for 1913:[1]

	Billions of marks
Personal services	5
Housing accommodation	4
Food	16
Drink, tobacco	5
Clothing	5
Household effects, luxury articles, and the like	5
New equipment (savings)	8
Total	48[1]

[1] Of the total income of 49,000,000,000 marks, the income from abroad has been left out of account in dealing both with production and with consumption, as, roughly speaking, the same amount is reinvested abroad.

New Plants and the Production of Producers' Goods.

It should be noted that "new equipment" is not synonymous with the total creation of fresh values in the shape of producers' goods, as might at first sight be supposed. For even in a stable economic community, where no increase takes place in capital wealth, producers' goods are continually produced, for the purpose of making good the constant depreciation which production involves. Old buildings, locomotives, bridges, etc., must continually be replaced. Such production, however, is essentially nothing but repair work, and expenditure thereon represents, in the form of a sinking fund, part of the costs of production as they figure on the industrial balance sheet; it enters into

[1] Based on calculations which the author intends to publish in detail elsewhere. For the sake of simplification, only round figures are given, especially as our only object at present is to illustrate our principle of classification.

the price of consumers' goods and thus ultimately appears as consumption expenditure—just as do the raw materials which have to be worked up in order to make consumers' goods. The cost of producers' goods of this kind can scarcely be separated from consumption expenditure. The case is quite different where new equipment is created instead of old equipment being replaced—as, for instance, where fresh railway lines are constructed, or the soil is improved, or where new urban districts and new branches of industry spring up, and concurrently with the increase in population fresh working and living accommodation is created or the accommodation for the already existing population is increased and better workshops and dwellings are constructed. This increase, representing the creation of new equipment or the formation of new capital, may be estimated at 8,000,000,000.

Foreign Trade.

We have hitherto refrained from considering foreign trade. The part played by this item in the circular flow of goods may be expressed by the statement that of the total production of finished commodities about 5,000,000,-000 marks' worth is diverted (in so far as we leave out of account the exchange of finished commodities themselves between the home and foreign countries) in payment for imports of food stuffs, raw materials, and half-finished goods to about the same amount—that is, for productive values which we have included among the items of consumers' expenditure, as above defined. The following are the figures for 1913, in billions of marks:

	Imports	Exports	Excess of imports (−) or exports (+)
Live stock....................	0.3	....	−0.3
Food and drink................	2.8	1.1	−1.7
Raw materials and partly finished commodities..................	6.3	2.3	−4.0
Finished commodities...........	1.4	6.7	+5.3
Total......................	10.8	10.1	−0.7

Storage.

An important part is also played in the circular flow of goods by storage.   All goods undergo some form of storage when they leave the hands of the producer and before they enter into consumption.   Goods are held in "storage" both while they are being transported (as water may be said to be "stored" in the pipes through which it passes from the reservoir to the consumer) and while they are actually deposited in warehouses or shops.   The volume of goods in storage fluctuates continually and at very brisk rates of change, both as a whole and in detail.   The accumulation and consumption of crops cause violent seasonal fluctuations; but there are also very considerable cyclical fluctuations.   The investigation of these, however, belongs not to statics but to economic dynamics, with which we shall have to deal at a later stage.

Public Administration.

This analysis does not show the contribution to production and the consumption of the public administrative departments.   It is difficult, generally speaking, to bring public administration into the scope of any survey of economic circulation, as it is, for the most part, covered by the separate items in the general table.   The receipts of the Reich, the states, and the local authorities for the financial year 1913–1914 were as follows:

	Billions of marks
Taxes and customs duties	4.0
Administrative receipts	1.0
Surplus on commercial operations	1.0
Loans, etc	1.3
Total	7.3

Against the above, the following expenditure must be set:

	Billions of marks
Salaries and pensions	2.3
Current expenditure	2.0
New buildings	1.6
Social and miscellaneous objects	0.5
Debt service	0.9
Total	7.3

The surplus from commercial operations (or earned income) may be regarded as payment for the productive activities of the state; in our diagram of production, such surplus figures among the productive values created by various branches of productive activity.[1] But we also regard the activities of public officials, in general, as a form of state production (see above), for which 2,300,000,000 marks are paid. A further portion of the receipts serves to pay for such activity of other branches of industry as is called into existence by the state; these are devoted partly to developing the national productive mechanism (roads), partly to developing the mechanism of consumption (schools, barracks), the remainder being devoted to non-economic objects (welfare work, unkeep of prisons, etc.).

For the purpose of our diagram of production, therefore, the state's activities may be classified as follows:

1. Direct contributions by the state to production:
   a. Governmental administration (salaries and pensions). To be classified under "personal services."
   b. Commercial services (earned income). To be included among "productive values from which the trade surplus is derived."*
2. Productive activity of other branches of industry called into existence by the state and serving the development:
   a. Of the mechanism of production.
   b. Of the mechanism of consumption. To be classified particularly under "production of industrial producers' goods."
3. Unproductive functions of the state, represented by expenditure on:
   a. Social welfare.
   b. Interest on unproductive state loans. Not to be classified among the items in national production.

* The bulk of the state's activities in this sphere figure not under this head but above, under "transport and communications," as the costs of the commercial services are entered up separately from the trading surplus.

Against the above, we have to set state consumption; though any clear-cut statistical separation of this factor from the general figures is impossible, if only for the reason that the prices, on the basis of which those figures are established, already include taxes. Its inclusion within the schematic analysis of consumption, in general, may be effected as follows:

[1] Its proceeds may be said to serve the purpose of paying interest on public loans.

1. Consumption of services of officials. Included in "personal services."
2. Consumption of producers' goods:
   a. For the development of the mechanism of production and consumption (included under the heading "investments in material goods").
   b. For the replacement of worn-out material utilized by the administration (concealed particularly among producers' goods).
3. Consumption of consumers' goods (such consumption, in so far as it proceeds from the agency of the officials or the creditors of the state, is, of course, not to be considered as consumption by the state) arises from the rationing of the army and, also, from public welfare work (seeing that we have agreed to consider all income which is not based on any corresponding productive services as derivative) above all, however, from real expenditure for administrative purpose (so far as these are not covered by 2b).

Thus, the public administration is intimately associated in all the main subdivisions both of production and of consumption; its share cannot at the present stage be expressed statistically with greater precision.

THE CIRCULAR FLOW OF MONEY

The metaphorical expression "circular flow of money" helps us to form a schematic picture of the almost infinitely numerous payment processes in a national economic system.

The Meaning of Money.

We may interpret the meaning of "money"[1] as follows: Money is essentially not a form of material property. It represents no labor value, no intrinsic value. Where it takes the form of coin, it carries with it, of course, a labor value based on the precious metal of which it consists. Such material consolidation of the standard of value may be convenient for particular purposes of financial policy; it may, however, be omitted without affecting the essential nature of money. Fundamentally, money belongs rather to the category of book values, from the main body of which it stands out owing to its inherent purchasing power. Property values may thus be classified as follows:

---

[1] Cf. WAGEMANN, "Allgemeine Geldlehre," vol. 1, Theorie des Geldwerts und der Währung, especially pp. 93 ff.

I. *Material property* (intrinsic values, labor values, *i.e.*, the sum total of economic goods possessed by the nation, to be interpreted statistically on real or objective lines):
   A. Land and soil.
   B. Buildings.
   C. Plant.
   D. Commodity stocks.
   E. Surplus from foreign credits and investments.
II. *Monetary property* in the widest sense (extrinsic values, book values), *i.e.*, the total economic power to dispose of material property (to be interpreted statistically on individual or subjective lines; danger of counting the same item twice). Fundamentally, the nation's monetary property equals its material property, in so far as debit or credit relations with foreign countries are left out of account.

Monetary property is either

A. Independent of documents (conferring direct purchasing power on the holder) or
B. Based on
   1. The register of landed property, etc.
   2. Documents deriving their monetary worth from their connection with some unit of value.

Values based on documents may be further subdivided into

1. Individual titles to property, tied to some specific property value or representing a specific share in proceeds (mortgages, shares) and (in contrast with these)
2. Abstract extrinsic values, which are not dependent on any specific source of wealth (not to be confused with abstract property rights in the legal sense). These include claims founded on a bill of exchange or on a book debt, as against a specific debtor but not a specific source of wealth; public loans, in regard to which the taxpayer is responsible for payment of interest and redemption; and, above all, money.

Abstract monetary property based on documents may be divided according to its purchasing power into

A. Values based on documents possessing no, or no legally recognized, purchasing power:
   1. State loans (temporary).
   2. Bills of exchange and checks (in part).[1]
   3. Bank deposits.
B. Values based on documents with legally recognized purchasing power (money). The following subdivision, based on the extent and degree of the legally recognized purchasing power in each case, may be made:

[1] So far as these are not reckoned under *A* 3.

1. Optional currency.
2. Compulsory currency:
   a. Provisional currency.
   b. Definitive currency.
      (1) Accessory currency.
      (2) Standard currency.

The circular flow of money may be diagrammatically represented in all sorts of ways. Attempts to draw up such diagrams have been made repeatedly.[1] The following diagram appears to be appropriate for the purpose of business-cycle investigation:[2]

THE CIRCUIT OF PAYMENTS

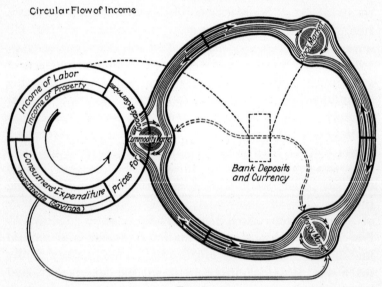

FIG. 2.

Classification of Payment Processes.

This diagram is based on the classification of payment processes, in general, in five main groups:
1. Income.
2. Expenditure and savings.

[1] For example, LAHN, "Kreislauf des Geldes," Berlin, 1903; FOSTER and CATCHINGS, "Money," 2d ed., New York, 1924.

[2] Already published by the author in *V.z.K.*, vol. 1, No. 3, pp. 10, 11.

3. Turnover of commodities (prices).
4. Credits.
5. Turnover of securities.

These groups are interconnected by many links.

The Circuit Flow of Income (the Business Equation).

The circular flow of payments takes place particularly along two main streams. One of these streams is the flow of payments from income through expenditure and savings to prices. Every income, and, consequently, the sum total of incomes, is either spent or saved. Expenditure is converted into the prices paid for consumers' goods (food stuffs, clothes, etc.) or personal services (for example, theater tickets, hairdressers' charges). Savings are, as a rule, "invested" at interest. "Hoarding" in the old sense of the word now occurs, if at all, only among peasants, though at the present time the increased amount of cash in hand that is maintained is temporarily exerting an influence. Investments are partly "direct"—as, for instance, when a tradesman buys new stock or a manufacturer installs new machinery. In such a case, purchasing power reaches the commodity market direct from the business undertaking, passing through the "income" stage only on paper, as it were (accumulation out of trading profits). For the most part, however, savings pass by way of income, from which they are shorn away in order to flow straight to the credit markets (money and capital markets) in the most diverse forms. Thence, they finally reach the stage of investment in the commodity and labor markets (passing, to some extent, by way of the stock market). Thus, they end by being transformed into prices—that is to say, they are used by the entrepreneur to buy raw materials or pay wages. Income, therefore—whether saved or spent—constantly transforms itself into prices paid for goods and services, these, in turn, are transformed into costs of production, which, finally, are simply the income of the individual business. This circular flow has been expressed in a formula: Income =

expenditure + savings = prices = costs of production = income (the equation of exchange).[1]

The Flow of Finance Capital.

The above circulatory system is affected by another flow of payments; these are the payments which pass from one gainful economic unit to another, constituting what we may call the "flow of finance capital," the latter being defined as monetary property which is in operation on the markets. This important flow of payments, involving a turnover far greater than the flow of income, is connected therewith, as we have seen, by a channel leading straight from savings to the money market. Their special point of interconnection, however, is situated at the commodity market. In this market is spent not merely income but also the entrepreneur's working capital—not only "consumers' money" but also "producers' money," to borrow Adolf Wagner's terms. The commodity market is, in turn, closely connected with the credit markets (the money and capital markets); for it is partly with credits obtained in these markets that the entrepreneur buys commodities, while part of the receipts of the commodity market flow back immediately to the credit markets. On the other hand, both these markets are closely connected with the securities market, in which both fixed-interest bearing bonds and shares are constantly changing hands.

The notion of the double stream of payments is and will always be no more than a metaphorical figure, which at best reflects the course of payments in a national economic system in the same way as double-entry bookkeeping reflects the course of business in a commercial undertaking, namely by the aid of dummy entries. Our diagrammatic representation of the circular flow both of goods and of money is, moreover, of course, only a very rough reproduction of the reality; for a living and growing national economic system presents the aspect of a circular flow at most for brief periods. In reality, the circulation of

[1] See WAGEMANN, "Allgemeine Geldlehre," vol. 1, p. 149.

goods and payments in such a system undergoes constant expansion and contraction.

Bibliography

WAGNER, ADOLPH: "Sozialökonomische Theorie des Geldes und des Geldwesens," 1909.

FISHER, IRVING: "The Purchasing Power of Money."

WAGEMANN, ERNST: "Allgemeine Geldlehre," vol. 1, Berlin, 1923; "Kreislauf und Konjunktur der Wirtschaft," Münster, 1927.

LAHN: "Kreislauf des Geldes," 1903.

WILKEN, FOLKERT: "Der Kreislauf der Wirtschaft," Jena, 1928.

FOSTER and CATCHINGS: "Money," New York, 2d ed., 1924.

CHAPTER III

THE BASIC FORMS OF ECONOMIC MOVEMENT

We have now reached a point in our investigation at which we must pass from the realm of statics (or kinetics) to that of dynamics. Originally, the German word *Konjunktur*, which roughly corresponds to the English term "business cycle" and is usually so translated, was regarded as referring to all economic fluctuations, without distinction.

ETYMOLOGICAL NOTE.—The word *Konjunktur* is derived from the Latin, but indirectly, seeing that it is a linguistic innovation which appears first in medieval astrology, being used in much the same sense as the word "constellation." By the seventeenth century, it had passed into the language of everyday life, with the meaning "state of affairs" or "contemporary conditions." From the end of the seventeenth century, it is used in commercial language with essentially the same significance as it has at the present day, namely, as an expression denoting the up-and-down movement of business. In the nineteenth century, the word established its position in German economic science (Lassalle, 1864, Schäffle, 1878). In everyday speech, and, also, in the language of literary discussion, the word has lately assumed a one-sided significance, for people speak simply of a *Konjunktur* when they mean a favorable "conjuncture," the peak of the cycle—as, for instance, in the phrase *Verbrauchskonjunktur* (consumption conjuncture). In scientific terminology, the word has, as we shall see, undergone a contraction of significance of another kind, having come to be used as a pregnant expression for a specific kind of economic fluctuation. When, however, we use the term *Konjunkturlehre* to describe the subject of the present study, we are employing the term in its wider meaning, as covering the whole interplay of economic forces.

Bibliography

LASSALLE, FERDINAND: Herr Bastiat Schulze von Delitzsch, "Reden und Schriften," Berlin, 1864.

SCHÄFFLE, ALBERT: "Bau und Leben des sozialen Körpers," Tübingen, 1878.

RÖPKE, WILHELM: "Die Konjunktur," Jena, 1922.

The Underlying Principle of Classification.

One of the most important foundations for the construction of a theory of business cycles (or "conjuncture")

50

was laid when means were discovered of dividing up the vast and, at first sight, dizzying complexity of economic interaction into a number of heterogeneous movement forms. At the present day, following the lines laid down by the Harvard Business School, such movement forms are usually classified as follows:

1. The fundamental course of movement (or secular trend).
2. Seasonal fluctuations.
3. Cyclical fluctuations ("conjuncture," in the narrower sense).
4. Miscellaneous random fluctuations.

Cyclical movements are frequently still further subdivided into long- and short-wave fluctuations or, in some cases, even into short-, medium-, and long-wave fluctuations.

This classification is, in the main, based on the formal distinctions of statistical science; it is unsatisfactory, however, because the underlying principle of classification is not clear. We prefer to rely on the contrast established above between changes in economic structure and cyclical fluctuations and to classify movement forms as follows:

1. Isolated changes (changes in structure), *viz.:*
   a. Discontinuous changes (*i.e.*, changes involving a breach in the course of development: displacements, collapses, dismemberments).
   b. Continuous changes (*i.e.*, changes involving no breach in development: expansion, transformation, regression).
2. Periodical fluctuations, *viz.:*
   a. Fluctuations occurring in a fixed rhythm (seasonal fluctuations).
   b. Fluctuations occurring in a free rhythm (business cycles—"conjuncture" in the narrower sense).

The great practical importance of distinguishing between the various movement forms is immediately evident. As soon, for instance, as one has identified an upward movement as an isolated continuous change, one can be certain that, while the movement will sooner or later come to a standstill, it does not conceal within itself the seeds of a consequent regression. It is no less important to be clear as

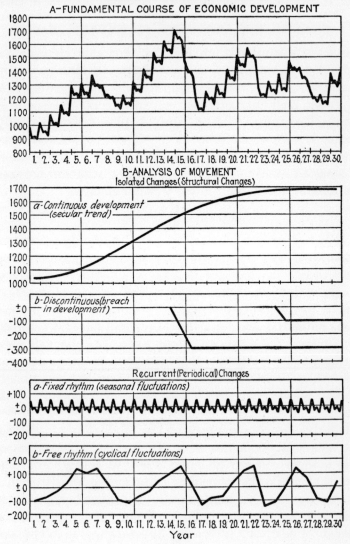

DIAGRAMMATIC ILLUSTRATION OF THE FORMS OF ECONOMIC MOVEMENT

A—FUNDAMENTAL COURSE OF ECONOMIC DEVELOPMENT

B—ANALYSIS OF MOVEMENT

Isolated Changes (Structural Changes)

a-Continuous development (secular trend)

b-Discontinuous (breach in development)

Recurrent (Periodical) Changes

a-Fixed rhythm (seasonal fluctuations)

b-Free rhythm (cyclical fluctuations)

Year

FIG. 3.

to whether a movement is seasonal and, therefore, bound to recur at a fixed interval of time or whether it is cyclical— *i.e.*, is certain to recur but at an uncertain interval of time.

1. ISOLATED, NON-RECURRENT (STRUCTURAL) CHANGES

As we postulate that isolated economic changes are subject to a system of laws analogous to that governing the birth and growth of organisms, we are accustomed to say that they are organic, constitutional, or structural. As we observe that such changes take place either gradually, and as it were in obedience to the dictates of some internal law, or suddenly and, for the most part, under the pressure of some external influence, we draw a distinction between continuous and discontinuous isolated changes.

A. DISCONTINUOUS CHANGES

It is relatively easy to detect and isolate discontinuous organic changes. For instance, it is fairly easy to represent statistically the changes undergone by the German economic system in consequence of the cession of territory under the Versailles treaty. The reduction in population, industrial and agricultural production, and turnover consequent on such an amputation can be expressed arithmetically. Again, the collapse of the Russian market in consequence of the revolution has had plainly visible effects on the importation of foodstuffs from Russia and the export to Russia of manufactured articles. Similarly, the consequences of the production of artificial nitrogen can be determined. In making calculations of this kind, a certain difficulty arises, of course, from the fact that, while the immediate consequences of discontinuous changes can be mechanically determined, it is not so easy to estimate their indirect effects. For instance, the cession of territory under the peace treaty involved not only the loss to Germany of specific economic activities but also a disturbance in communication and a displacement of centers throughout the whole country which necessitated expenditure on the part of the national economic system and, thus, resulted in an indirect loss of capital.

B. CONTINUOUS CHANGES

Continuous organic changes—whether defined as consisting in development, expansion, transformation regression or any other such modification—result from the most diverse causes. The problem is one which obtrudes itself at a thousand points of practical experience. Where an undertaking observes an upward movement in its turnover, it is of the greatest importance for it to find out definitely whether this is part of a general progressive development— a rising standard of life in an increasing population, let us say—or whether the phenomenon is merely one of a rhythmical character, which will later on be compensated by a corresponding downward movement. A similar problem may present itself—to take another example— in regard to the price situation. Is the downward tendency of the price level which we are at present experiencing in Europe and America an organic, constitutional change, specially connected with, for example, the rationalization of industry and business, or are we confronted by something of a cyclical character, by a phenomenon which may be, for instance, connected with a temporary process of liquidation, and which is bound, at a later stage, to recoil in a contrary direction? To take another case: If orders start coming in in increased numbers, and production can, in consequence, be expanded, the question necessarily arises whether the determining impulse is due to some rhythmic change either in income or in national stocks of commodities, so that the increased buying is due simply to an effort to replenish supplies which had been reduced during a period of liquidation by export or by unloading on the home market, or whether the demand for additional production is to be attributed to permanent necessities and interests—for example, the acquisition of new markets abroad or a modification in consumption (a change in dress fashions or new tastes in diet).

In many cases, the causal connection is so plainly recognizable that it is fairly easy to decide how far it is a question of some organic transformation—for instance, in the case of phenomena consequent on growth of population. But what are we to think of the powerful upward tendency of industrial production in the United States during the recent years? Is it due mainly to an altered division of labor in world economy, or has a cyclical upward movement in the American home market been, to a far greater extent, responsible? In other words, how far are we witnessing nothing but a development toward self-sufficiency, which is bound to come to a standstill within a measurable period of time, or an expansion of production of an entirely cyclical character?

As causal connections can only rarely be discovered with certainty, a formal arithmetical investigation is all that is usually attempted; an effort is made, that is to say, to establish a basic course of movement, or *trend*, with which the fluctuations observed may be related. A number of methods for determining trend are at our disposal.

A very frequently practicable though primitive one is the so-called "freehand" method; a smoothed line (either straight or curved) is drawn freehand so as to follow the main course of the line which represents the actually observed movements, without following its detailed fluctuations.

A more exact method consists in the use of *moving averages;* that is to say, averages are calculated in a specific manner from the numerical values for a series of years— for example, from the aggregate values for years 1 to 8, years 2 to 9, years 3 to 10, and so on. This gives a curve which, while avoiding the numerous small fluctuations of the purely empirical curve, shows the general direction of the curve's course.

The methods of determining trend, borrowed from *analytical geometry*, represent a further refinement. Such methods are employed in order to discover a basic curve

DIFFERENT METHODS OF REPRESENTING TREND

INDEX FIGURES OF PRICES OF RAW MATERIALS OF INDUSTRY
FOR GERMANY 1851-1913
1913=100

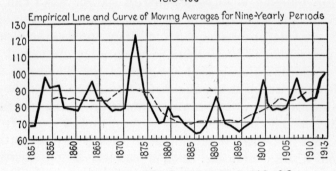

Empirical Line and Curve of Moving Averages for Nine-Yearly Periods

RAILWAY FREIGHT TRAFFIC 1890-1913

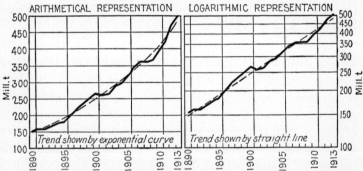

ARITHMETICAL REPRESENTATION   LOGARITHMIC REPRESENTATION

Trend shown by exponential curve   *Trend shown by straight line*

INDEX FIGURES OF PRICES OF INDUSTRIAL COMMODITIES FOR
ENGLAND, ACCORDING TO SAUERBECK, 1854-1913

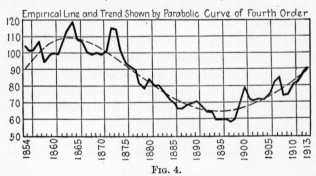

Empirical Line and Trend Shown by Parabolic Curve of Fourth Order

Fɪɢ. 4.

which obeys a simple mathematical law or, in other words, can be expressed in a simple mathematical equation (as for a straight line, a parabola, an exponential curve, etc.). Which function is to be selected in specific cases can be decided only separately for each individual case. Straight lines are frequently adequate, and they are also the easiest to determine. The deciding consideration in regard to the trend equation is that the sum of the squares of the differences between the empirical results and those shown by the trend should be a minimum—that is, the principle known as the "method of least squares" is taken over from the theory of errors of observation. A way of representing trend which suits this method consists in representing it by orthogonal functions; the use of these for calculating trend equations has been set out in detail by Dr. Lorenz in Suppl. 9 of *V.z.K.*

The very multiplicity of the possible methods of determining trend is an indication of the inherent difficulty of the operation. It is always, to some extent, a matter of arbitrary choice whether trend is to be expressed as a straight line (that is, a first-degree parabola) or as a parabola of the second, third, or higher degree. Trend, moreover, often wears a very different appearance according to the period for which it is to be determined. Even where we ascertain it for 10-year periods, our analysis can hold good only for the past, and the basic direction and course of the trend may vary in each future year—may, at any moment, slow down, come to a standstill, or revert to a contrary tendency. Thus, the trend curve does not signify the real ecliptic, around which the planetary curve of the business cycle fluctuates; it can never be anything but an arithmetical computation. Experience shows, however, that its use yields very valuable results.

2. PERIODICAL MOVEMENTS

While we have characterized isolated changes as organic, constitutional, or structural, we may venture, in many cases, to establish a contrast between them and periodically recurrent movements, calling the latter "functional phenomena," subject to the reservations required in using such a metaphorical expression—in this case, taken over from medical terminology. In any case, a whole series of those phenomena which we have called "isolated changes" have as it were the character of organic disturbances in contrast to the functional disturbances, which come under the heading of "recurrent movements." Thus, for example the loss of the Russian export market has the appearance of an organic injury to the German economic system, while the temporary falling off of imports observable during a crisis appears like a functional disturbance in an otherwise healthy economic body.

We distinguish between seasonal and cyclical fluctuations according to the time interval by which they are successively separated. Seasonal fluctuations succeed each other in fractions of a year; their rhythm is more or less fixed, like that of a pendulum or like the stroke of a machine. Cyclical fluctuations, on the other hand, stretch out beyond the limits of the year and occur in waves, with a free rhythm.

A. Fixed-rhythm Movements (Seasonal Fluctuations)

By "seasonal" fluctuations is meant periodical movements tied down to fixed chronological terms and owing their origin to the fact that economic processes and activities are distributed over the year in a definite order of time, just as the times for meals are spread over the day. They are, in part, "artificially" tied to particular terms or seasons by institutions, customs, or regulations; there is also a certain "natural" distribution of economic processes and activities over the year, determined by seasonal changes.

"Artificial" Seasonal Fluctuations.

Those processes are dependent on institutions and regulations—and are, therefore, "artificial" in character—which are bound up with the system by which payment transactions are regulated (settlement of accounts by stock exchanges and banks on the last day of the month or on quarter day, involving regularly recurring fluctuations in the note circulation and money rates). Under the same head may be classified, for example, increases in consumption due to specific habits and customs (as at Christmas, Easter, and Whitsuntide).

"Natural" Seasonal Fluctuations.

Those fluctuations are of "natural" origin which are due to the influence of meteorological factors—for example, seasonal movements in tourist traffic, retail trade in textiles, fuel consumption, building-trade activity. The harvest produces the most widespread effects; it affects railway traffic figures, and the labor market, its financing influences the money market; it also influences the price level and foreign trade. It is difficult enough in all the above cases to trace the connection between cause and effect, and it is absolutely impossible to isolate the various intermediate factors which intervene between cause and effect, in cases where various kinds of seasonal influences are at work simultaneously. This happens where direct meteorological influences and the effects of the harvest unite with the "artificial" moments to form annually recurring seasonal fluctuations. The curves of the money market and of foreign trade are thus affected. Such fluctuations can be expressed only in a formal, arithmetical manner. A number of methods are available for this purpose.

Short-period Seasonal Rhythm.

The group of fixed-rhythm movements includes, in addition to "seasonal movements" properly so-called in different branches of economic phenomena, various periodical movements of *briefer duration* the investigation of which has lately been taken in hand. The special obstacle to any precise determination of these fluctuations consists in the fact that observations involving consecutive notations for extremely brief units of time—the day or even the hour—lie, to some extent, outside the normal business procedure of an undertaking and presuppose calculations of an extremely complex character.[1]

On the basis of detailed business reports, Grünbaum has succeeded in establishing the following short-period fluctuations in retail-trade activity:

1. *The Movement within Each Month.*—The activity represented by a day's sales in a normal month (with 25 selling days) rises, in typical cases, to a very high peak on the last day of the month and then falls away, at first somewhat sharply and then by degrees more gradually. The downward movement in turnover, after a brief check about the middle of the month, continues immediately after the fifteenth day of the month and reaches its lowest point on about the twenty-second selling day. The last two days before the last day of the month already begin to show a certain revival.

2. *The Movement within Each Week.*—The activity represented by a single selling day in a normal week undergoes, in typical cases, a revival around the week-end (Friday, Saturday, and Monday). The middle of the week is characterized by particularly small sales. The intensity of the weekly rhythm varies according to the social classification of the customers; it is most pronounced in businesses with a purely working-class clientele and for commodities intended mainly or exclusively for male buyers.

3. *The Movement within Each Day.*—The activity during the separate selling hours of a normal selling day shows, in typical cases, a temporary liveliness in the late morning hours, a sharp fall round midday, and a maximum activity in the evening hours. The daily rhythm also varies in intensity according to the class of customer.

The motive factor, in the case of the monthly rhythm, consists in the buying habits of the salaried classes, that

[1] A detailed study of short-period fluctuations is contained in a work by Heinz Grünbaum, "Die Umsatzschwankungen des Einzelhandels als Problem der Betriebspolitik" (fluctuations in retail-trade turnover as a problem of industrial policy), Berlin, 1929.

of the weekly rhythm in those of the wage-earning classes, together with the increased time facilities for buying enjoyed by employed persons on Saturday afternoon. The determining factors in the daily rhythm consist essentially in the restrictions placed by employment on time facilities for buying and in certain buying habits of the consumers.

Short-period fluctuations—plainly perceptible fixed-rhythm movements within the month, the week, or the day—are characteristic of those branches of economic activity which are in the closest touch with the ultimate consumer and, therefore, especially of retail trade, transportation, and the electricity-supply industry; they also regularly affect such sensitive elements in the economic system as money rates and the note circulation.

There are a number of methods available for the *arithmetical measurement of seasonal normal values*. Apart from the simple computation of averages, these methods can be classified in two groups—those in which the percentual ratio of the value for each month to a specific average is calculated and those in which the ratio is calculated from month to month. In employing the first group of methods, the average taken may be the yearly mean, or a moving 12 months' average, or a trend. A method which is frequently used on account of its simplicity consists in relating the monthly values to the mean for the year; this process, in many cases, yields very useful results. A method in the second group is the "link-relative" method expounded by Professor Persons in vol. I of the *Review of Economic Statistics*.

Alterations in Seasonal Fluctuations.

The measurement of seasonal movements gives rise to difficulties similar to those encountered in determining trend; for just as the basic direction of the series as expressed in a trend may change at any moment, so the seasonal movement, also, can never be said to have been determined once and for all. Both the "natural" and the "artificial" seasonal influences may undergo modifications, either through a displacement of chronological terms or

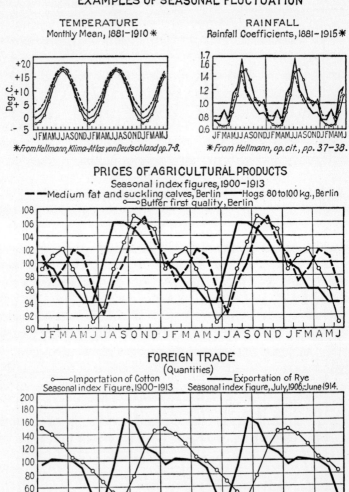

EXAMPLES OF SEASONAL FLUCTUATION

TEMPERATURE
Monthly Mean, 1881–1910 ✳

RAINFALL
Rainfall Coefficients, 1881–1915 ✳

✳from Hellmann, Klima-Atlas von Deutschland pp. 7-8.

✳ From Hellmann, op. cit., pp. 37-38.

PRICES OF AGRICULTURAL PRODUCTS
Seasonal index figures, 1900–1913
– –Medium fat and suckling calves, Berlin ——Hogs 80 to 100 kg., Berlin
o—o Butter first quality, Berlin

FOREIGN TRADE
(Quantities)
o—o Importation of Cotton   —— Exportation of Rye
Seasonal index Figure, 1900–1913   Seasonal index Figure, July,1906–June 1914.

Fig. 5a.

through an increase or a decrease in the deviation from the norm. Such modifications involve a change in (so to speak) the structure of a seasonal movement—to use a somewhat paradoxical expression.

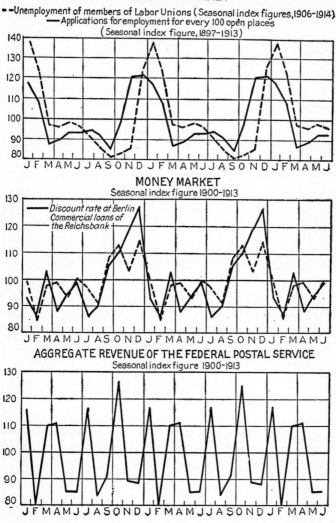

LABOR MARKET

– –Unemployment of members of Labor Unions (Seasonal index figures,1906-1914)
—— Applications for employment for every 100 open places
(Seasonal index figure, 1897-1913)

MONEY MARKET

Seasonal index figure 1900-1913

—— Discount rate at Berlin
Commercial loans of
— — the Reichsbank

AGGREGATE REVENUE OF THE FEDERAL POSTAL SERVICE

Seasonal index figure 1900-1913

FIG. 5*b*.

In the first place, the artificial seasonal influences are, as will be readily understood, liable to modification.

An example may help to make this clear. In the prewar period, the flow of payments was far greater in Germany on quarter days than at any other time. This pendulum-like deviation has since undergone a remarkable transformation, and a specifically quarterly movement in the flow of payments is at present perceptible only to a slight extent. It is clear that payment by the month has taken the place of payment by the quarter not only in the case of civil servants' salaries but also in many other fields of economic life (rents, for example)—apart from the fairly numerous quarter-day payments which have altogether disappeared (for example, a large proportion of interest payments on mortgages).[1] It is noteworthy that business practice failed to discover this important transformation in the payment system for itself but persisted for a long time in methods based on the requirements of the old system. In proportion as quarterly payments are again increasing, a more marked quarterly movement is once more gradually— since the middle of 1927—making its appearance.

The postwar period has, however, also involved changes in the "structure" of seasonal fluctuations in many other fields, and fresh changes of this kind are taking place under our eyes. After the inflation of the currency, the seasonal fluctuations had, to a very great extent, receded into the background, in contrast to structural and cyclical movements. They are now once again securing a much firmer footing. A particularly clear example of the manner in which the whole system of economic movement is gradually reassuming a more markedly seasonal character is afforded by the curves for the textile industry. Retail trade in textiles, which by its nature is necessarily—under any circumstances—seasonal, transmits the seasonal movement, under normal conditions, to the clothing trade and the textile industry as well. After the inflation, this transmission practically ceased. The curves show that seasonal fluctuations have lately become more noticeable again in the clothing trade and are gradually beginning

[1] See *V.z.K.*, vol. 1, No. 3, p. 20 (results of Dr. Hermann's researches).

to reappear in the textile industry.[1] Another excellent example is afforded by the changes in the balance sheet of the bank of issue. The movement of business credits is, however, highly instructive on yet other grounds, for it shows us that seasonal movements are, in turn, also influenced by the cyclical situation, just as cyclical movements are influenced by structural changes (see above, p. 25 *ff*). During the revival of 1924, and, also, during the sharp recession which took place during the crisis of 1925 to 1926, the seasonal movement was practically washed out by the cyclical wave, to reappear in a more strongly marked form both during the depression of 1926 and, also, during the periods of prosperity in 1925 and, more particularly, in 1927 to 1928—so much so that it becomes very difficult to separate the seasonal and cyclical fluctuations. It is, thus, clear that seasonal fluctuations are more clearly perceptible wherever economic activity remains at a steady level.

While, therefore, the various economic movement forms are, at times, inextricably entangled in each other, the measurement of seasonal fluctuations is, nevertheless, in general, of very great practical value—even though it can be carried out in only an inadequate and a makeshift manner. A reminiscence from the prewar period may help to show how indispensable is the fundamental differentiation between seasonal and cyclical fluctuations. Before the World War, a special tightness in the money market was always observable round quarter day, in consequence of the seasonal expansion in payment transactions at such times. Bendixen used to point out that it was absurd automatically to raise the bank rate on that account. He might have said, in the language of business-cycle theory, that the manipulation of the bank rate was justified only if it took place with a view to checking or accelerating cyclical reactions and that seasonal fluctuations, being more or less automatic, had absolutely no need of an artificial corrective.

---

[1] See *V.z.K.*, vol. 2, No. 4, pp. 14 *ff*. (results of Dr. Donner's researches).

A contemporary instance may also be quoted. The press, at the moment of writing (end of July, 1928), is pointing out that the interim balance sheets published by the credit banks show a remarkably heavy falling off in the number of debtors; and the conclusion is being drawn that this represents an essential easing in the cyclical situation. As a matter of fact, this phenomenon is of a purely seasonal character and may be observed every year at midsummer.

"Sliding" Seasonal Fluctuations.

The fundamental principle already laid down applies, also, to the case of seasonal fluctuations; the student should endeavor not to measure them on purely diagrammatic lines but, so far as possible, to investigate their causes. Thus, in the case of foreign trade, for instance, the "seasonal peaks" which stand out during the summer and autumn months may be observed to shift frequently in the course of a number of years from one month to another. A purely arithmetical treatment of the curve of foreign trade would, therefore, easily lead to false conclusions in regard to the seasonal fluctuation. Not so, however, if one bears in mind that the above-mentioned variation depends, for the most part, on what countries are, respectively, prominent as sources of imports or as destinations for exports; for seasonal fluctuations in foreign trade are determined primarily by buying and selling conditions abroad, so that the moment at which a commodity crosses the frontier depends on the distance between the exporting and importing countries.[1]

Bibliography

From the very comprehensive literature regarding the calculation of seasonal alterations and trend, reference may be made to:

ALTSCHUL: "Berechnung und Ausschaltung von Saisonschwankungen," Karlsruhe, 1927.

BOWLEY and SMITH: Seasonal Variations in Finance, Prices, and Industries. *Special Memorandum* 7, London and Cambridge Economic Service, July, 1927.

[1] According to the studies of Dr. Bühler and Dr. Bauer in *V.z.K.*

BOWLEY, A. L.: "Element of Statistics," 5th ed., London, 1926.

DONNER, OTTO: Die Saisonschwankungen als Problem der Konjunktur-forschung, *V.z.K.*, suppl. 6, where further references are given.

CHADDOCK, R. E.: "Principles and Methods of Statistics," New York, 1925.

CRUM, W. L., and PATTEN: "An Introduction to the Methods of Economic Statistics," Chicago, 1925.

DAY, E. E.: "Statistical Analysis," New York, 1925.

HENNIG, HERMANN: Die Ausschaltung von saisonmäszigen und säkularen Schwankungen aus Wirtschaftskurven, *V.z.K.*, vol. 1, suppl. 1; Die Analyse von Wirtschaftskurven, *V.z.K.*, special issue, 4.

KING, W. I.: "Elements of Statistical Methods," New York, 1924.

LORENZ, P.: Der Trend, ein Beitrag zur Methode seiner Berechnung und seiner Auswertung für die Untersuchung von Wirtschaftskurven, *V.z.K.*, special number 9.

MILLS, F. C.: "Statistical Methods Applied to Economics and Business," New York, 1924.

PERSONS, W. M.: Explanation of the Data and Methods Used in the Index of General Business Conditions, *Review of Economic Statistics*, 1919. Comparison of an Individual Concern with the Harvard Index of General Business, Harvard Economic Service, Cambridge, 1924.

VANDERBLUE, HOMER B.: "Problems in Business Economics," Chicago, 1924.

See, also, various articles in:

RIETZ, H. L. (ed.): "Handbook of Mathematical Statistics," New York, 1924.

B. FREE-RHYTHM MOVEMENTS (BUSINESS CYCLES)

Negative Definition.

When we have eliminated from the general complex of economic movements the isolated changes (continuous and discontinuous) and from the periodically recurrent movements which remain the seasonal fluctuations, a series of movements remains which are called "business cycles" (or "conjuncture," in the true sense of the term). The foregoing represents a negative definition of business cycles—they are brought to light as something that remains after a process of elimination has been carried out. Such a method of definition is unsatisfactory as long as no possibility exists of determining the course of cyclical movements directly and positively.

Positive Definition.

In order to form a positive conception of business cycles by a purely abstract method, we must begin by presupposing a perfect circulation of money and goods in the national economic system. Business cycles are disturbances in this "state of equilibrium"—however caused—which lead to a corresponding deviation in the opposite direction or, in other words, proceed in accordance with the law of reaction. Isolated organic changes are not covered by this definition, because they are, in a certain sense, final. Seasonal fluctuations resemble cyclical movements in respect of their recurrent character but, as has already been stated, differ from them fundamentally (a) in respect of the duration of the fluctuations, the former being based on fractions of a single year and the latter extending beyond the year, and (b) in respect of their character, seasonal fluctuations recurring in a fixed, and business cycles in a free, rhythm, so that the former are chronologically determined with almost complete rigidity, while the latter succeed each other at fairly indeterminate intervals. This superficial contrast is based on more profound differences. Seasonal fluctuations proceed from a distribution of economic activities over a period of time; this distribution is fully realized in advance and is, moreover, generally speaking, well adapted to circumstances. Persons engaged in the building industry, farmers, persons who earn their living in the dressmaking trade, all accommodate themselves in their work and their general arrangements to the seasonal character of their employment. A business cycle, on the contrary, takes place in an altogether planless fashion and leads to situations of tension and difficulty which urgently require solution. As every cyclical movement issues in a recoil—as has been said above, the problem of final causation does not concern us here— the business cycle may be defined as the *total complex of economic reaction phenomena*.

Seasonal Fluctuations and Business Cycles.

The distinction between seasonal fluctuations and business cycles assumes special significance if one agrees, for instance, with Prof. Henry L. Moore, the American investigator,[1] in attributing the business cycle to Venus' revolution about the sun once every eight years, which in his view exercises a decisive influence on weather and harvests. Even if one accepted the view that business cycles are marked by a fixed periodicity of this kind, one would not be justified in assimilating them, so far as their essential nature is concerned, to seasonal fluctuations. For seasonal fluctuations arise from a distribution of economic transactions over a period of time directly necessitated by the seasons of the year, while business cycles, on the contrary, are forced on the economic system indirectly by the occurrence of periods of economic tension which press for relaxation or, conversely, by the surplus forces which are set free in a period of relaxation and which lead to a fresh period of tension.

Economic Reactions.

Among the most important achievements of the earlier political economists—to some extent the mercantile school, but more particularly the classical economists—was the discovery of this kind of reaction. After Adam Smith had brought to light the miracle of the adaptation of supply to demand, notwithstanding anarchical productive methods, through the regularizing influence of prices, further examples of such reactions were constantly discovered and were assembled into a picture of harmonious interplay among the various economic forces. Ricardo drew attention to the existence of a "mechanism" by which the movement of foreign trade was connected up with the supplies of gold held by the central bank and showed how the differences between the home and foreign price levels brought about a balancing movement. He perceived similar connections between wage changes and the movement of population figures. Further examples are the connection between interest rates and commodity prices, the interdependence of commodity prices, and the relation between commodity prices and wages.

[1] "Generating Economic Cycles," 1923.

The earlier political economists have identified the majority of the reaction phenomena which occur in the economic system, for they have perceived the "automatism," or the self-regulation, of the system in almost all its details. They contented themselves, however, with demonstrating the existence of such an "automatism" and made no attempt to investigate the manner in which reactions succeeded each other. They wished only to show that disturbances in equilibrium were overcome without outside intervention by the dispensation of the economic principle and that tension must always end in relaxation. They never looked into the resultant movement processes as such. The fact is, however, that these vary in intensity and duration most essentially; for action and reaction succeed each other in some cases with great rapidity, in others at an interval of months, years, or even decades. A change in money rates usually leads very rapidly to an alteration in the rate of exchange; for instance, if the bank rate in London rises above the Berlin rates, funds flow so rapidly from Germany to England that in respect simply of the displacement of interest a good hundred million marks get transferred in Germany to the other side of the balance sheet—which must exercise a considerable influence, seeing that Germany's turnover of international payments amounts in normal circumstances to only a few hundred million marks each week. A change in wholesale prices influences the cost of living with distinctly less rapidity; and changes in the cost of living also react only after some considerable time on wholesale prices, by way of reduced consumption. The position as between interest rates in the money and capital markets, respectively, is similar; before the World War, the reaction interval usually amounted to some eight or ten months. The reaction interval in the mutual interplay of the money market, the commodity market, and the stock market is at present still longer.

The total complex of reaction phenomena forms a complete general notion, so that the business cycle stands out in a definite form, which, of course, has no final or absolute character but holds true only for a given form of economic organization; for the particular reaction phenomena vary considerably in character from one national economic system, or one epoch, to another.

Bibliography

On reactions, see:

SMITH, ADAM: "The Wealth of Nations," 1776.

RICARDO, DAVID: "Principles of Political Economy and Taxation," London, 1817.

MILL, JAMES: "Elements of Political Economy," London, 1821.

SCHUMPETER, JOSEPH: "Wesen und Hauptinhalt der theoretischen Nationalökonomie," Munich, 1908.

WALRAS, B.: "Elements d'économie politique pure," 4th ed., 1900.

BRIEFS, G.: "Untersuchungen zur klassischen Nationalökonomie," Jena, 1915.

SECTION II

PHASES OF THE BUSINESS CYCLE

CHAPTER IV

THE TRADITIONAL CLASSIFICATION OF THE PHASES

The Problem of Classification.

The main object of business-cycle theory is to investigate cyclical (or "conjunctural") movements in the narrower sense—that is, variations of the economic elements recurring in free rhythm.

The business-cycle rhythm consists in the regular recurrence of specific economic configurations and is thus made up of movement divisions which, in accordance with ordinary scientific terminology, we shall call "phases." The different phases together form a single cycle. We have, therefore, now to face two groups of questions:

1. What are the determining characteristics of these configurations and phases, and how are they to be demarcated from each other?

2. What is the position as regards the duration of the various phases, and at what intervals do they usually recur?

These questions, though they specially concern business cycles and not economic movements as a whole, had, of course, been considered before economists had learned how to separate business cycles from other movement forms. Starting from the primitive vocabulary of the stock exchange, with its "booms" and "slumps," the scientific economists have gradually elaborated methods of constantly increasing precision and scope for the definition of the separate phases. In the beginning, however, attention was concentrated on the cyclical phase which possesses the greatest dramatic interest, namely, the economic crisis.

Juglar's Threefold Classification.

If we agree to disregard certain *obiter dicta* of previous authors, we may say that Juglar was the first investigator to make a thoroughgoing attempt to fit the crisis into the framework of the business cycle as a whole and to treat it as one of the constantly recurring phases in the wavelike movement of economic life. He divided the business cycles into the following three phases: prosperity, crisis, and liquidation.

Among the results of the more modern investigation of crises and business cycles—the attempts made during the intervening period need not be considered here, especially as they did not lead to the discovery of anything really new—we may next refer to two subdivisions: (1) Spiethoff's "theory of economic alternation" and (2) the Harvard analysis of the business cycle.

Spiethoff's Classification.

Like Juglar, Spiethoff distinguishes between stagnation, prosperity, and crisis; but he renders this classification more subtle by further subdividing, so as finally to distinguish six separate phases: decline, first upward movement, second upward movement, full prosperity, capital shortage, crisis. His outline is as follows:[1]

Stagnation:
>   *Decline.*—Fall in capital investment, consumption of iron, production of iron, interest on loans.
>   *First Upward Movement.*—Fall in production of iron, consumption of iron and capital investments ceases, and a slight upward movement begins.
>   *Second Upward Movement.*—Considerable increase in capital investments, and especially share investment. Consumption of iron approaches the peak of the previous period of prosperity.

Prosperity:
>   *Full Prosperity.*—Rising interest on loans, consumption of iron.
>   *Capital Shortage.*—Difficulty in obtaining capital, fall in capital investments, rise in rate of interest on loans, recession in security prices, decline in house building, fall in the consumption of iron.

[1] See SPIETHOFF, article on crises in "Handwörterbuch der Staatswissenschaften" 4th ed.

Crisis:
Collapse of credit, mass suspension of payments.

The Harvard Committee's Five Phases.

The Harvard Committee has put forward the following fivefold classification of phases in the business cycle:[1]

Phase 1. Depression:
  a. Security prices begin to advance; speculative activity increases.
  b. Commodity prices begin to decline; business activity is sluggish.
  c. Rates on commercial paper decline; bank reserves increase.

Phase 2. Recovery:
  a. Speculative activity is marked.
  b. Business activity recovers; commodity prices begin to advance.
  c. Rates on commercial paper begin to advance late in this phase of the cycle.

Phase 3. Business prosperity:
  a. Speculative activity is checked.
  b. Business activity and commodity prices continue to increase.
  c. Rates on commercial paper continue to advance while bank reserves decrease.

Phase 4. Financial strain:
  a. Security prices decline sharply; speculative activity is depressed.
  b. The upward tendency of business activity and commodity prices is checked.
  c. Rates on commercial paper remain high or stiffen, and the banking situation is strained.

Phase 5. Industrial crisis:
  a. Prices of securities reach bottom, and speculative markets are panicky.
  b. Commodities are liquidated, prices fall, and business activity slumps badly.
  c. Rates on commercial paper reach maximum, and bank reserves reach minimum. The crisis breaks.

The differences of classification are due mainly to differences in the emphasis laid on various characteristic features in the business cycle. In Juglar's view, the most important feature is the part played by the banks of issue; for Spiethoff, it is capital investments, which according to him are reflected in interest rates on loans and production of iron and, also, in consumption of iron; while in that of the Harvard Committee it is the interrelationship among the three markets (security, money, and commodity).

[1] *Review of Economic Statistics,* 1919.

The Classification Established by the Institut für Konjunkturforschung.

It seems more appropriate to select a method of subdivision implying the least possible connection with any specific theory of business cycles or any particular feature in the process of economic movement. In distinguishing the various phases, we should take account of the processes which take place under both aspects of the economic system (industrial and financial); we should consider the facts in regard both to movements of capital and to variations in income, as well as those concerning production, storage, consumption, and foreign trade. The outline of the course of the business cycle established by the author in *V.z.K.* is based on the results of business-cycle observation in Germany during the last few decades, in other words, both during the period just before the World War, and since the stabilization of the currency. It pays no attention to particular deviations from the general rule, nor is it intended to suggest that the business-cycle rhythm is always identical. Both the intensity and the duration of the fluctuations may vary.

OUTLINE OF THE COURSE OF THE BUSINESS CYCLE IN GERMANY

1. Depression

Financial aspect:

The Markets.—Commodity prices vary only slightly, but downward rather than upward; prices rise, those of fixed-interest-bearing securities moving in advance of dividend-bearing stocks; the money market is in a thoroughly fluid state.

The Flow of Income.—The income and (so far as it is elastic) the expenditure both of the entrepreneur and of labor are at a minimum.

Industrial aspect:

Production.—The production of commodities reaches a minimum, the production of producers' goods falling in advance of that of consumers' goods.

Foreign Trade.—Stagnant imports, but rapidly increasing exports.

2. Recovery

Financial aspect:

The Markets.—Rising commodity prices; boom in the stock market; which, toward the end of this phase, turns into a downward movement;

at first, the money market remains fluid; money rates rise only as the phase proceeds.

The Flow of Income.—The entrepreneur's income begins to increase sharply, labor's income slowly follows, elastic expenditure begins to increase.

Industrial aspect:

Production advances all along the line.

Foreign Trade.—Imports increase, exports oscillate about the level already attained.

3. Full Prosperity

Financial aspect:

The Markets.—Considerable hardening of the money market; financing and credit difficult to obtain; further downward movement in stock prices; commodity prices stable or tending to crumble; partial but pronounced displacement in price relations (as between consumption and capital goods).

The Flow of Income.—Entrepreneur's income stops increasing and, toward the end of this phase, begins to fall. Labor's income, also elastic expenditure, remains for a time, generally speaking, at the level already attained.

Industrial aspect:

Production.—Production stops increasing; production of producers' goods begins to fall, while that of consumer's goods goes on increasing for a time.

Foreign Trade.—The increase in imports is arrested; exports continue to fluctuate about the level already attained.

4. Crisis

Financial aspect:

The Markets.—Commodity prices drop; slump on the stock market; extremely severe credit and financing conditions, leading to collapse of numerous businesses; the money market relaxes.

The Flow of Income.—Sharp drop in entrepreneur's income; more gradual fall in labor's income and elastic expenditure.

Industrial aspect:

Production.—Sharp drop in production of producer's goods, and, later on, in consumer's goods.

Foreign Trade.—Sharp drop in imports.

More recent reflections have led me, as I shall explain, to take account of yet another principle in classifying the phases of business cycles. Before dealing with this subject, however, we shall have to consider the question of the so-called "long-wave" economic movements, which dominate the whole problem of phase classification.

CHAPTER V

LONG-WAVE ECONOMIC MOVEMENTS[1]

The Problem and the Method of Measurement.

While each business cycle may be considered as representing a wave—with a wave crest and a wave trough—the separate cycles appear to constitute together a further and wider rhythmical movement, in the same way as short waves together constitute a long wave or swell. If one limits one's observations to a few decades, one may easily confuse this long-wave movement with trend. We must, however, be clear as to the clearly marked logical distinction between the long-wave movement and trend (and isolated variations, in general), for it definitely belongs to the class of recurrent economic movements; it is a cyclical phenomenon and is dominated by the reaction principle. It must, however, be admitted that our information in regard to these movements is very defective, especially as we cannot carry our observations back even so far as 150 years, so that we can consider only less than three of these long waves.

The problem of long-wave movements has been investigated with great thoroughness by De Wolff and Kondratiev. For the purpose of measuring waves, they began by smoothing out the fluctuations of the business cycle by means of moving averages[2] for periods covering

[1] Based, for the most part, on matter already published by the author in *V.z.K.*, vol. 3, No. 1A.

[2] Kondratiev reaches the conclusion for England, France, the United States, and Germany, that three long waves can be distinguished since the early nineties of the eighteenth century, namely:

1. Upward movement to 1810–1817, downward to 1844–1851.
2. Upward movement to 1870–1875, downward to 1890–1896.
3. Upward movement to 1914–1920, probable downward movement from then onward.

9 years—this period being selected because the duration of the business cycles during the last century was generally from 7 to 11 years. This method of measurement, however, involves a considerable risk of obliterating the characteristic demarcations between the various cycles, as the averages mechanically overlap or fall short of the limits between the business cycles. It might, therefore, be better to compute an average for each separate cycle. If this method be adopted, each average will cover a greater or smaller number of annual index numbers, according to the duration of the respective cycles. It must, of course,

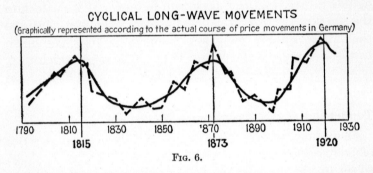

CYCLICAL LONG-WAVE MOVEMENTS

(Graphically represented according to the actual course of price movements in Germany)

Fig. 6.

be presupposed that the precise duration of each cycle is known, for the course of the curve thus obtained depends essentially on the exact years covered by the average in each case. If we measure the long waves on these lines, we shall find that, as far as German economic conditions are concerned, the phenomena of long waves is observable only for the money-volume series and not for the physical-volume series.

(See *Archiv für Sozialwissenschaft und Sozialpolitik*, vol. 56, Part 3, p. 590, 1926.)

De Wolff distinguishes the following cycles:

Ebb tide..................................	1826 to 1850
Springtide...............................	1851 to 1873
Ebb tide..................................	1874 to 1895
Springtide...............................	1896 to 1913

(See "Der lebendige Marxismus," pp. 30 *ff.*, Jena, 1924.)

1. THE PHYSICAL-VOLUME SERIES

The Movement of Physical-volume Series.

Let us begin by considering the physical-volume series, on the lines laid down above. The development of industrial production is, to a certain extent, well represented for longer periods by the consumption of coal and pig iron. Both series—consumption of coal and consumption of pig iron—show, however, an upward movement so rapid and constant that we shall succeed better in bringing out the cyclical fluctuations and other wave movements if we base our examination on the per capita figures rather than the aggregate figures. If we calculate the average per capita quota for each cycle, we shall see that these quotas increased from cycle to cycle down to the outbreak of the World War. The drop which took place after the collapse has, since the stabilization of the currency, been pretty well smoothed out.

Tendencies of the Quantitative Movement.

Should one decide to assume that from now on a series of increases similar to that of the prewar period is about to set in, the average yearly percentage increase might be reckoned at about 4 per cent for consumption of coal and about 5 per cent for consumption of pig iron. The World War has, of course, involved the most important structural changes in this connection. The industrial expansion of the nineteenth century was primarily an extending process, rendered possible not only by progress in technique and organization but also by the opening up of new markets. This development has now, to some extent, come to an end, particularly since the great fields of economic activity overseas have begun to direct their energies toward the attainment of economic self-sufficiency. Europe, moreover, has, for the time being, surrendered the lead in economic progress to the United States. The view can nevertheless hardly be accepted that the development which characterized German economic life before the war is to be regarded as terminated; for there are, in any case, still certain strongly progressive forces inherent

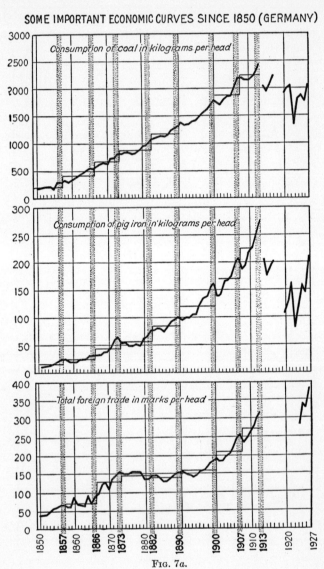

SOME IMPORTANT ECONOMIC CURVES SINCE 1850 (GERMANY)

Consumption of coal in kilograms per head

Consumption of pig iron in kilograms per head

Total foreign trade in marks per head

FIG. 7a.

in the German economic system (technique, professional education, organization), though it is, of course, possible

that these forces may tend toward internal economic
expansion rather than to the development of foreign

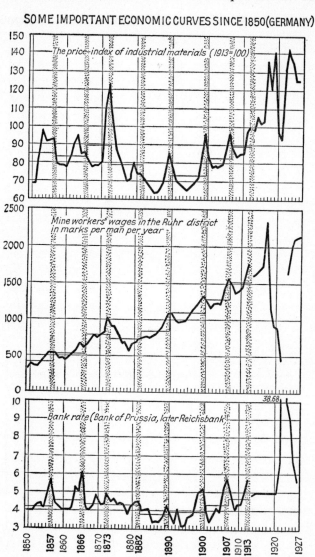

FIG. 7b.

trade. Such tendencies may, for the present, and particularly for the duration of the reconstruction period, find

expression in an average annual increase in industrial production of several per cent.

2. THE MONEY-VOLUME SERIES

The Movement of Price Series.

The course taken by money values during the last century was quite different. Whereas in the case of physical quantities the averages vary from one cycle to another only as regards the degree of expansion which they show (so that the resultant movement is, perhaps, in the nature of a trend but is not a "long-wave cyclical movement"), in the case of money values, on the other hand, the averages sometimes show a rise but sometimes a distinct fall. Their variations plainly reveal a movement over and above the ordinary business cycle, with phases of from 25 to 30 years. In England, according to Sauerbeck's figures, the index of commodity prices rose from about 1790 to 1815 and fell from 1815 to 1850. In Germany, a similar movement may well have taken place. From 1850 to the seventies, the average of money values (prices, wages, interest rates) for each cycle moved upward, to fall sharply during the next two cycles. The last three business cycles of the prewar period were again accompanied by a sharp upward movement in money values, so that in the years immediately before the war the price level of the seventies had just about been recovered.

Causes of the Long-wave Movement in Money Values.

At the present stage of investigation, it does not appear possible to account fully for the phenomenon of long-wave movements in money values. A certain number of interconnections do, however, obtrude themselves. In the first place, it can be shown that the great European wars have begun the upward course of the long-wave movements and that the downward movement has set in after the end of each respective war (Kondratiev has also noted this fact). This statement applies equally (a) to the Napoleonic wars, (b) to the period of the Crimean

War, the American Civil War, the Austro-Prussian and the Franco-Prussian War, and (c) to the period of time covering the Spanish-American War, the Boer War, the Russo-Japanese War, the Balkan War, and the World War. Secondly, it has been pointed out (by Sombart) that the price movement which began in the seventies is to be accounted for by reference to gold production and the gold standard; the spread of the gold standard throughout the world from the seventies so intensified the demand for gold (it is said) that the price of gold rose and general prices fell in consequence. Conversely, the extremely rapid increase in the production of precious metals from the nineties, in conjunction with the immense expansion of the credit system, is held to have been responsible for the rise in prices during recent decades. A connection may be established between the depression in Europe during the seventies and eighties (and the low level of prices during the same period) and the opening up of fields of colonization overseas.

The establishment of these interconnections must satisfy us for the present. It is, of course, by no means certain how far they are purely fortuitous. But even supposing the phenomena referred to have been respectively connected by the operation of some natural law, it would still be scarcely possible to say how far the appearance of long-wave cyclical movements has been due to some part or to the sum total of the associated phenomena in question or, indeed, to form any adequate idea of the nature of the chain of causes. In any case, it is not altogether improbable that we may be justified in counting on a general tendency toward falling prices for some considerable time, as from the end of the World War. A *prima facie* argument in favor of this view is afforded by the observation that industrialization in the greatest oversea economic areas is advancing continually and that, in general, the technique of industrial production is making further progress. Cassel assumes that a downward pressure on prices is also exerted from the financial side; he is expecting a fall in the production of gold in the Transvaal in proportion as price conditions there adapt themselves to those on the world market and as the mines are exhausted. On the other hand, it should be noted that since the World War the transition from a gold-currency system to a gold-reserve system has been universally completed and that credit systems have been so developed that adjustment to a rising demand for currency has become progressively easier.

Bibliography

Van Gelderen: Springvloed beschouwingen over industrielle entwikkling en prisbeweging, *De Nieuwe Tijd*, pp. 253–277, 369–384, 445–464, 1913.

Sombart, Werner: "Der moderne Kapitalismus," vol. 3, Part 2, p. 564.

Aftalion, Albert: "Les crises périodiques de surproduction," 2 vols., Paris, 1913.

Spiethoff, Arthur: Krisen, "Handwörterbuch der Staatswissenschaften," 4th ed.

De Wolff: Prosperitäts- und Depressionsperioden, "Der lebendige Marxismus," pp. 13 *ff.*, Jena, 1924.

Kondratiev: Die langen Wellen der Konjunktur, *Archiv für Sozialwissenschaft und Sozialpolitik*, vol. 56, Part 3, 1926. See, in this connection, Oparin's critical analysis of the "long waves of cyclical fluctuations" of Professor Kondratiev in the publications of the Economic Institute, Moscow, 1928.

Parvus: "Handelskrisis und Gewerkschaften," 1902.

Kitchin: Cycles and Trends in Economic Factors, *Harvard Business Review*, 1923.

Tugan-Baranowsky, Michael von: "Studien zur Theorie und Geschichte der Handelskrisen in England," German ed., Jena, 1901.

Mitchell, Wesley C.: "Business Cycles," 2d ed., vol. 1, pp. 226–231, 1927.

CHAPTER VI

PREWAR BUSINESS CYCLES

A Brief Outline of the History of Business Cycles

Since the first half of the nineteenth century, cyclical fluctuations, the duration of which was at first about eleven years but in course of time gradually became much shorter, stand out with far more clearness than do the "long waves" dealt with in the preceding chapter. These are the wave movements which one has in mind when one refers simply to business cycles. They have hitherto been relatively easy to distinguish from each other, because their course has been plainly divided into sections by business crises.

Forerunners of the Business Crisis.

We may see forerunners of the peculiar phenomenon known as the "business crisis" in the sensational panics which accompanied the introduction of the stock-exchange system. Such a panic arose, for instance, out of the well-known tulip boom on the Amsterdam stock exchange, which was at its height in the years 1634 to 1637 and ended in a large-scale smash. This was not a business crisis in the proper sense of the term, as its effects on "market economy," in general, were slight and on production still slighter, seeing that in those days production was, to a large extent, carried on independently of any market. The consequences of the notorious financial operations of the Scotchman, John Law (who founded the Mississippi Company in France in 1716, along with a bank of issue by means of which he intended to revive business and thus restore the state finances, which under Louis XIV had been severely strained) resembled a business crisis more closely. The note issue rose to the (for those times) enormous sum of 3,000,000,000 *livres;* these notes could be forced into circulation only by means of mass sellings of Mississippi Company shares, in order to provide an investment for them. The shares and the notes were like playing cards which were constantly exchanged against each other. The manipulations, in this case, had effects which definitely spread outside the walls of the stock exchange; for commodity prices were also driven upward, building activity increased, and industrial production expanded considerably. When the crash came in 1720, many persons were ruined; transfers of property had taken place on a large scale. Thus, the collapse of the Mississippi Company—like the great South Sea Bubble crash which occurred simultaneously on the London stock exchange—had definite effects on the economic system. It cannot, however, be classified as a proper business crisis, as it took place independently of the production and distribution of commodities and so developed without any inherent connection with the general economic conformation.

It was only when market economy has been developed, and the economic division and association of labor within the nation evolved, that the economic elements acquired that inherent interconnection which is a prerequisite condition for the appearance of typical cyclical movements. Then, and not till then, emerged the phenomenon now known as the "business cycle"; then, and not till then, occurred business crises of an organic character, generated by the internal forces in a business economy. The gradual development of such internal interdependence of the individual economic elements can be clearly traced in the course of the eighteenth century. At first, however, it is scarcely possible to detect a distinctly cyclical rhythm. According to Tugan-Baranowski, we can distinguish a whole series of crises during the eighteenth century, which had much in common with those of the nineteenth century. But in one respect modern crises are clearly distinct from all others the earlier crises were brought about by exceptional circumstances, generally of a political character, and there is no periodicity in their recurrence. The periodical recurrence of crises, in his view, began in England, starting with the crisis of 1825. The crises of 1811, 1815, and 1818, he groups with those of the preceding century, as being non-periodical and attributable solely to the Napoleonic wars. As to that, the question, of course, remains open how far the political rhythm may not correspond to the economic rhythm; as we have seen above, the phenomenon of "long waves" appears to indicate such a correspondence. It does not make much difference in the end whether we agree with Bouniatian in identifying the great crisis of 1793 in England as the starting point of the modern industrial era, or whether we accept Tugan-Baranowski's view that the round of business cycles opens with the English crisis of 1825. It is, in any case, noteworthy that England, the country in which the economic association of the nation's labor forces first took shape, was, also, the land in which a series of business cycles first made its definite appearance.

The Crisis of 1825.

The course of events during the crisis of 1825 shaped itself—according to Tugan-Baranowski's analysis—as follows: in the second half of 1825, commodity prices began to crumble. Stock-exchange quotations came to a temporary standstill and then, amid the competition of bulls and bears, began to fall and proceeded to tumble sharply, causing the collapse of the speculative concerns which had flooded the London Exchange. Numbers of speculators were ruined. As the industrial firms were at the beginning able to hold out, bankruptcy made its appearance first among the banks, which were heavily involved in the speculations that had been going on and which had landed themselves in a dangerous position by issues of £1 bank notes, as, in accordance with the mercantile financial system[1] of the time, these notes possessed the character of credits rather than currency. According to Tugan-Baranowski, as the holders of £1 bank notes

[1] See WAGEMANN, "Allgemeine Geldlehre," I, chap. 10.

were, for the most part, not rich people but small manufacturers, shopkeepers, farmers, etc.—people who were
easily carried away by panic—the danger was, in consequence, increased. In October, five provincial banks
crashed, and the strongest banks found themselves in
difficulties. A strong demand for specie arose. The flow
of gold abroad was transformed into a flow from London
to the provinces. The insolvency of the banks, which
persisted throughout the whole of the first half of 1826,
resulted in the bankruptcy of their clients—traders and
manufacturers. English trade and industry as a whole
were by now affected—especially large firms of exporters
numbers of which came to grief.

The only external feature which distinguishes this
from later crises consists in the monetary phenomena
by which it was attended and which arose out of the
mercantilist basis of money—later replaced by the charter-
and-balance-sheet system. It was essentially akin to
later crises in so far as it represented a reaction following
an upward movement which had profoundly affected
English economy. The extent to which it was a link
in the chain formed by a cyclical movement similar to
those of modern times is also shown by the fact that it
was followed by a depression marked by the same features
as those of the present day: minimum note circulation,
increase in private deposits, considerable unemployment,
small commodity sales.

Crises like that of 1825 followed in 1836 and 1847.
We need not consider their history in detail, as it is of
little interest. Their only peculiar feature consists in
the fact that in each case the interval between crises was
exactly 11 years—which, later (1875), led the English
political economist Jevons to connect economic crises with
sunspot cycles.[1] A rhythm so strict no longer appears
in subsequent decades; this is, perhaps, connected with the
fact that about the middle of the century a great structural
change in national and world economy took place.

[1] JEVONS, W. S.: "The Solar Period and the Price of Corn," 1875.

The Break in Continuity about 1850.

It was at this juncture that Germany and, still more, France, which had hitherto remained distinctly behindhand in the development of a market economy as compared with England, began to develop into full-fledged capitalistic states. Some investigators (led by Sombart) attribute this forward movement primarily to the increased production of gold, consequent on the discovery of the gold fields of California (1848) and Australia (1858). Others refer it to the stimulating influence of the Crimean War (1853). Others, again (Cassel, etc.), emphasize the extremely rapid progress in technique and organization made about this time; for this was the period which witnessed the beginnings of the development and intensification of transportation in consequence of the use of the railway and the steamship. The credit system underwent epoch-making transformations (1852, Crédit Mobilier founded in Paris; 1853, Bank für Handel und Industrie founded in Darmstadt). The crisis of 1857, which, on this occasion—a significant symptom in regard to the development of world economy—had its origin in the United States, put a check on the upward movement. The ensuing depression lasted until 1862, when a new period of prosperity set in, which, again, was connected with a war (the American Civil War, 1861–1865). The failure of American cotton supplies brought to the fore new and important overseas countries (Egypt, the East Indies, and Brazil) which were in a position to turn to cotton growing. Foreign trade also made important progress in other fields. A further extension of railways took place. A slight setback occurred in 1866 to 1867, but this was definitely not a proper crisis, although, cyclically speaking, a crisis was due at about the same time.

The Crisis of 1873.

The forward movement of Europe and of world economy again set in. In the midst of it, the war of 1870 to 1871 broke out. The only national economic system which for a few years was unfavorably affected by this event was that of France; in Germany, on the contrary, a rapid upward movement set in at the termination of hostilities. The indemnity paid by France occasioned a fever of company promotion, with the usual accompanying symptoms—boom on the stock exchange, increased prices, and rapid accumulation of fortunes. The spring of 1871 marks the culminating point of the speculation period—the point at which rates began to crumble. The crisis began in 1873—May in Vienna, June in Berlin, September in New York, November in London.

The "Structural" Depression of 1874 to 1895.

The long economic wave movement which had set in in the forties of the nineteenth century thus broke up early in the seventies. The period of depression, which followed, lasted in Europe for 21 long years, from 1874 to 1895. It is true that during this period industrial production on the whole increased rapidly, and the population of Germany grew considerably—from 42,000,000 to 52,000,000. Technical progress was, however, obtained in the face of difficulties, for money values had a continual tendency to fall. This is true not only of industrial prices but also and especially of agricultural prices. Rye fetched 170 marks per ton in the seventies, 150 marks in the eighties, and as little as 118 marks in 1894. Economic pressure drove a million individuals to emigrate from Germany in the five years 1881 to 1885, while in the same period Europe as a whole must certainly have lost several millions from the same cause. These emigrants flocked to underpopulated America, to plough up areas as yet uncultivated; with the result that the production of wheat in the new world increased enormously and began to compete dangerously with European agriculture. It is, of course, hard to distinguish cause and effect in this movement; but we are, in any case, safe in asserting that it was "structural" rather than cyclical in character. Personally, I am inclined to view this long-drawn-out depression as mainly indicative of the fact that the center of gravity of agricultural production had shifted more definitely from Europe to the New World. So strongly marked was the long-wave depression between 1874 and 1895, that the business cycle proper almost disappeared. During the whole period, only a few faint upward movements can be discerned.

The "Fever" of Development in the Nineties.

About the middle of the nineties, the process of international displacement came to an end, and from about 1895 the great turn for the better set in in Germany and Europe. A strong upward movement began practically throughout the world and lasted until the World War. The precipitating impulse came from the progress made in the field of electrical technique. The passing over to electrical motive power by the factories, and to electric lighting and electric tramways by the cities, gave rise to a rapidly increasing demand for electrical supplies, which was passed on to the engineering and extractive industries and thence, in turn, proceeded to affect the whole of economic life. The whole world, and particularly Germany, fell into the grip of a perfect fever of development. This was a period in which men saw no limits to the possibilities of economic and technical progress, in which Malthus' law of population, according to which humanity could rely only on a limited supply of food stuffs, was treated as a joke; a time in which even the idea of a world war inspired no alarm, for it was assumed that such a war could last for only a few weeks. German exports, which in the eighties had moved steadily around the figure of 3,250,000,000 marks, rushed up from 3,000,000,000 in 1894 to 5,000,000,000 in 1904 and 10,000,000,000 in 1913. Imports increased still more notably, for Germany, in order to pay for them, had at her disposal not merely the proceeds of her export trade but also the freights earned by her rapidly growing merchant fleet, the earnings of her insurance companies and banks, and the like. Industry made enormous strides forward; production of pig iron rose from

5,000,000 tons in 1892 to 15,000,000 in 1912, while that of coal rose during the same period from 71,000,000 to 175,000,000 tons. In a time of such headlong progress,

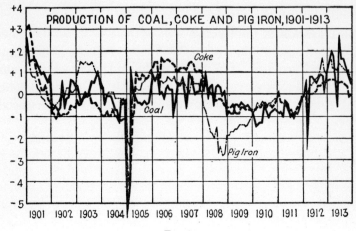

FIG. 8a.

even the crises took on a special character; that of 1900, and, again, that of 1907, appeared like a sudden reining in of business in the course of its gallop forward, which, after a brief breathing space, it once more resumed.

FIG. 8b.

In 1913, a kind of peak was reached. Owing to the outbreak of the World War, it is unfortunately impossible for us to judge whether the cyclical recession which is to be observed during the first half of 1914 might have turned into a crisis or whether it would merely have prepared the way for a new period of prosperity even without the stimulus which the placing of the economic system on a war footing gave to industry.

The Duration of the Cycles.

We can summarily divide the course of business development in Germany from 1848 to the outbreak of the war into the following cycles, each beginning with a depression and closing with a more or less definitely pronounced crisis:

Period	Duration, years
1848 to 1857	10
1858 to 1866	9
1867 to 1873	7
1874 to 1882	9
1883 to 1890	8
1891 to 1900	10
1901 to 1907	7
1908 to 1913, 1914	6 to 7

In order to make this analysis, it is necessary to rely not merely on the separate records of economic history but also on a few statistical series. This gives us, of course, a result which varies somewhat, according to the series selected; for, as the diagrams on pp. 80, 81, 92, and 94 show, there is absolutely no congruence between the variations of the various economic elements. Thus, our results will differ according as we regard pig-iron consumption and the bank rate as the determining features in cyclical movements (in agreement with Spiethoff[1]) or base our investigation on industrial commodity prices or even on stock-exchange quotations. The primitive method, moreover, of relying on separate records of conditions or crude statistics, in order to represent cyclical fluctuations, which has been the one usually adopted hitherto, is inadequate for a thorough observation of economic variations,

---

[1] See SPIETHOFF, Krisen, in "Handwörterbuch der Staatswissenschaften," 4th ed.

such as theory and practice alike really require. The modern study of business cycles, though still in its infancy, relies on definitions and methods of far greater precision.

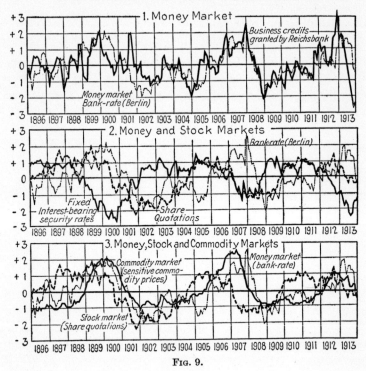

BAROMETER FOR THE THREE MARKETS 1896-1913

FIG. 9.

Bibliography

TUGAN-BARANOWSKI, M. VON: "Studien zur Theorie und Geschichte der Handelskrisen in England," Jena, 1901.

BOUNIATIAN, M.: "Studien zur Theorie und Geschichte der Wirtschaftskrisen," 2 vols., Munich, 1908.

ESZLEN, J. B.: "Konjunktur und Geldmarkt, 1902–1908," Berlin, 1909.

FEILER, A.: "Die Konjunkturperiode, 1907–1913," Jena, 1914.

HERKNER, H.: Krisen, "Handwörterbuch der Staatswissenschaften," 3d ed.

JEVONS, S. W.: "The Solar Period and the Price of Corn," 1875; "Investigations in Currency and Finance," London, 1884.

MOMBERT, PAUL: "Einführung in das Studium der Konjunktur," 2d ed., Leipzig, 1925.

WIRTH, MAX: "Geschichte der Handelskrisen," 3d ed., Frankfort, 1883.

OECHELHÄUSER, W.: "Die wirtschaftliche Krisis," Berlin, 1876.

SOMBART, WERNER: "Die Entwicklung der deutschen Volkswirtschaft im 19. Jahrhundert und im Anfang des 20. Jahrhunderts," 6th ed., 1927; "Der moderne Kapitalismus," vols. 1–3.

CASSEL, GUSTAV: "Theoretische Sozialökonomie," Bk. IV, 4th ed., Leipzig, 1927.

Harvard Review of Economic Statistics, 1919 *ff.*

V.z.K., vol. 1, No. 1.

Schriften des Vereins für Sozialpolitik, vols. 105–113.

Other references in Herkner and Spiethoff.

CHAPTER VII

CYCLICAL POSITIONS AND CYCLICAL TENSIONS

Each phase in the business cycle presents a double contrast with the preceding phase, (*a*) in virtue of those factors which constitute what we may call the course or level of business and economic affairs—what we may define as the cyclical position—and (*b*) in virtue of those factors which I venture to group together under the single term "cyclical tensions." Thus, each phase in the cycle is characterized by two features—namely, the position and the tension which it involves. The position may be estimated by a comparison of the situation of the various moving economic elements with that for preceding periods; such a comparison will show the level of business as relatively high or low, the course of affairs as rising or falling. The tensions are shown by the configuration of the economic elements at any given moment; the various incongruences which exist at any given time in the business firmament are so many tensions, which necessarily tend toward compensation—that is, tend to pull the system in another direction.

CYCLICAL POSITION

The cyclical position may be divided into four fundamental forms, or stages, as follows:
1. Depression.
2. Recovery.
3. Prosperity.
4. Recession.

It is frequently possible without great difficulty, with the aid of comprehensive indices—such as those for employment, totality of turnover, or the national income—to arrive at a general result recognizable as indicating one of these fundamental stages. All four stages are, however, naturally not always unmistakably recognizable in every series taken; for it is not merely possible, but absolutely the rule, that the various sections of the national economy should, respectively, show different tendencies and different levels of prosperity.

In many cases, it is even very difficult to decide as between the two opposing tendencies. Thus, in Germany immediately after stabilization, there was a pronounced industrial depression, and unemployment, in particular, was considerable; on the other hand, the money market was in a quite abnormal state, in consequence of the after effects of stabilization on credit and currency policy— a state which rather resembled one of high prosperity. It is also difficult to classify the American economic position since 1924 under any one of the above forms, since the various branches of business have developed very unevenly. Thus, in 1925 and 1926, the industries producing producers' goods, led by the building and automobile-manufacturing industries, enjoyed great prosperity, while during the same period the industries producing consumers' goods, particularly the textile, boot-and-shoe, and leather industries, were generally in a depressed condition, and agriculture was hit hard by bad harvests. These difficulties should warn us that the "four stages of the business cycle" do not represent a framework into which all cyclical movements must necessarily fit, for the level of prosperity and the tendency of development need not always vary in a uniform manner throughout the economic system; full prosperity may be followed by a sudden collapse as well as by a slow decline; or a period of recovery may be immediately succeeded by a decisive relapse, without any intervening period of full prosperity. Experience so far shows that business cycles usually proceed in a regular manner through the stages laid down above, though the duration of the respective stages may vary widely.

In spite of the enormous structural changes in German economy since the inflation period, we can quite clearly recognize even in the last few years the progress of the business cycle through the normal stages. The unemployment and price figures show the following vicissitudes:

Depression, November, 1923, to June, 1924.
Recovery, July, 1924, to January, 1925.
Prosperity, February, 1925, to September, 1925.
Recession, October, 1925, to January, 1926.
Depression, February, 1926, to October, 1926.
Recovery, November, 1926, to August, 1927.
Prosperity, September, 1927, to November, 1927.
Recession, from December, 1927.

This table shows the duration of the various stages of the business cycle as distinctly shorter than before the World War. While in the period from 1848 to 1913, the business cycle in Germany had a duration of 6 to 10 years, and the separate stages lasted about 1 to 3 years—only the actual crisis was liable to be got over more rapidly—since the inflation period (down at least to the middle of 1927), no stage has lasted longer than a year. Now, however, the stages appear to be lengthening.

CYCLICAL TENSIONS

The degree of regularity with which the business cycle tends to pass through the four consecutive stages described above is closely connected with the complex of factors which we have grouped under the term "cyclical tensions." Here, again, four basic forms can be distinguished:

1. Negative tensions (slackness).
2. Relaxations of negative tensions, tightening process begins.
3. Positive tensions (high tension).
4. Relaxation of positive tensions, reaction in negative direction (liquidation, possibly crisis[1]).

Such a subdivision takes no account of the possibility of a state of complete absence of tension, which would be equivalent to the static condition described in a previous chapter. The sole significance is that of an

[1] Contrary to the view of Juglar, who characterized the depression stage as the period of liquidation, I prefer to regard the crisis as primarily a liquidation process.

imaginary limiting case; in a living economic system it could never occur, as positive or negative tensions will always be present at some point in the system. Such a state, could it be attained, would mean the realization of a completely non-cyclical economy—a possibility which, for practical purposes, can be left out of account.

Let us trace these changes in tensional conditions in two important elements in the business cycle—the accumulation of goods in storage and long-term borrowings.

As a general rule, the tensional stage of *slackness* runs parallel to that of depression in the business situation. Slackness manifests itself as far as long-term borrowings are concerned in the falling of undertakings heavily into debt, which forces them to take on new business in order to pay the interest on borrowed capital. In this they can succeed, however, only if they make full productive use of such capital. Further slackness is caused by the unloading of stocks in the preceding (liquidation) phase; stocks have now to be replenished, as, in most cases, they have fallen below the safety point.

A *positive reaction* (involving a recovery in the business situation) occurs when the negative tensions are relaxed or—as we may alternatively put it—when they begin to tighten; this happens, for example, when undertakings begin to increase their production and accumulate fresh stocks.

The state which we have termed *high tension* usually coincides with a state of full business prosperity, for the upward-soaring tendency, manifested in increased production and the replenishing of stocks, generally overshoots the mark. The capital borrowed during the depression and even during the recovery is insufficient. Additional credit must be obtained, for instance, by drawing bills of exchange or borrowing foreign capital. As there are limits set to the possible expansion of credit, this causes a positive tightness or tension of credit. Where, in addition, stocks become congested—that is, where the proportion of stocks to turnover becomes so high that it increases costs beyond a certain limit—the tension is so increased that a slight impulse from without is sufficient to compel liquidation.

The process of *liquidation*, which consists in the unloading of commodity stocks or securities at falling prices, causes *recession* in the state of business. This process may take the form of a crisis—in other words, it may begin suddenly and involve the collapse of numerous undertakings, as, for example, in Germany in 1857 and 1873, in the United States in 1907 and, in the postwar period, in a number of countries in 1920, and in Germany at the end of 1925; or it may take place more gradually, as in Germany in 1882 and 1890. The recession of 1913 to 1914 may, perhaps, be regarded as an example under the latter head; the economic situation in those years was closely analogous to that of the present day in Germany, for the recession began without creating a crisis.

Where a gradual recession from a peak of prosperity occurs, we may deduce that the positive strains or tensions have been sufficiently moderate to allow undertakings to liquidate stocks in a quiet and unhurried manner.

Negative and positive tensions arise and are relaxed in many other ways. We shall come back to them later in dealing with specialized business-cycle theory.

SECTION III

THE RELATIONS OF CYCLICAL MOVEMENTS

CHAPTER VIII

THE FORMAL CLASSIFICATION OF SERIES

Series Based on Material Data.

So far, we have considered economic fluctuations from the point of view of (*a*) their forms and (*b*) their phases; that is to say, we have analyzed them morphologically and chronologically. We have now to investigate what we may call their substratum or their material content—that is, the tangled web formed by the interaction of the various economic elements. To do so, we must resolve the process of economic movement, and cyclical movement more particularly, into series of material data.

The series which have to be compared consist, for the most part, of *relative figures* and *index numbers*. Such figures are the numerical expression of changes in statistical series by comparison with some relative quantity set up as a standard. The term "relative figures" is applied, generally speaking, to figures resulting from simple series, while the term "index number" is usually employed to denote a compound series derived from several simple series (for example, the cost-of-living index, derived from the figures for the price of bread, of meat, etc.).

For the purpose of composing a single index number from several statistical series, the question of *weighting* the various series is of special importance. Thus, if we wish to form an index of wholesale prices, it will scarcely help us to take all the price series considered at their simple or face value; what we must do before we fit them into the compound series is to weight them according to the importance of the branch of production to which they apply (this can probably be estimated from the statistics of sales).

If we form a collective notion of the economic series, we can immediately distinguish between those which are more and those which are less constant or, as we may alternatively put it, between those which react strongly and those which react feebly; between series which in the course of their movement show small and those which show large variations in either direction. Thus, we may contrast the comparatively constant interest rates in the capital market with the highly variable rates in the money market or the widely fluctuating prices in the main raw-material markets with the relatively stable cost-of-living figures.[1]

Constant and Variable Series.

The distinction between relatively constant and relatively variable series is of special importance for quantitative analyses, particularly where we are in a position numerically to resolve a given movement group on such a basis into its component parts. The national income can be analyzed in this manner without difficulty; on the (more or less) constant side we may group officials' salaries, house rent, and, in general, a large part of income derived from property; while we shall, of course, classify business profits as variable income, and we shall also group wages under the same head in view of the extent to which these fluctuate according to the state of trade and the rates current.

Thus regarded, Germany's national income would appear at first sight to be predominantly composed of variable items (cf. pp. 32 *ff.*). In reality, however, the constant portion of the national income is very much more considerable than such an analysis would indicate. Large sections of the income groups which, on the whole, must be classified as variable are revealed, on closer analysis, as in themselves possessing a considerable degree of stability, as we shall

[1] Lederer, in particular, draws attention to the great importance of this distinction; "Grundriss der Sozialökonomik," vol. 4.

realize if we examine more closely the way in which income is expended; for expenditure, as a closer reflection on the notion of circular flow will make clear, turns again into income. The average annual expenditure for the years 1925 to 1927 may, on a rough estimate, be divided up as follows:

		Per cent
Predominantly constant expenditure:		
Food, drink, and tobacco[1]		43
House rent, including heating and lighting		14
Total		57
Comparatively variable expenditure:		
Public expenditure[2]		9
Reserves (savings, etc.)		9
Clothing		13
Domestic equipment		3
Miscellaneous		9
Total		43
Grand total		100

[1] Viewed inductively, drink and tobacco must be classified as representing fixed expenditure, no less than food.

[2] Only half of the total proceeds of taxation is revealed under this head; the remaining half is concealed under the other items, since taxation is, to a great extent, not to be separated from prices.

Such a dissection, notwithstanding its rough and approximate character, nevertheless permits the drawing of useful conclusions. It shows us, for instance, that a reduction in the national income by a certain percentage will react on specific items of expenditure and so on specific trades by a multiple of that percentage. It reveals to us, for example, the reason why the decline in the business done by the retail clothing and furnishing trades from 1925 to 1926 exceeded the simultaneous decline in the national income.

CHAPTER IX

PARALLEL AND "RADIATORY" FLUCTUATIONS

The relationship among the cyclical fluctuations in the various series takes various forms. If we agree to disregard entirely irregular relationships, we may classify these forms as follows:

1 Parallel fluctuation (fluctuation in the same direction and to the same degree).

2. "Radiatory" fluctuation (fluctuation in the same direction, but to an unequal degree).

3. Sequence.

4. Countervariation (scissor movement).

THE CONFIGURATION OF THE SERIES
(The 4 Basic Forms)

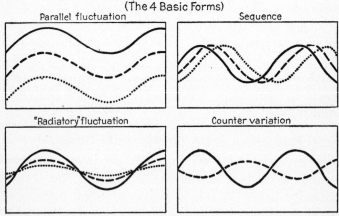

Fig. 10.

Parallel Fluctuation.

It is extremely important, not only for theoretical but also for practical work, to discover series the curves of which are parallel to each other. A most interesting example is afforded by a comparison of the index figures for the influx of orders and imports of raw materials with those of sensitive commodity prices. The reason for the parallelism in this case would appear to be the fact that fluctuations in the business activity of undertakings are reflected in the same manner both in purchases of raw materials and in the passing on of orders to other undertakings. The oscillation of raw-material prices, as shown by the collective index of sensitive commodity prices, may, perhaps, be regarded as a direct consequence of the above-named cause.

In order to obtain an accurate means of measuring parallel fluctuation, the mathematical notion of *correlation* is employed. Correlation means correspondence, to a greater or lesser degree, of the progression of different statistical series. The degree of correlation is expressed in a coefficient, known as the "coefficient of correlation," which varies between +1 and −1. The positive sign implies that the several series at any given point are moving parallel; the negative, that their movement is opposite. The nearer the coefficient of correlation approaches to +1 or −1 the fuller is the correlation in a positive or negative sense; while the nearer it approaches to zero the slighter is the correlation. By +1 is implied complete correspondence; −1 implies complete opposition; while zero implies a complete lack of dynamic relationship.

Parallel Fluctuation in the Circulation of Goods.

If we investigate the correlation in the relations between the influx of orders, raw-material imports, and sensitive commodity prices in recent years, we shall immediately observe a closer resemblance between the respective courses of the curves for the influx of orders and raw-material imports than between the courses of these and that of the curve representing the index of sensitive commodity prices. This, however, is due to the fact that the influx of orders and raw-material imports shows a rising tendency in the period under investigation, while sensitive commodity prices tended to fall. If these tendencies are eliminated from the curves, by calculating for each value in each curve the corresponding value for a straight line to represent trend (to be obtained in the usual manner), the relations among the three curves assume another aspect, which may be expressed as follows:

The closest correspondence (in deviations from the trend line) is now found to exist between the curves representing imports of raw materials and the index figure of sensitive commodity prices (coefficient of correlation = +0.78). The correspondence between the raw-material-imports and influx-of-orders curves is somewhat less

VOLUME OF ORDERS, IMPORTATION OF RAW MATERIALS AND PARTLY MANUFACTURED GOODS AND INDEX OF SENSITIVE COMMODITY PRICES

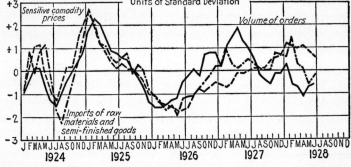

FIG. 11.

marked (coefficient of correlation = +0.68). The lowest coefficient of correlation (+0.50) is found as between the orders and sensitive commodity price curves.

The establishment of such parallel fluctuations is extremely valuable for practical work, if only on account of the fact that the series can with some confidence be substituted for each other where the statistical material for one or other of the series is defective or has become available too late. When, for instance, an attempt has to be made to form an idea of the movement of the balance of trade—and this may be of great importance with a view to decisions on economic policy—more rapidly than the speed with which trade statistics are compiled would permit, one can fall back on the immediately available index of raw-material prices, as representing raw-material imports. As in the case of Germany, exports are less liable to cyclical fluctuations than imports, a rising price index indicates an increasingly adverse trade balance, while, conversely, a falling index indicates a decreasingly adverse balance. The kind of forecasting thus made possible by the price index might be termed "counterfeit forecasting."

"Radiatory" Fluctuation.

Parallel fluctuation of a less perfect kind, where the direction alone is identical—the degree of fluctuation being different—takes on what we have called a "radiatory" appearance. Such a group of curves is formed, for instance, if we compare cost of living, wholesale prices, and sensitive commodity prices—each of which represents a commodity market. It is true that the series differ to some extent according to the particular articles selected for observation; such variations are, however, accidental and not essential. The differences in the respective quantities of trade done are of more importance. The cost-of-living index represents roughly the small-commodity market, that of wholesale trade the medium-commodity market, while the curve of sensitive prices represents the great comprehensive commodity market, dependent on the stock exchange and directly subject to international influences. The different magnitude of the transactions involved confers on these three markets, which are closely connected with each other by their dependence on commodities and which, therefore, tend to reach their peaks and troughs simultaneously, an unequal degree of sensitiveness, which is expressed in differences in the extent to which they fluctuate. A more fundamental cause of divergence lies (as we shall have to demonstrate at a later stage) in the special differences between the funds (income or finance capital) on which the effective demand is based. Under certain circumstances, the extent of the divergence between the three curves permits us to draw valuable conclusions in regard to the business situation, in so far as we can recognize specific tensions or relations behind their fluctuations.

Vertical and Horizontal Connections between Markets.

If we describe markets based on the same articles of commerce as *vertically* connected, it is permissible to consider as being in *horizontal* relationship with each other these markets which are differentiated sharply as regards the articles handled and are, therefore, brought into communicative relationships with each other solely through the circulation of money and not through the nature of the commodities in which business is done. In the case of horizontally related markets, we observe not so much a divergent degree of sensitiveness as a definite consecutiveness in their fluctuations, with which we may now proceed to deal.

CHAPTER X

SEQUENCE

It is, perhaps, of still greater importance, from the point of view of knowledge, to establish the existence of regular consecutive fluctuations as between different series.

Correlation and Time Lag.

The mathematical notion of correlation may also be employed in order to measure more accurately the relationship between consecutively fluctuating curves. In applying this notion, one proceeds by attempting to discover the time lag between the points at which the curves under comparison show the highest coefficient of correlation.

Further, the measurement of correlation need not be limited to the comparison of two series; it is also possible to express mathematically the dependence of one series on several others. The process known as "multiple correlation" is, for instance, employed in order to determine the influence of various market conditions on the fixing of the price of a product.

The Deployment of Economic Forces.

The discovery of regular consecutive fluctuations frequently brings facts to light which are of interest from the point of view only of a relatively small department of economic investigation. Should it, for instance, be proved —to take a single case chosen at random—that the fluctuations of the curve of employment in the bookbinding trade follow at an interval of some months those of the curve of production in the publishing trade, the observation of the movements of the latter curve would naturally be of great importance for bookbinding. These are, however, cases of sequence which are also of the greatest significance

109

for the diagnosis of the cyclical business situation in general. Thus, the consecutive fluctuation as between the curves for the circular flow of goods published by the Institute for Business Cycle Research (see p. 130) is of evident importance. These curves show us that the rate of influx of orders, which, as we have seen above, moves more or less parallel to raw-material imports and sensitive commodity prices, usually moves ahead of production of raw materials, which, in turn, moves ahead of employment. This consecutive order of movement permits us as it were to survey the deployment of the various economic forces. The observation of such sequences may help us considerably in business forecasting, for it supplies a basis for estimating the probable course of employment for weeks if not months ahead. A forecast based on such evidence will not, of course, be absolutely infallible; but, in the nature of things, business forecasting can in no case lay claim to infallibility (see chap. **XX**). There is nothing inevitable in the consecutiveness of the series' movements, if only because orders, which in any case can be statistically treated only by taking representative series, may be fulfilled out of stock instead of by fresh production, because raw-material imports may be stored instead of being turned to productive uses immediately, because rationalization may involve organic changes in the relations between the economic elements, and, possibly, for many other reasons as well. In forecasting, one must be careful to allow for such disturbing factors; but the fact that they may divert the cyclical process from its normal course does not lessen the value of the knowledge which we may obtain from observing sequential movements.

The Three Markets.

More problematical is the use of another case of sequence for the purpose of analyzing the cyclical business situation—a case which frequently arises from the relations of the various markets with each other. It has been shown that, at various periods in various countries, a characteristic sequence appears, as we have seen above, among the respective movements of the money market, the stock market, and the commodity market. This fact leads us to picture finance capital as flowing in a mighty undulatory movement from one market to another. After a crisis, the money market immediately becomes saturated; it relaxes and interest rates fall. Capital, therefore, flows out into the stock market, where business increases and prices rise, without causing the fluidity of the money market immediately to disappear. In the course of time, the available money supplies overflow the stock market and pour into the commodity market, causing a considerable increase in business activity and, generally speaking, an upward movement in prices. The tide then turns, finance capital rushes torrentially away from the stock and commodity markets, prices and rates weaken, and dealings in stocks and commodities fall off; the money market again fills up, in so far as the flow of money is not checked by a restriction of credit.

Does the Stock Exchange Draw Finance Capital Away from the Commodity Market?

Such is the mental picture which we are apt to form; the real facts assume, of course, a different appearance. When, for instance, we say that capital flows into the stock market, what we really mean is that business is being done on the stock market at rising prices. The quantity of stocks available in a national economic community is not increased thereby, nor is the amount of cash available diminished, for the immediate signification of the process in question is simply that an exchange takes place between securities and currency. This consideration has led a political economist so eminent as Gustav Cassel to conclude that a boom on stock exchange cannot draw any finance capital away from the commodity market, as if increased turnover on the stock exchange did not necessarily tie up a certain quantity of currency and, therefore, of working capital. If business could be done without reference to circulating medium, the whole of the payments in a national economic system could be covered by a single mark; for—as Wicksell has said—one pfennig would suffice, if its velocity of circulation could be increased indefinitely. The commodity market is stripped of finance capital, more particu-

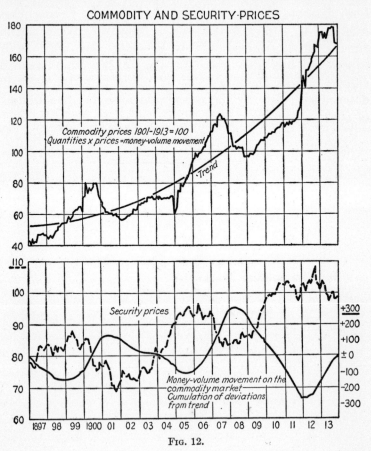

FIG. 12.

larly, when the stocks are bought by the producers from whom orders for raw materials emanate and by the traders who stock the products; for in such a case, finance capital is as it were removed from the sphere of economic activity and is temporarily withdrawn from the economic process of commodity production. The diagrams reproduced above, illustrating the interconnection between the commodity and stock markets, seem to me to be most instructive.

There is, thus, undoubtedly a connection between the various markets, and finance capital serves as the link. The relationship between movements of the markets, therefore, deserves the most careful observation. Consecutive fluctuation, as described above, is, however, by no means rigidly predetermined.[1] This is clear not only from experience but also from the simple fact that finance capital enjoys great freedom of movement; its path is determined solely by the actual and probable possibilities of profit in various markets.

[1] See *V.z.K.*, vol. 3, No. 2A, p. 30 (paper by Dr. Donner and Dr Hanau).

CHAPTER XI

COUNTERVARIATION (SCISSORS MOVEMENT)

The establishment of the existence of counter- or "scissors" movements throws light of a quite different kind on the problems with which we are concerned. Such movements are of great interest, because, in particular, they frequently indicate the existence of tensions which are pressing for relation.

The Trade Balance and the "Storage Scissors."

One of the most important examples of countervariation on the commodity side of economics consists in the results which we secure if we compare series which indicate an increase in the nation's commodity supplies with those which indicate a decrease therein. The scissors movement as between imports and exports, to look no further, is instructive; for if, for example, imports increase and exports fall, this points to an increase in the quantity of goods either consumed or stored in the home country. If we take further representative series covering supplies— if, for instance, we combine the curve of reproduction of important basic materials with that of imports and series reflecting home consumption with the curve of exports— we shall obtain a kind of gage of the quantity of goods in storage in the national business system. As, however, the quantity of goods in storage has an upper and a lower limit, a comparison of movements such as described above supplies us with valuable information on which to base forecasts. A surfeit of goods in storage is a symptom which warns us of the approach of a crisis; while depleted stocks mean that the way is clear for a revival. The range of a forecast based on such data is, of course, restricted by the fact that we are ignorant of the absolute limits beyond which the quantity of goods in storage cannot rise or fall, especially as those limits are constantly shifting. An example may be quoted from war-time economics to show how careful one must be in estimating these limits. During the World War, the question of what were called "stocks in movement" was of great importance for diagnosing the situation in regard to supplies. The German Reichs-getreidestelle, in its public management of wheat supplies, had to reckon on a certain minimum quantity being necessarily retained at any given moment by the machinery of distribution—like water in pipes—if the supply was not to suffer a disastrous interruption. In the early days, the minimum "stock in movement" was estimated at 300,000 tons; it turned out later that the country could get along with only 100,000. The upper limit of quantities of goods in storage is, perhaps, even more difficult to estimate; this limit is a function more particularly of the capital wealth of the country, but it also simultaneously depends on a number of other factors.

The Scissors Movement of Credit.

On the money side, the countervariation notionable as between credits granted by the banks of issue and drawings of bills of exchange appears to me to be particularly instructive (see pp. 155 *ff.*, 161, 185 *ff.*). A comparison of these two series shows, for instance, that during a period of full prosperity, that is, before a decisive recession, credits drop temporarily while bill drawings rise or remain stable. This was the case alike in 1900, in 1906 to 1907, and in 1911 to 1912. Even during the high-tension period of 1925, we had a rising curve of bill drawings combined with a falling curve of bank credits. Immediately before the crisis, however, the latter usually rises abruptly—as a candle flares up before going out—while bill drawings do not start falling off until the crisis actually breaks out. The processes underlying these graphic phenomena are probably as follows: The quantity of credit granted is determined mainly by the lack of currency experienced at the consumption end of the economic system, as expressed in the note circulation. Bill drawings, however, are an expression of the business activity in the region lying beyond consumption—that is in the sphere of the entrepreneur. In a period of high prosperity, such activity is particularly intense. When, however, at such a time consumption falls off, thus entailing a slackening in the issue of bank notes we may infer the existence of a state of tension which is, perhaps, the forerunner of a crisis.

It is, of course, true, in this case, also, that the value for forecasting purposes of comparing the curves is diminished by our ignorance, at any rate under present circumstances, of the possible limits of economic tensions.

Bibliography

On statistical methods in the business-cycle field:

BORTKIEWICZ, L. VON: Kritische Betrachtungen zur theoretischen Statistik, *Jahrbuch für Nationalökonomie und Statistik*, 3d ser., vol. 10, 1894, 1895; "Iterationen, eine Betrachtung zur Wahrscheinlichkeitstheorie," Berlin, 1917; Der gegenwärtige Stand des Problems der Geldwertmessungen, "Handbuch der Staatswissenschaft," 4th ed., vol. 4; Zweck und Struktur einer Preisindexzahl, *Nordisk Statistik Tidskrift*, vol. 2, 369, 1923; vol. 3, pp. 208, 494, 1924.

FISHER, I.: "The Making of Index Numbers," New York, 1922.

YOUNG, A. A.: Index Numbers, in H. L. Rietz, "Handbook of Mathematical Statistics," Boston, 1924.

MILLS, F. C.: "Statistical Methods Applied to Economics and Business," London, 1925.

MARCH, L.: Les modes de mesure du mouvement général des prix, *Metron*, vol. 1, p. 57, 1921.

CHUPROV: "Grundbegriffe und Grundprobleme der Korrelationstheorie," Leipzig, 1925; Ziel und Wege der stochastischen Grundlegung der statistischen Theorie, *Nordisk Statistik Tidskrift*, vol. 324.

PERSONS, W. M.: Indices of General Business Conditions, *Harvard Review of Economic Statistics*, 1919.

JOHANNSEN: "Elemente der exakten Erblichkeitslehre," 2d ed., Jena, 1913.

YULE: "Introduction to Theory of Statistics," 7th ed., London, 1924.

BOWLEY: "Elements of Statistics," 5th ed., London, 1926.

BAUER, F.: "Korrelationsrechnung," Leipzig, 1928.

EXNER, F. N.: "Über die Korrelationsmethode," Jena, 1913.

TUGWELL, R. G.: "The Trend of Economics," New York, 1924.

See, also, numerous papers in the *Journal of the American Statistical Association* and the *Journal of the Royal Statistical Society*.

Additional references in:

ALTSCHUL, E.: Konjunkturtheorie und Konjunkturstatistik, *Archiv für Sozialwissenschaf und Sozialpolitik*, vol. 55, No. 1.

ZIŽEK, F.: "Statistische Mittelwerte," 1908.

Works in Russian:

JASTREMSKI, CH.: Methods of Indirect Determination of Stability or Instability of Statistical Series; The Development of the Trends of a Statistical Series; Statistics and Dynamics in Research in Mathematical Statistics, all in *Vestnik Statistiki*, 1919, 1923, 1927.

CHETVERIKOV: Contributions to the Technique of Parabolic Curves, *Vestnik Statistiki*, 1926.

IGNATIEV: Some Fundamental Questions of Method in Business Cycle Research, *Vestnik Statistiki*, 1926.

SLUTZKI: The Coincidence of Chance Causes as a Basis of Cyclical Changes, *Business Cycle Review*, 1927.

ROMANOVSKI: "The Theory of Statistical Constants," *Vestnik Statistiki*, 1927.

BOBROV: Some Serious Problems of Our Handling of Indexes, *Price Movement*, 1928.

BOOK II
BUSINESS-CYCLE THEORY IN APPLICATION

SECTION IV

ECONOMIC BAROMETERS

CHAPTER XII

GENERAL ECONOMIC BAROMETERS

The comparison of movement processes is an important element in the construction of what are called "business" or "economic barometers." These are graphic representations of time series, which can be combined in the most varied ways with the aid of certain mathematical or arithmetical devices. The idea of a "barometer" is based on the notion that such graphic methods facilitate the forecasting of the course of business. It is true that the term is also used of diagrams which express only a certain position or constellation of movements at a given moment, without offering any indication as to their future course. Although in this case it would be more correct to speak of an "economic thermometer," it seems preferable to fall in with the accepted usage.

In the following pages, economic barometers are considered from the point of view of their technical construction. I propose to group them according to their economic scope, beginning with those which aim essentially at covering the whole field of economic movement and proceeding, subsequently, to investigate those which aim simply to cover special or sectional movements.

The forerunners of modern business-cycle theory devoted a great part of their attention to finding a single formula or general index for the course of business—thus falling in with the monistic tendencies which always characterize the beginnings of any branch of scientific study.

GENERAL INDEXES

Neumann-Spallart.

One of the first attempts of this kind is embodied in a study published by Neumann-Spallart in 1887.[1] His object was to obtain a general index of the *état économique, social, et moral* for a country. To do this, he combined a number of separate indexes, having first—though by comparatively primitive methods—eliminated seasonal fluctuations and trend. He went outside the sphere of purely economic phenomena, for he relied, also, on demographic and moral statistics (marriages, births, suicides, etc.) in order to form his index. By representing unfavorable factors (such as bankruptcy) as "inverse," that is, by treating them as minus quantities, he succeeded in constructing an unweighted general index out of the separate index series.

Julin.

Julin proceeded on similar lines[2]. Taking account, to a certain extent, of seasonal fluctuations and trend, he constructed a general index, by combining 43 separate series on the basis of which he obtained four group indexes. He calculated the variations in industrial production on the basis of 7 series, those in commerce and transport on the basis of 15, and those in consumption and income on the basis of 12. In the fourth group, he combined 9 series representing demographic and moral-statistical factors.

Mortara.

Similarly, Mortara[3] calculated a general index, based on 8 entirely heterogeneous series.

[1] NEUMANN-SPALLART, Mesures des variations de l'état économique et social des peuples, *Bulletin de l'Institut International de Statistique*, vol. 2, p. 150, 1887.

[2] JULIN, The Economic Progress of Belgium from 1880 to 1908, *Journal of the Royal Statistical Society*, February, 1911; Les indices des progrès économiques de la Belgique de 1880 à 1908, *Revue des questions scientifiques*, April and July, 1911; "Précis du cours de statistique," p. 109 *ff*., 3d ed., 1912.

[3] MORTARA, Numeri indici delle condizioni economiche d'Italia, *Bulletin de l'Institut International de Statistique*, pp. 663 *ff*., 1915.

The object of a general index, according to all the three authors mentioned above, is to find a means of measuring the variations in the economic situation of a country.

Such indexes are criticized on two main grounds: In the first place, their technical construction is attacked. No choice of series and no method of combining them could be at all convincing. Some critics have even gone so far as to suggest that, if a perfect combination of all the relevant series could be achieved, no fluctuations whatever would appear; according to this theory, economic variation consists solely in a shifting of balance as between the various branches of the economic system all traces of which would disappear if a perfect combined picture should be obtained.

If, however, we begin by postulating that business cycles consists in the expansion and contraction of the economic process as a whole, including both business activity and employment, and if we agree to assume that a general index can be found to reflect this up-and-down movement, our attempts to treat such an index as affording a gage for measuring economic variation will still come up against an insuperable obstacle, namely, the difficulty of determining the relative conditions under which it is to be employed. Does there exist a normal line, calculable in advance, about which the state of business oscillates?

The Babson Chart.

The Babson chart certainly represents an interesting attempt to get over this difficulty.[1] It consists in a general index, in which are artfully—not to say artificially—combined a large number of indexes and series based on population, price, and quantity movements. This general index (the "compositplot") is represented as a simple curve, fluctuating upward and downward. Babson endeavors to extract a meaning from his general index by assuming as an axiom that in economics as in physics (in

[1] BABSON, R. W., How the resultant line of net growth "*xy*" on the Babson chart is located, *pamphlet*, "Business barometers," 17th ed., 1925.

the case of the pendulum, for example) "to every action
there is always opposed an equal reaction." The two
movements may, of course, be of very different duration
from each other, such differences being compensated by
inverse differences in intensity. Thus, the duration of an
upward movement multiplied by its intensity would be
equal to the product of the duration and intensity of
the subsequent depression. Babson represents these products by areas, proceeding as follows: He relates the general
business index to a normal line, which he calls the "xy
line," and which he identifies with the trend of bank clearings outside New York City; this gives a general index

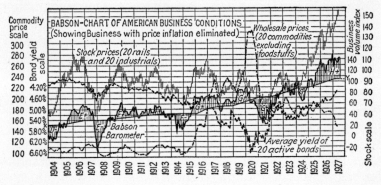

FIG. 13.

fluctuating about the normal line in such a manner that
the total areas above and below the line are equal.

The original Babson chart has evidently not been found
satisfactory, for it has undergone frequent modifications.
Since the World War, an effort has been made to eliminate
price movements. In its latest form, the chart aims more
and more at independence of all price series and at relying
as far as possible solely on physical-volume figures. Thus,
Babson has moved steadily away from a "business-value
index" to a "business-volume index." The scientific value
of such methods is problematical, especially as there can be
no proof that the xy line is a genuine and normal line.
The object of the chart is not merely to establish the course
of business activity down to the present (as in the case

of the general indices of Neumann-Spallart, Julin, and Mortara) but also to provide a basis for forecasting. In the latter respect, however, it may easily prove an untrustworthy guide, if only for the reason that it is extremely difficult to project trend into the future (see pp. 53–57).

The Necessity of a General Expression for the Course of Business.

We may admit, however, that the Babson chart possesses at least a certain illustrative value. Even though most modern investigators reject the principle of a general index, the need of a comprehensive quantitative expression for cyclical fluctuations within a national economic system still exists. In practice, we possess a certain quantity of statistics for Germany which may be used for this purpose; the general cyclical movement of the commodity side of the economic system can, to some extent, be measured for relatively short periods by the fluctuations in the employment index, while on the money side the statistics of business transactions—which in Germany can be obtained by a proper enlargement of the returns for the turnover tax—together with the figures for the note circulation and for bank clearings afford a comprehensive expression which can be turned to excellent use for a variety of purposes.

BAROMETERS CONSISTING OF SEVERAL CURVES

A closer insight into economic dynamics, and particularly into the business cycle, is made possible by barometers illustrating the interplay of various time series.

EARLIER EXPERIMENTS

De Foville.

The earliest experiment of this kind—if we agree to exclude Juglar's work—was made by the French statistician De Foville.[1] He declared, in a lecture delivered in 1887, that economic meteorology should be based on methods

[1] DE FOVILLE, Essai de météorologie économique et sociale, *Journal de la Société de Statistique de Paris*, pp. 243 *ff.*, 1888.

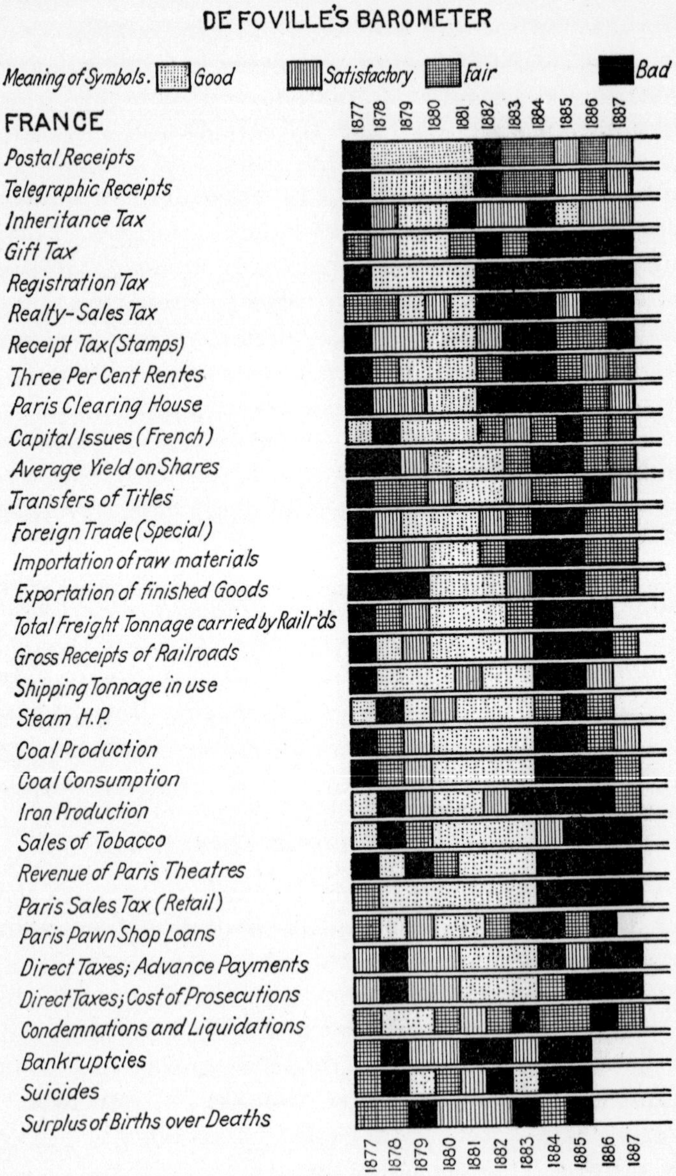
DE FOVILLE'S BAROMETER
Meaning of Symbols. Good
Satisfactory
Fair
Bad
FRANCE
1877
1878
1879
1880
1881
1882
1883
1884
1885
1886
1887
Postal Receipts
Telegraphic Receipts
Inheritance Tax
Gift Tax
Registration Tax
Realty-Sales Tax
Receipt Tax (Stamps)
Three Per Cent Rentes
Paris Clearing House
Capital Issues (French)
Average Yield on Shares
Transfers of Titles
Foreign Trade (Special)
Importation of raw materials
Exportation of finished Goods
Total Freight Tonnage carried by Railr'ds
Gross Receipts of Railroads
Shipping Tonnage in use
Steam H.P.
Coal Production
Coal Consumption
Iron Production
Sales of Tobacco
Revenue of Paris Theatres
Paris Sales Tax (Retail)
Paris Pawn Shop Loans
Direct Taxes; Advance Payments
Direct Taxes; Cost of Prosecutions
Condemnations and Liquidations
Bankruptcies
Suicides
Surplus of Births over Deaths

FIG. 14.

corresponding to the barometer, the thermometer, the hygrometer, and all the other instruments used in the physical world. He constructed a combined instrument in the basis of 32 series in the following manner: He gives a mark to the figure for each year and reproduces the marks in a diagram—red = good, pink = fairly good, gray = moderate, black = bad. The marks are allotted according to social significance—that is, he gives a bad or moderate mark in respect of declining or sluggish business activity, high suicide figures, or slow progress in natality as compared with deaths. The method is, generally speaking, quite primitive but, as a first attempt, deserves to be rescued from oblivion.

The results of similar investigations for Italy were published in 1892 by Benini.[1]

Sorer.

A study published in 1913 by Sorer[2] on some index numbers illustrating Austria's economic development represents a certain progress in the same direction. He combines the separate indexes in specific groups. In a further study, he goes on to calculate the correlation between various series. He compiles three group indexes—a "total index for all production data," a transport-group index, and a consumption-group index.

More Modern Experiments

A far higher stage in scientific method is represented by a barometer consisting of several curves, which also aims at covering the whole field of economic fluctuations and which is, therefore, also to be counted among the general economic barometers; this is the Harvard barometer the readings of which we have quoted as examples of sequence.

[1] BENINI, Il totalizzatore applicato agli indici del movimento economico, *Giornale degli Economisti*, pp. 131 *ff.*, 1892.

[2] SORER, RICHARD, Einige Wirtschaftszahlen zur wirtschaftlichen Entwicklung Österreichs, *Bulletin de l'Institut de Statistique*, vol. 20, No. 2, pp. 772 *ff.*, 1915.

Brookmire's Three-market Barometer.

James H. Brookmire,[1] founder of the Brookmire Economic Service, as a matter of fact forestalled the Harvard Committee in establishing the fact that over a number of years three series show a definite consecutive fluctuation. He showed that in the prewar period, at any rate since 1900, the undulations of the curve representing "banking factors" preceded those of the curve representing "specula-

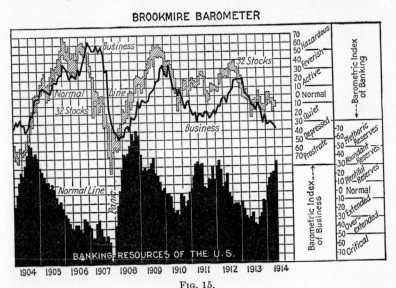

BROOKMIRE BAROMETER

Fig. 15.

tive factors" by a certain interval of time and that the latter, in turn, preceded those of the "general business factors" curve. During the World War, of course, and even in the postwar period, such consecutive fluctuation has, in many cases, failed to manifest itself, so that the Brookmire Economic Service has been gradually abandoning its earlier methods of investigation.

The Harvard Barometer.

The Harvard Committee has, however, investigated the relations among the three markets on a new basis, proceed-

[1] See VANCE, RAY, "Business and Investment Forecasting," 2d ed., 1925.

ing in the following manner: It begins by a thorough examination of 23 statistical series, for which monthly figures covering a considerable number of years are available; a careful effort is made to eliminate trend and seasonal fluctuations

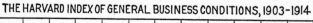

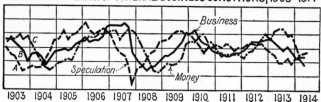

FIG. 16a.

from these, and they are then subjected to a certain process with a view to smoothing out the resultant curves (representation in units of standard deviation). Of the 23 series thus treated, 20 were found to exhibit a rhythm in their

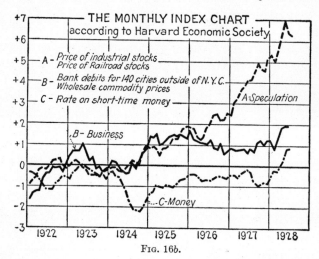

FIG. 16b.

fluctuations such as to make them appear comparable. Series with an approximately equal lead or lag, as compared with the index of wholesale prices, are combined in groups by the method of correlation measurement and the components of each group averaged. This gives five quite heterogeneous groups (for example, iron production and bank clearings outside New York City are included in a single group). A further rearrangement and shifting of the groups gives a diagram showing curves very similar to the Brookmire barometer. Since 1923, the curves have been based on the following elements:

Speculation (curve A):
  New York bank debits.
  Price of industrial stocks.
Business (curve B):
  Bank debits outside New York City.
  Wholesale commodity prices.
Money (curve C):
  Commercial-paper rates.

This barometer has since been further modified. In particular, fresh calculations of trend have been made.[1] Notwithstanding all these efforts, the barometer's curves since 1924 no longer show the sequence which was previously in evidence.

We have already seen above (pp. 109 *ff.*) the limitations to which the forecasting possibilities of the Harvard barometer are necessarily subject. These limitations are due essentially to the fact that it claims, without proper scientific justification, to fulfill the function of a general barometer, covering economic fluctuations as a whole—even if only by way of illustration. Such a claim is bound to fail, in view of the fact that business, like all other vital processes, cannot be compressed within the limits of a single formula. However hard one tries to prove that there is a strictly regular sequence of markets in a particular direction, using cunningly contrived methods such as trend determination and interpolation, one can never succeed in laying bare more than a single cross-section of the dynamic process of economics, whereas our need, theoretical as well as practical, is for numerous sections taken both crosswise and lengthwise. The truth

[1] See, especially, BULLOCK, C. J., W. M. PERSONS, and W. L. CRUM, The Construction and Interpretation of the Harvard Index of Business Conditions, *Review of Economic Statistics*, April, 1927.

is that the Harvard barometer fully justifies its existence only when it is put into its place as one among a multiplicity of barometers. The Harvard Committee itself has not shut its eyes to the truth of this assertion, and for some considerable time past it has been buttressing up its forecasts with a considerable variety of data.

Spiethoff and Singer's Barometer.

The *reductio ad absurdum* of the single-barometer idea is still more clearly demonstrated in a business barometer which was published for some time from June, 1926, by *Wirtschaftsdienst*. This barometer was constructed by Singer on the basis of a theory put forward by Spiethoff[1] concerning the causation of the business cycle and was introduced with much éclat as a diagrammatic representation of "the relationship between capital investments and consumption of construction goods which is the basis of the whole course of business development in our time."[2] The barometer consists of two curves, one representing iron and steel consumption ("approximately represented by the production of crude steel, hematite, and foundry pig iron, plus the excess of imports over exports shown in respect of certain specific items in the trade returns") and the other capital accumulation, shown by share issues. Singer ascribes extraordinary forecasting efficiency to the barometer, for he writes:

If capital accumulation progresses more rapidly than the consumption of iron, this means that the conditions necessary to bring the motive impulses for prosperity into action are on the increase; while, in the contrary case, we may deduce a situation unfavorable to a revival.[3]

It is true that in the next sentence Singer renounces any claim to prophetic possibilities for his graphic diagram; and the readings of such a barometer are, in fact, by no means sufficiently clear and definite to permit continuous and trustworthy business forecasting. This is evidently why

[1] *Wirtschaftsdienst*, No. 1, p. 3 *ff.*, 1926.
[2] *Wirtschaftsdienst*, No. 24, p. 819, 1926.
[3] *Schriften des Vereins für Sozialpolitik*, vol. 173, Part II, p. 330.

it has been dropped since the middle of 1927, so that in
the accompanying diagram the author has had to supply
the portion referring to the subsequent period.

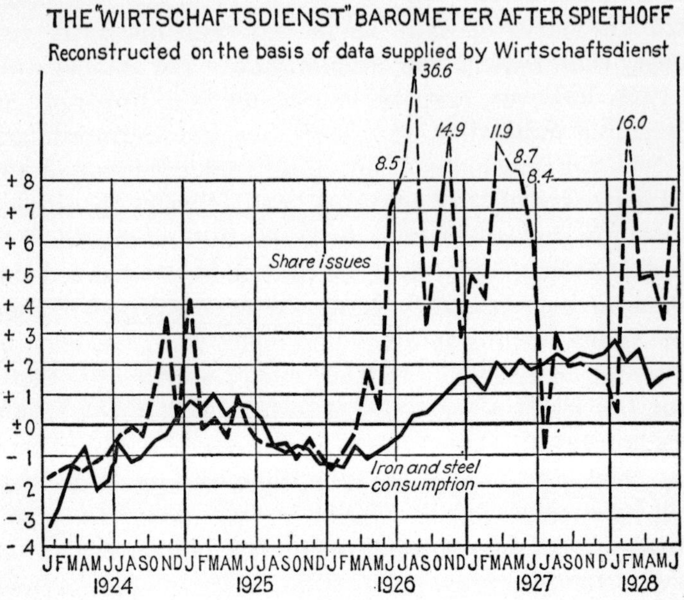

THE "WIRTSCHAFTSDIENST" BAROMETER AFTER SPIETHOFF
Reconstructed on the basis of data supplied by Wirtschaftsdienst

FIG. 17.

The curves are based on (*a*) home consumption of iron and steel (production of
foundry pig iron, crude steel, and hematite, plus the excess of imports over
exports in respect of the revelant items in the trade returns) and (*b*) the nominal
value of share issues by German joint-stock companies according to *Frankfurter
Zeitung*.   Average per month for 1925 equals 100; unit-average deviation of the
percentage figures for each month in 1924 to 1925 from the average per month
for 1925.   It has proved impossible to obtain exactly the same curve as that
shown by *Wirtschaftsdienst;* the latter has not published sufficient information
as to the method by which its curve is calculated.

In June, 1926, *Wirtschaftsdienst* inferred from its
barometer that a revival in the near future was out of the
question[1]—contrary to the opinion formed by the Institute
for Business Cycle Research, which in May, 1926, declared
that the trough of the depression had been reached and in
August predicted the impending revival.   In November,
1926, the institute registered the beginning of a revival
phase, yet in December, 1926, *Wirtschaftsdienst* was still

[1] *Wirtschaftsdienst*, No. 24, p. 819, 1926.

maintaining that, apart from fortuitous developments (the English coal strike), the German business situation was unchanged. As a matter of fact, the latter was not doing justice to its own barometer, for in the first half of 1926, the curve of share issues had risen distinctly more steeply than that of iron consumption. For the beginning of 1928, however, even the barometer fails to supply any intelligible indication, and, moreover, the extraordinarily uncertain movement of share issues about the end of 1926 and beginning of 1927 anything but facilitates the drawing of unequivocal conclusions as to the future course of the business cycle. Such, then, are the results of what Spiethoff proclaims as "an easily read and easily digested chart, from which surplus data have been eliminated, which aims rather at managing with the least possible quantity of data, but which selects its data systematically."[1] It must be admitted, in justice to the inventors of the barometer, that their own theory is better than the methods which they have employed to "verify" it; for it is, of course, a mistake to consider share issues as supplying a satisfactory index of the accumulation of capital, and even the consumpton of iron and steel only imperfectly expresses the creation of productive equipment. Opponents of the study of "symptoms"—by which alone these facts can be demonstrated—naturally could not be expected to realize this.

Even the theoretical foundations of Spiethoff and Singer's work, moreover, are inadequate to support it. The motive forces of business are far too numerous and too powerful to be expressed by means of the relation between accumulation of capital and the production of producers' goods. To imagine that "the whole course of business development in our time" can be judged from the relations between share issues and consumption of iron is almost as wild as the medical theory that all physical ailments can be diagnosed from the condition of the eyes.

[1] *Wirtschaftsdienst*, No. 1, p. 3, 1926.

Spiethoff and Singer's comparison of movements is, however, undoubtedly as fully justified as the Harvard barometer of the three markets, provided that it takes its place modestly in a more comprehensive scheme of investigation. In this connection, it may be mentioned that the relation between capital accumulation and the production of producers' goods has, also as a matter of fact, been kept under observation for a long time past by the Institute for Business Cycle Research, but its methods have been purged of the statistical defects inherent in *Wirtschaftsdienst's* curves.

Only a system of barometers which throws light from a number of angles on the whole business organism can permit us to form some sort of interpretation of the business situation. Before expounding such a system, however, we must first consider the different methods of constructing barometers which are appropriate to the investigation of sectional cyclical fluctuations.

Bibliography

NEUMANN-SPALLART: Mésures des variations de l'état économique et social des peuples, *Bulletin de l'Institut International de Statistique*, vol. 2, p. 150, 1887.

JULIN, A:. The Economic Progress of Belgium from 1880 to 1908, *Journal of the Royal Statistical Society*, 1911; Les indices des progrès économiques de la Belgique de 1880 à 1908, *Revue des questions scientifiques*, April and July, 1911; "Précis du cours de statistique," 3d ed., 1912.

MORTARA, G.: Numeri indici delle condizioni economiche d' Italia, *Bulletin de l'Institut International de Statistique*, p. 663, 1915.

SORER, R.: Einige Indexzahlen zur wirtschaftlichen Entwicklung Österreichs, *Bulletin de l'Institut International de Statistique*, p. 772, 1915.

DE FOVILLE: Essai de météorologie économique et sociale, pp. 243–247, *Journal de la Société de Statistique de Paris*, 1888.

BENINI: Il totalizzatore applicata agli indice del movimento economico, *Giornale degli Economisti*, pp. 131–137, 1892.

PANTALEONI: Observations sur la sémiologie économique, *Revue d'Economie Politique*, pp. 106 ff., 1892.

BERNHEIMER: Zur Frage der Berechnung von Totalindizes in der Semiologie, *Statistische Monatsschrift*, New ser., vol 19, Brünn, 1914.

BABSON, R. W.: "Business Barometers," 1925.

VANCE, RAY: "Forecasting Business Conditions," 2d ed., 1925.

HARDY, CHARLES O., and G. V. COX: "Forecasting Business Conditions," New York, 1927.

Harvard Review of Economic Statistics, 1919 ff.

GINESTET, P.: "Les indices du mouvement général des affaires," Paris, 1925.

MITCHELL: "Business Cycles, the Problem and Its Setting," New York, 1927.

KARSTEN, R. G.: The Theory of Quadrature in Economics, *Journal of the American Statistical Association*, March, 1924.

KARSTEN, R. G.: The Harvard Business Index, A New Interpretation, *Journal of the American Statistical Association*, December, 1926.

BOBROV: Problem der ökonomischen Barometer, *Die Planwirtschaft*, 1926.

OPARIN: Ökonomische Analyse des Harvard-Barometers, *Die Planwirtschaft*, 1926.

CHAPTER XIII

BUSINESS BAROMETERS FOR SEPARATE SECTIONAL FLUCTUATIONS

Brookmire's Forecasts of Commodity Prices.

Brookmire has for some time been using a barometer based on a peculiar combination of various principles for the forecasting of commodity prices.[1] The basis of this barometer is a general index derived from a combination of four groups of important time series. The first group covers the physical volume of production in primary basic industries (production of pig iron, steel, and lumber and consumption of cotton); the second covers foreign trade (ratio of imports to exports); the third covers the turnover of bank deposits; and the fourth, commercial paper rates. These four factors are weighted according to a special system, which is subject to modification under certain conditions, and then combined to produce a general index. The Brookmire Service has succeeded, with the help of this barometer, in forecasting the movement of commodity prices from 4 to 6 months ahead. Brookmire lays particular stress on the idea that only important and considerable fluctuations can be foreseen. He, therefore, relies on a number of "safeguards"—as, for example, a so-called "neutral zone" inside which fluctuations are left out of account—and, also, on certain technical devices in drawing his curves, which express only considerable fluctuations lasting over a comparatively long period. On the same basis, he also constructs a number of barometers for the industrial stock market, etc. It may incidentally be noted that early in 1927 Brookmire, after having for months prophesied a business crisis in America for the first half of 1927, abandoned, in the face of uninterrupted prosperity,

[1] See VANCE, op. cit., p. 80.

the forecast which he had established on the basis of his barometer.

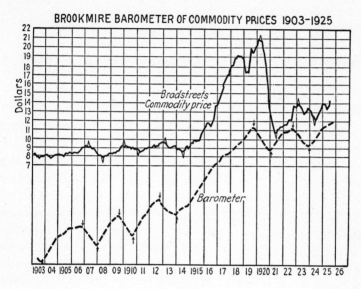

BROOKMIRE BAROMETER OF COMMODITY PRICES 1903-1925

Fig. 18.

Haney's *PV* Line.

The principal barometer of the Franklin Statistical Service, constructed by Prof. Lewis H. Haney,[1] appears so far to have been more successful. Haney believes that his barometer is capable of indicating the general trend of business from 5 to 7 months ahead. This barometer, known as the "*PV* line," reflects the relation between commodity prices and the volume of business transacted. The relation between prices *P* and the volume of goods disposed of *V* shows whether or not the market is capable of absorbing any more goods at existing prices; if, that is to say, the *PV* line shows a downward movement over several months in succession—as, for instance, since the middle of June, 1928—Haney infers that on the basis of previous experience the purchasing power of the market no longer

[1] A barometer constructed on the same principles is also published by Haney in the *Iron Age* and the *Textile World*.

suffices to enable the volume of goods produced to be absorbed, so that a kind of overproduction exists.

The stock-market barometer, also constructed by Haney, represents by means of a *"PVM* line," an extension of the above principle. In this barometer, the *PV* line is combined with factors indicating demand in the capital market, and conclusions are drawn from the behavior of this line as to the future course of the stock market. Thus, since the beginning of 1928, the *PVM* line shows a falling tendency. From the fact that since February, 1923, no sharp change similar to that which took place in January, 1928, has been observable, the conclusion

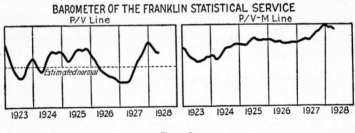

BAROMETER OF THE FRANKLIN STATISTICAL SERVICE

Fig. 19.

was drawn in May that the falling tendency of the stock market would probably continue through June and July.

Karsten's Cumulation Method.

The American statistician Karsten has carried out a fresh investigation of the relations among the three markets, for the special purposes of forecasting movements on the stock market. Karsten prefers not to consider the three markets from the standpoint of consecutive fluctuation, for, as he points out, modern methods of communication involve a very swift reaction in market movements. In contrast to the Harvard Committee, which regards the stock-market curve as the leading curve, and other investigators, who attribute a determining influence to the money-market curve, he considers the fluctuations in the commodity-market curve (curve *B*) as the leading factor.[1]

Curve *B* (deviations from trend)	Curve *A*	Curve *B* (deviations from trend)	Curve *A*
40	40	−250	190
120	160	80	270
210	370	50	320
−120	250	100	420
480	730	340	760
90	820	90	850
100	920	40	890
70	990	−120	770
−280	710	−240	530
−270	440	−230	300

Karsten links the commodity market up with the stock market, for he bases his method on a kind of quantity theory. Every outflow of finance capital from one market must make itself as an inflow into another market, and to every contraction of one market must correspond an expansion of other markets. In order to ascertain how far this is the case, he employs a mathematical method built up on Edge's principle of cumulation or quadrature. He plots the stock-market curve (curve *A*) from the commodity-market curve (curve *B*) in the following manner: The deviations of curve *B* from its trend are given a minus sign and then successively cumulated. This gives a curve which for him represents the movement of the stock market. As long as curve *B*, inverted, lies above the trend line—even though it is already falling—curve *A* moves upward, and *vice versa*. Thus, these two curves show a marked sequence, the commodity market curve, inverted, moves some time ahead of the stock-market curve. According to Karsten, the stock-market curve thus calculated is

[1] KARSTEN, K. G., The Theory of Quadrature in Economics, *Journal of the American Statistical Association*, vol. 19, pp. 14–29, March, 1924; *id.*, The Harvard Business Indexes—A New Interpretation, *loc. cit.*, p. 409 *ff.*, December, 1926; see, also, *V.z.K.*, vol. 2, No. 1. But see also the paper of Max Sasuly in the *Journal of the American Statistical Association*, March, 1930.

roughly parallel to the actual cyclical fluctuations of that
market, as represented by the Harvard Committee's

HARVARD AND KARSTEN INTERPRETATIONS OF THE "A" CURVE
(from the Journal of the American Statistical Association)

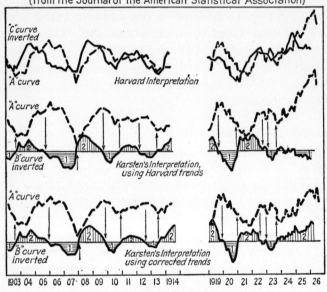

FIG. 20.

DIAGRAM SHOWING RELATIONS BETWEEN A BASIC
CURVE(B) AND ITS CUMULATION CURVE(A)

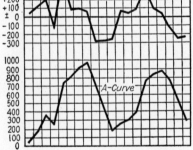

FIG. 21.

curve *A*. The question arises whether Karsten's measurement of trend is not to some extent arbitrary. A source

of special difficulty lies in the fact that Karsten presupposes that a nation's finance capital represents a constant reservoir, by reference to which the ebb and flow to the two other markets are regulated. This is clearly not the case; Karsten's method of determining trend appears to involve neglecting to some degree the changes which take place in the level of the reservoir.

A barometer for a narrowly limited market—hogs—has been constructed in the Business Cycle Research Institute by Dr. A. Hanau.[1]

Forecasting the Price of Hogs.

Hanau proceeds on the basis of an analysis of the statistics of cyclical fluctuations in the price of hogs in

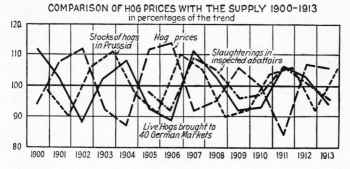

COMPARISON OF HOG PRICES WITH THE SUPPLY 1900-1913
in percentages of the trend

Fig. 22.

the prewar period, separating the apparently quite incalculable variations in such prices into regular seasonal movements—of great importance to the farmer—and cyclical fluctuations of from 3 to 4 years in length, whereupon the cycle of 3 to 4 years in hog prices emerges with amazing regularity.

If the movement of prices be compared with that of supplies (as shown by the statistics of live stock, hogs driven to market, or slaughterings), the dependence of the former on the latter is at once apparent.

As it would thus appear that supply is the determining factor in the hog market, while variations in demand

[1] See Chap. X.

inside comparatively brief periods are practically impercep-
tible, the farmer's policy in the production of hogs clearly
exercises a decisive influence on the movement of prices.
Farmers usually make the size of their stock of pigs depend-

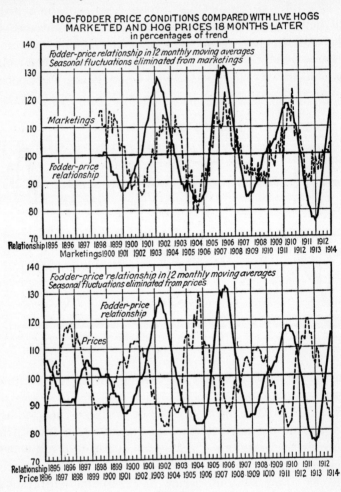

Fig. 23.

ent on current conditions as to profit. Statistical
analysis also shows that favorable conditions in the matter
of hog-fodder prices (that is, a favorable relationship of
the price of hogs in regard to barley, corn, and potato prices)

are followed 18 months later by plentiful supplies and low prices, while unfavorable conditions are followed 18 months later by scarcity and high prices.

A knowledge of these relationships makes it possible at any time to predict the broad lines on which prices will develop. The period of 18 months is explained by the natural period which elapses between the fertilization of the sow and the completion of the fattening of the young pig—on an average, about 14 to 15 months. This period is extended to about 18 months, because farmers usually

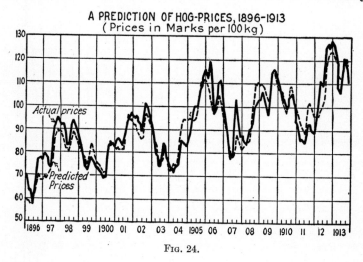

A PREDICTION OF HOG-PRICES, 1896–1913
(Prices in Marks per 100 kg)

Fig. 24.

take some time to react to the changing prospects of profit.

The forecasting process can be still further refined by bringing in additional factors in order to estimate the future market situation. Thus, the Institute for Business Cycle Research utilizes the following three factors—the value of which for forecasting hog-price movements has been demonstrated—in order to forecast prices at a given moment relying upon the coefficient of correlation:

1. Hog-fodder price relationship 18 months previously.
2. Fodder prices (potatoes, barley, corn) 11 months previously.
3. Tendency of stocks of brood sows (that is, present stocks as a percentage of the previous year's stocks) 12 months previously.

On the basis of these data, a forecast can be made for
the whole year at any time after the publication in February of the live-stock census figures. How far such forecasts coincide with the actual price movements can be
judged from the diagram given below. Even though, as
is only natural, deviations occur in the various months, the
main significance of the movement of prices (that is,
whether a profit or a loss is to be expected) has hitherto
always been correctly estimated; even the unfavorable price
situation in 1927 and the first half of 1928 was expected.

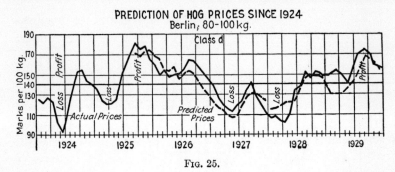

PREDICTION OF HOG PRICES SINCE 1924
Berlin, 80-100 kg.

Fig. 25.

Bibliography

VANCE, RAY: "Business and Investment Forecasting," Brookmire
Economic Service, 2d ed., New York, 1925.

Brookmire Forecaster (weekly).

WALLACE, W.: "Business Forecasting and Its Practical Application,"
2d ed., London, 1927.

Franklin Statistical Corporation, *Franklin Statistical Service*, New York
(in accordance with the methods of Prof. Lewis H. Haney).

KARSTEN, KARL G.: The Theory of Quadrature in Economics, *Journal
of the American Statistical Association*, March, 1924.

BULLOCK, PERSONS, CRUM: The Construction and Interpretation of the
Harvard Index of Business Conditions, *Harvard Review of Economic Statistics*,
April, 1927. *V.z.K.*, vol. 2, No. 1.

HANAU, A.: Die Prognose der Schweinepreise, *V.z.K.*, special Nos. 2 and 7.

HAAS, G. C., and M. EZEKIEL: Factors Affecting the Price of Hogs,
Department of Agriculture *Bulletin* 1440, Washington, D. C., November,
1926.

EZEKIEL, M.: Two Methods of Forecasting Hog Prices, *Journal of the
American Statistical Association*, 1927.

CHAPTER XIV

THE BAROMETERS OF THE INSTITUTE FOR BUSINESS CYCLE RESEARCH

Rejection of Single Formula.

Experience has shown that the movement of business can be neither adequately estimated nor correctly understood so long as we rely solely on some single formula, even though that formula be based on a wealth of statistical material, like the general indexes and some of the general plural-curve barometers described above. Every attempt which has hitherto been made to discover such a formula has failed. General indexes have, for long past, been laid aside as inadequate—unjustly, in so far as such indexes, if rightly used, certainly make a real, though limited, contribution to knowledge. The great plural-curve barometers, particularly those of the Brookmire and Harvard services (Spiethoff's and Singer's experiment can be left altogether out of account) have also failed. The various forecasting services have, therefore, been tending more and more to utilize a number of barometers for practical forecasting purposes.

It has been the constant endeavor of the German Institute for Business Cycle Research to build up a regular system of economic barometers. From the beginning, this institute has resolutely avoided pinning its faith to any single principle, such as that on which the Harvard barometer is based, or to any isolated theorem, such as Spiethoff's theory of the decisive significance of the iron-consumption curve.[1]

[1] Contrary to the unproved (and unprovable) statement in *Schriften des Vereins für Sozialpolitik*, vol. 173, Part II (cited above, p. 14).

The Principle of Classification.

Such a system of economic barometers ought to be based on a principle of classification of the sort described in our statistical consideration of economic circulation. We must keep in mind that on the commodity side, those interrelations, in particular, are to be investigated which are discernible between production and consumption, both in general and with reference to specific lines as well as the interrelations between these factors, on the one hand, and storage and foreign trade, on the other; while, on the money side, the interrelation between the markets and the relation between these and the flow of income are of the greatest importance. In the course of its aim to investigate the cyclical fluctuations which affect these interrelations, the institute has so far constructed the barometers listed below, which experience has shown to be the most important. The institute has thus been enabled to make analyses and even forecasts which have heretofore been abundantly confirmed by the subsequent course of the business cycle. Its analyses have, of course, frequently had to be restricted to narrowly limited objects, for under present conditions such work is necessarily limited in two directions: (*a*) The course of business can be predicted only some 3 months ahead, and (*b*) it can be forecast in respect of a single field (though a field of decisive importance) namely, in regard to the domestic-employment curve. Perhaps a further development of the system may gradually render more comprehensive forecasting possible.

A Survey of the Barometers.

At present the system consists of the following barometers:

1. A barometer of production, by which the following factors are compared:

    a. Inflow of orders.
    b. Imports of raw material.
    c. Production.
    d. Employment.
    e. Exports of finished goods.

2. An employment index for industries producing consumers' and producers' goods.

3. A barometer of storage movements.

4. Foreign trade as a barometer of the home market.

5. A barometer of business transactions, by which the following factors are compared:

    a. Long-term credits.

    b. Inflow of orders.

    c. Employment.

6. A barometer of credit, by which credits granted by the bank of issue and bill drawings, debtors and deposits, and issues of fixed-interest and dividend-bearing securities are compared with each other.

7. A barometer of the three markets, by which price movements in the security, commodity, and money markets are contrasted.

8. A barometer of commodity prices, covering:

    a. Sensitive commodity prices.

    b. Prices of industrial raw materials and semifinished goods.

    c. Prices of finished industrial commodities at wholesale.

    d. Retail prices.

Details in regard to the construction of these barometers are given below. In the next chapter we shall proceed to consider how they are used for business diagnosis.

1. THE BAROMETER OF PRODUCTION

The barometer of production is constructed on the principle of parallel and consecutive fluctuation and covers the following factors:

a. Inflow of orders.

b. Imports of raw materials.

c. Production.

d. Employment.

e. Exports of finished goods.

a. The index figure of the *inflow of orders* is a combination of nine separate series, taken from the iron, engineering, building, textile, and paper industries. Weighting is based on the money volume of production in the respective industrial groups. So far as it has been possible to distinguish between home and foreign orders, only domestic orders have been taken into account for the purposes of the index. Statistics based on selling prices are converted into quantity statistics by a process of reduction with the aid of appropriate price index figures. Seasonal

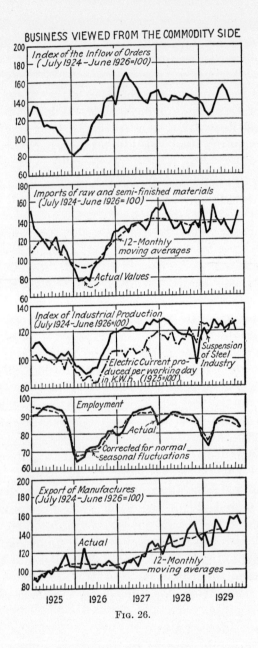

FIG. 26.

fluctuations are as far as possible eliminated. The index has been calculated on the basis of July, 1924, to June, 1926 (= 100).

b. Imports of raw materials and semifinished goods: money volume at present prices on the basis of the official monthly figures for Germany's foreign trade. For the purpose of eliminating fluctuations due to the varying length of the different months, the monthly totals are converted into daily averages. The results are shown in a scale of relative figures on the basis of July, 1924, to June, 1926 (= 100).

c. For the purpose of calculating the index figure of *production,* eight kinds of commodity were taken for the primary basic industries and six for the secondary or transforming industries (forming, with their subcategories, 19 separate series). Primary basic production is represented by coal, lignite, pig iron, steel ingots, rolling-mill products, potash, lime, and cement; and secondary production by cotton yarn, linen yarn, hemp yarn, semifinished paper material, cardboard, and paper. The monthly physical-volume production is first reduced to a daily average. For commodities belonging to the same industrial category, a general weight is adopted, calculated according to the money volume of the production of the industrial group concerned. The money volume of production is estimated on the basis of the physical volume for 1913 (present German territory) and 1925 and the prices for 1913. The general weight is distributed over the separate series according to the proportion which the subcategory represents of the total money volume of the production of the whole industrial group. The separate series are combined into a general index figure on the basis of the weighted arithmetic mean. The index is based on July, 1924, to June, 1926 (= 100).

d. The index figure for *employment* is calculated in the following manner.

The bases adopted are:

1. The monthly returns by the trade unions of their members wholly unemployed or working short time.

2. The occupational and industrial census (June 15, 1925) figures for the number of persons employed in the various economic groups.

The number of "fully employed" persons is obtained for the various branches by subtracting the number of unemployed and short-time workers from the total membership, short-time workers being converted into wholly unemployed for the purpose of this calculation on the basis of the reduction in weekly hours worked (according to whether the reduction is from 1 to 8, from 9 to 16, from 17 to 24, or over 24 hours). The number of fully employed persons thus calculated is expressed as a percentage of the membership of the unions.

In order to eliminate seasonal influences, the building-material industry, the building trade, and the clothing trade are excluded; the food, drink, and tobacco trades are also left out of account.

The significance attributed to the several industrial branches in estimating the level of employment in industry as a whole is determined by reference to the number of persons employed in the respective branches. The method employed is to multiply the percentage figure of fully employed persons for each group by the number of persons employed in the group (as revealed by the occupational and industrial census) and then to add the products thus obtained and to divide the total by the total number of persons employed. The result is a figure less than 100, which indicates the level of employment at any given moment.

e. *Exports of finished goods:* money volume at present prices, on the basis of the official monthly figures for Germany's foreign trade. For the purpose of eliminating fluctuations due to the varying length of the different months, the monthly totals are converted into daily averages. The results are shown in a scale of relative figures, on the basis of July, 1924, to June, 1926 (= 100).

2. THE EMPLOYMENT INDEX FOR INDUSTRIES PRODUCING PRODUCERS' AND CONSUMERS' GOODS

The employment figures, as determined for the various branches of industry by the method described under 1 *d*, above, are, at the same time, arranged according to the groups of industries producing consumers' and producers' goods, respectively. The groups are considered as consisting of the following trades:

1. Industries producing producers' goods: mining, iron and metal industries, chemicals, paper, leather, timber, and

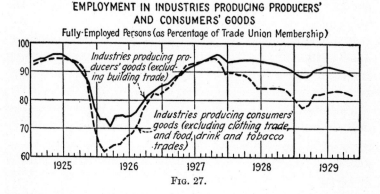

EMPLOYMENT IN INDUSTRIES PRODUCING PRODUCERS'
AND CONSUMERS' GOODS
Fully-Employed Persons (as Percentage of Trade Union Membership)

Fig. 27.

woodworking materials, and the engineering and electro-technical industries.

2. Industries producing consumers' goods: textiles, woodworking, leather, and pottery.

3. THE BAROMETER OF STORAGE MOVEMENTS

This barometer compares with each other the representative factors in the movement of commodities to and from storage. The following are taken as factors in the movement *to* storage: the production index figure, imports of raw materials and finished or semifinished goods (per calendar day), the percentage of trade-union members in full-time employment, and debtors in current account for the ten principal banks. The following are taken as factors in the movement *from* storage: retail-trade turnover in clothing, domestic equipment and furniture (subject to elimination of seasonal fluctuations), cooperative-societies turnover (average weekly turnover per member), exports of raw materials and finished or semifinished goods (per calendar day), and currency in circulation at the end of the month. Each series is reduced to a relative figure, on the basis of the average for July, 1924, to June, 1926 (= 100). With a view to eliminate seasonal fluctuations as far as possible, the retail-trade turnover figure is, in each case, divided by the wholesale index number for finished goods (consumers'-goods group), the cooperative societies' turnover figure by the cost-of-living index number

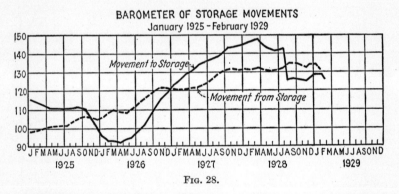

BAROMETER OF STORAGE MOVEMENTS
January 1925 – February 1929

Fig. 28.

(dwelling accommodation excluded), and the currency-circulation figure by the inclusive cost-of-living index number.

The separate series thus transformed are, by ascertaining the arithmetic mean of the respective relative figures, combined into representative series for the factors in the movement of commodities to and from storage, and these two series are further smoothed by calculating moving averages for 3 months, so as largely to eliminate, also, the influence of random disturbances.

4. FOREIGN TRADE AS A BAROMETER OF THE DOMESTIC MARKET

The calculation of the excess of imports of raw materials and semifinished goods over exports and of the exports of finished goods over imports is based on the money-volume figures, at present prices, for the exchange of commodities only, on the basis of the international classification of merchandise (Brussels Convention of Dec. 31, 1913). In the case of raw materials and semifinished goods, exports are subtracted from imports, and a balance-sheet value for the demand for imports is thus obtained. In the case of finished goods, imports are subtracted from exports, and the value is thus obtained of the commodities exported by Germany abroad under the production and consumption conditions obtaining at any moment. In plotting these

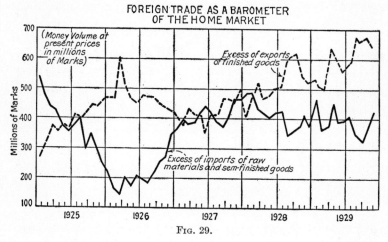

FOREIGN TRADE AS A BAROMETER
OF THE HOME MARKET

FIG. 29.

curves, it is necessary to correct the foreign-trade statistics for the months January to October, 1924, in order to eliminate errors due to the defective calculation of imports or exports, as the case may be, over the western frontier. With this object, the monthly figures shown by the foreign-trade returns have been increased by one-twelfth for imports and by one-eighth for exports.[1]

5. THE BAROMETER OF BUSINESS TRANSACTIONS

The barometer of business transactions has been constructed on the principle of sequence. It involves a comparison of the following items:

[1] See *V.z.K.*, vol. 1, suppl. 2, pp. 30 *ff*.

   a. Long-term credits.
   b. Inflow of orders.
   c. Employment.
   a. The long-term credits curve represents the provision of German business with capital on long terms, out of domestic or foreign resources. It is plotted on the basis (1) of the Federal Statistical Office's monthly figures for loan issues at home or abroad by the public authorities or by private undertakings (other than banks) together

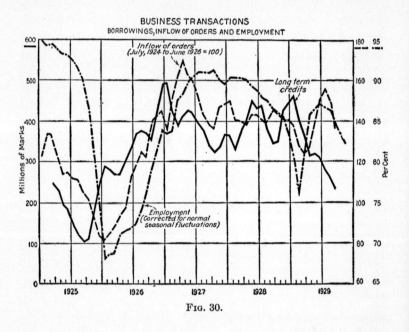

BUSINESS TRANSACTIONS
BORROWINGS, INFLOW OF ORDERS AND EMPLOYMENT

Fig. 30.

with share issues (exclusive of shares issued in return for surrender of property rights or in connection with amalgamations) at the price of issue; and (2) of the monthly increase in the amount of credits given on mortgages, (as far as compiled by the Federal Statistical Office). Under the latter head are included agricultural and urban mortgages, and the municipal loans granted by the land banks, savings banks, life-insurance companies, and the Salaried-employees' Insurance Association.

b. For index figure for the inflow of orders, compare 1 *a,* above.

c. For employment index figure, compare 1 *d,* above.

6. THE CREDIT BAROMETER

The barometer of credit covers the following items:

a. Bill drawings, calculated from the Treasury's monthly receipts under the tax on bills of exchange.

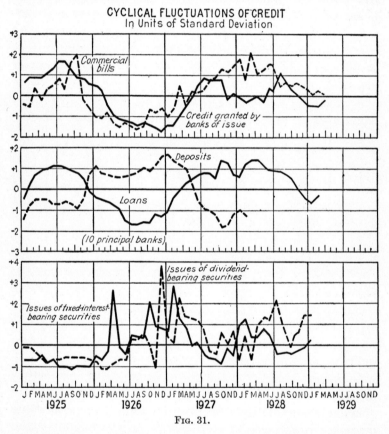

CYCLICAL FLUCTUATIONS OF CREDIT
In Units of Standard Deviation

Fɪɢ. 31.

b. Credits granted by the banks of issue, that is, advances by the Reichsbank, the four private banks of issue, and (down to November, 1927) the Rentenbank on bills or collateral; monthly averages are calculated from the four weekly statements issued in each month.

c. Debtors of the ten principal banks, that is, the advances on current account shown in the interim bank statements (position at the end of each month).

d. Deposits for the ten principal banks, that is, the sums deposited on account free of charge, as shown in the interim bank statements (position at the end of each month).

e. Issues of fixed-interest bearing securities, based on the statistics compiled monthly by the Federal Statistical Office of loans, industrial debentures and municipal and other bonds thrown open to subscription at home.

f. Issues of dividend-bearing securities, based on monthly statistics, compiled from the returns of the joint-stock companies, of share issues, reckoned at the price of issue, and excluding new shares issued in connection with amalgamations or in return for surrender of property rights.

7. THE BAROMETER OF THE THREE MARKETS

The barometer of the three markets registers the movement of prices in the security market, the commodity market, and the money market. Two different forms are used for representing this barometer:

1. A *single* representative curve is selected for each market. The monthly average values for these three curves are combined into a general diagram (the three-curve barometer)—trend and seasonal fluctuations being eliminated and the values being calculated in terms of the standard deviation, where necessary. The following factors are selected as representative:

Stock market: the level of stock prices.

Commodity market: the index of sensitive commodity prices.

Money market: interest rates on monthly loans, or an average money rate.

2. Each market is represented by *several* time series. The quotations for a selected day in each week, or the average daily quotations in each week, are brought into periodical relation with the average for a particular basic period (= 100), and the selected curves for each market

are combined to form a separate diagram. Trend and seasonal fluctuations are not eliminated; each curve represents the natural uncorrected movement of the figures.

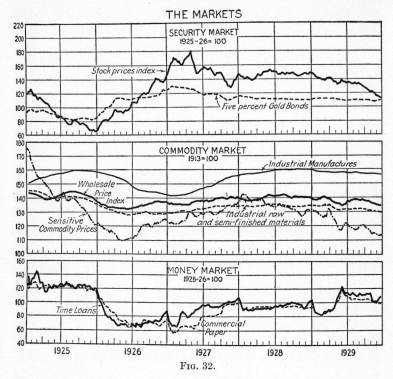

FIG. 32.

The following items are selected as respectively representative.

Stock Market.

1. *The average price level of* 229 representative *industrial stocks* quoted on the Berlin Stock Exchange. For the purpose of calculating the general average of the 229 stock prices, each trade group is given a weight corresponding to the nominal capital of all the companies to be included in the group. The price level represents the arithmetic mean of the prices actually quoted; the effect of preferential purchase rights and other technical factors influencing the average price are not eliminated.

2. *The index of 5 per cent gold bonds.* The average price level of ten gold bonds at a nominal rate of interest of 5 per cent, quoted on the Berlin Exchange. Weekly averages are calculated from the rates for each day.

Commodity Market.

1. *The index of sensitive commodity prices.* The geometric mean of the relative figures of ten price series: wool, flax, hemp, ox hides, calfskins, lead, medium plates, scrap iron, machine-foundry scrap, brass-plate chips.

2. *The wholesale-price index figure (general).* The weighted arithmetic mean of the relative figures of 800 price quotations, covering 400 different commodities.

3. *The index figure for the industrial raw-materials and semifinished-goods group*, included in the general wholesale price index. The weighted arithmetic mean of the relative figures of 170 price quotations for 120 different commodities.

4. *The index figure for the industrial finished-articles group*, included in the general wholesale price index. The weighted arithmetic mean of the relative figures of 545 price quotations for 230 different commodities.

Money Market.

1. *The commercial paper rate.* Calculated as an average from the daily quotations for bank-endorsed commercial paper on the Berlin Exchange.

2. *Average money rates.* Calculated from the daily quotations for call loans, 30-day loans, private discount (average for short and long dated bills), and commercial paper on the Berlin Exchange.

8. THE BAROMETER OF COMMODITY PRICES

The barometer of price movements comprises four price curves:

1. *Index of sensitive commodity prices.* The geometric mean of the relative figures for ten retail-price series.

2. *The index figure for the industrial raw-materials and semifinished-goods group, included in the general wholesale-price index.*

3. *The index figure for consumers' goods, from the industrial finished-articles group, included in the general wholesale-price index.* The weighted arithmetic mean of the relative figure for 260 price quotations covering 105 different commodities.

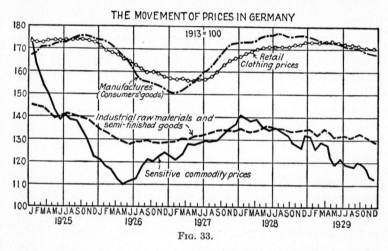

FIG. 33.

4. *Retail clothing prices.* Weighted arithmetic mean of the prices for 15 articles of clothing, average for 72 districts (*subgroup of the cost-of-living index number*).

Bibliography

"*Die weltwirtschaftliche Lage Ende* 1925," Treasury, Statistical Office, and Institute for Business Cycle Research, Berlin, 1926. *V.z.K.*, with supplements and special numbers, since May, 1926. Weekly reports of the Institute for Business Cycle Research, since April, 1928.

WAGEMANN: Deutsche und amerikanische Konjunkturforschung, *Deutsche Wirtschaftszeitung*, No. 13, 1926.

SECTION V

THE INTERLACING OF SPECIFIC FLUCTUATIONS

CHAPTER XV

PURPOSE AND METHOD OF CLASSIFICATION

Cyclical "Situations" and "Tensions."

If we bring together the readings obtained from our business barometer and attempt to derive from them a typical picture of the course of a business cycle, we shall obtain a result on the lines appearing in the diagram shown on the following page.

In this diagram, the characteristic features of the cyclical "situations" are set against those of the cyclical "tensions." Although tensions are themselves characteristic features in the situation, it appears better to draw a distinction between series (such as those representing the employment level, income, production, and turnover) which represent solely or primarily the progress of business or the development of prosperity (and so play the part of a thermometer rather than that of a barometer) and series which more definitely indicate maladjustments, disturbed relationships, or tensions (and so play the part of a genuine barometer or, if the term be preferred, of a pressure gage). Accordingly, the diagram of cyclical situations comprises series showing parallel or consecutive fluctuation, while that of cyclical tensions comprises series showing inverse or "radiatory" fluctuation.

Such a chart is no farther from reality, and no nearer to it, than a description of the seasons in which January is characterized by ice and snow and July by extreme heat

160

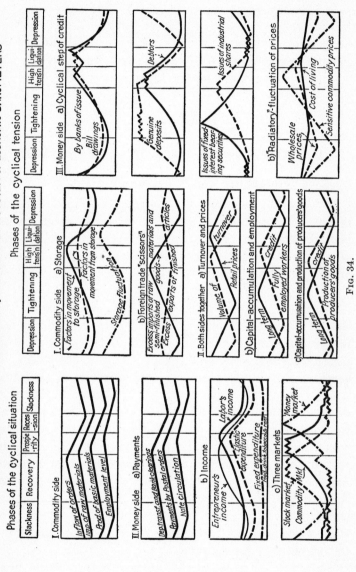

Fig. 34.

or than the description of a "typical" storm. It naturally does not pretend to represent the business cycle as pursuing an invariable course of development (this point has to be emphasized in view of the somewhat childish mentality of a certain school of critics). For just as warm, rainy weather may be predominant in January, rather than snow and ice, so the conditions shown in our chart of the business cycle are, also, subject to very considerable deviations. For the purpose of economic diagnosis, it is, therefore, not sufficient to identify on the chart the particular situation and tension which correspond to actual business conditions at any given moment; nor is it necessarily even possible to do so, for deviations from the chart (which should be regarded not as a norm but rather as a combination of phases as they present themselves in typical cases) will constantly make their appearance. In particular, the sequence of "situations" may easily get out of step with that of "tensions." Indeed, for the purposes of a diagnosis of business conditions it is often more important to observe the deviations than to establish the normal movement sequence; for they are, to some extent, an indication of the future course of the cycle— in so far as it is possible to forecast that course at all.

Analysis by Industries as a Basis of Classification.

The system of barometers shown in our chart is imperfect if only because satisfactory statistical series are not available for their construction. We can, however, form an idea of what a really comprehensive system would look like if we obtain a basis of classification which will permit us to arrange economic fluctuations as a whole according to subject. Such a basis is afforded by the business analysis of the individual undertakings, for these are as it were the cells of the economic organism and comprise the totality of the separate points on which the motive forces of the business cycle are exerted.

In its efforts to earn profits, the undertaking has, on the one hand, to obtain and, on the other, to dispose of goods and services. As this process of exchange takes place not as in a state of nature but under the conditions imposed by money economy, the former side of the undertaking's activities appears as a procuring of working capital (flotation, borrowing, profit earning) and as a purchasing of goods and services, and the latter as a disposal of finance capital (granting of credit, provision for depreciation, liquidation, etc.) and as a selling of goods and services. The activities of an undertaking may, accordingly, be classified, in the main, as follows (if we agree to exclude internal management and the technical side of production, which are only indirectly related with the business cycle):

1. Procuring and disposing of working capital.

2. Procuring and disposing of commodities and labor power (services).

These processes are reflected in the individual trading account of an undertaking in somewhat the following manner (if we confine ourselves to the main basic items):

Expenditure:
1. Raw materials and accessory supplies:
   a. Domestic.
   b. Foreign.
2. Salaries and wages.
3. Provisions for depreciation.
4. Interest and entrepreneurs' profits.

Receipts:
5. Domestic sales:
   a. Physical volume.
   b. Money volume.
6. Sales abroad:
   a. Physical volume.
   b. Money volume.

According as turnover is divided among these six basic items,[1] undertakings, in general, may also be classified

---

[1] A first attempt, admittedly of a very modest character, to bring to light a portion of the relationships in question for a number of important economic branches is embodied in the following survey, worked out by Dr. Ruberg on the basis of an analysis of profit and loss calculations or costs for *V.z.K.* The figures in parentheses are taken from the results of another study. The divergences between them and the other figures are an indication of the

within the national system according to whether they are predominantly dependent on

1. Raw materials.
2. Wages.
3. Producers' goods.
4. Credit and interest.
5. Domestic market, or
6. Exports.

Factors Affecting Cyclical Position of Businesses.

It goes without saying that there is scarcely any undertaking or branch of production which is not dependent in one way or another on all of these factors. Their position in relation to the fluctuation of business as a whole varies considerably, however, according to the nature and extent of their dependence. If it appears, for instance, that in a particular branch of business interest plays an important part in costs of production on account of the slowness of returns and that in consequence of a considerable reliance on outside capital, and especially on short-term loans, the fluctuation in money rates bulks largely in the balance sheet while the remaining items show only a slight tendency to vary, we may conclude that the branch in question is particularly dependent on interest and credit. An industry which tends to sell a good deal of its produce

---

inadequacy in this field of inquiry of the generally available material supplied by companies compelled to publish information concerning their activities. Incidentally, such material is not always typical for other forms of undertaking (particularly, in the case of the retail textile trade).

Particular Costs in Various Branches of Business as a Percentage
of Total Cost of Production

Branch	Raw materials, etc.	Wages and salaries (not incl. entrepreneurs salary)	Depreciation	Interest on outside capital	Miscellaneous
Coal mining.......	20 to 25 (30)	45 to 60 (68)	7 to 9 (8)	5 to 8 (2)	8 (2)
Lignite mining.....	20 to 25 (36.4)	24 to 30 (39)	20 to 25 (11.2)	6 to 10 (3.2)	18 (10.2)
Foundries.........	90 to 95	1 to 2	1 to 2	?	3
Rolling mills......	90 to 95	2	1 to 2	As little as 0.7	3 to 4
Textile industry...	60 to 70	10 to 15	2 to 5	1 to 3	17
Retail textile trade	70	8 to 9	1 to 2	1 to 2	8

in foreign markets would be, to a high degree, dependent on exports, and so on.

The bringing to light of all these forms of dependence will be one of the most important objects of our research work in the immediate future; for if we can succeed in so analyzing the whole national business process that all the "dependences" can be calculated, or even estimated, according to their volume and intensity—that is, according to their importance and to the limits within which they fluctuate—for every branch of business we shall obtain a conception of the intercomplexity of movements which will enable us to measure a variation at one point in the business process in terms of its reactions on other points, both in extent and, to some extent, in duration; while our principle of classification, based on individual business analysis, will automatically develop in the course of our investigations. We should thus build up a system of knowledge which would permit us to produce something rather more useful than the general and sterile deductions customarily put forward in such cases. It would be possible, for example, to determine the significance of a change in money rates or prices, or even of a technical improvement affecting the raw-material requirements of a given type of production. Investigation in this field is still in its infancy; but the Institute for Business Cycle Research has already begun the preliminary spade work. In this respect, I agree with Cassel that it is better

. . . to form a quantitative notion as a result of a proper manipulation of the available material than to formulate a random interpretation and then attempt to recommend it to the uncritical and sentimental judgment of one's readers by piling up masses of appropriate adjectives around it, in the manner of the authors of the various current textbooks.

A survey of the interlacing of movements possesses the advantage that it does not bind us to any single theory on the causation of business cycles; it thus permits us to vary the object of our study at will, so that we are, for instance, just as much at liberty to investigate the factors on which money rates depend as we are, conversely, to estimate the reaction of money rates on some other factor —such as exports or the labor market. A chart of the interlacing of movements signifies simply a chart of functional relationships between the separate factors in economic movement. The term "causal relationships" may be substituted for "functional relationships," if preferred; but it possesses the disadvantage that it indicates only the direction in which investigation is to be pursued, as determined by the object of study at any particular moment. We shall not succeed in revealing causal relationships between the separate economic factors in the true sense of the term, for we conceive the economic organism as an interdependent closed system (though in a different sense from Schumpeter and Löwe, who use this conception as signifying a mechanical interaction between the economic elements).

In the following pages, a number of important interlaced relations between movements are considered more closely, attention being directed more particularly to the level of employment in industry. This last is only one among an infinity of possible landmarks, but at the present moment it may be considered as the most important.

The first step is to separate the movement of business in agriculture from that of business in industry and, thus, to investigate the cyclical dependence of the latter on the former. We shall then proceed to consider, in the second place, the relations between industry and foreign trade; thirdly, the part played by credit in industrial fluctuations; and, fourthly, the interdependence of money-volume and physical-volume movements, so as to obtain an insight, at any rate, into the most important determinants of the industrial employment level.

CHAPTER XVI

THE RELATIONSHIP BETWEEN CYCLICAL FLUCTUATIONS IN AGRICULTURE AND INDUSTRY

Agrarian and Industrial States.

During the nineteenth century, the nations of western and central Europe completed their evolution from a predominantly agricultural to an industrial economy. This process of evolution can be excellently illustrated by a comparative investigation of marriage statistics (which may be taken as a characteristic expression of the economic prosperity of the national community) and time series

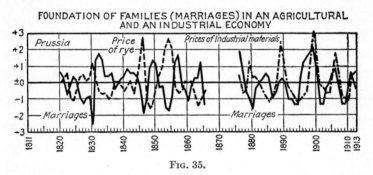

FOUNDATION OF FAMILIES (MARRIAGES) IN AN AGRICULTURAL AND AN INDUSTRIAL ECONOMY

FIG. 35.

adequately reflecting (*a*) agricultural and (*b*) industrial cycles.[1] The figures show that in England down to the twenties of the last century, the curve of marriages moved inversely as compared with that of wheat prices but that thereafter this inverse fluctuation disappeared and that from the thirties on, its place was taken by a very marked parallel fluctuation as between marriages and (*a*) prices of industrial materials and (*b*) exports, which, in the case

[1] Such an investigation has been conducted, on the model of previous researches (by Süssmilch, Quetelet, Engel, Von Mayr, Tönnies, and others) by Dr. Bramstedt in the Institut für Konjunkturforschung.

of England, comprise almost exclusively industrial products (the price series is available only from the fifties on). In Prussia, as the diagram shown above indicates, the inverse fluctuation between cereal prices and marriages lasted until the sixties and then disappeared, giving place to a pronounced parallel fluctuation as between marriages and prices of industrial materials.[1]

Cyclical Fluctuations in Industry and Agriculture before the World War.

A comparison for the last ten years before the World War of a few series representing cyclical fluctuations in industry (number of demands for employment registered at the employment exchanges, sensitive commodity prices) with others similarly representative for agriculture (gross yield in money of the rye, wheat and potato harvests, and value of hogs and cattle slaughtered, which together reflect the fluctuation of agriculture's gross receipts)[2] shows the following results:

After a decline in the business year 1905–1906, agriculture's gross receipt rose fairly considerably until the business year 1907–1908. During this period, industry went through three successive phases of the business cycle—revival, high tension, and crisis. During the industrial revival, agriculture's gross receipts underwent a decline in 1905–1906. The high tension and crisis in industry failed in 1906–1907 and 1907–1908 to check the rise in agriculture's gross receipts, which continued, though slowly, from 1907–1908 to 1909–1910, although these were years of industrial depression. In 1910–1911, a fairly sharp decline set in, while industry, on the other hand, entered a distinct phase of revival. In 1911–1912, agricultural gross receipts and business conditions in industry moved upward simultaneously; but agricultural net receipts did not rise in proportion, as, owing to the bad

---

[1] For further details, see *V.z.K.*, vol. 3, No. IA, pp. 37 *ff.*

[2] This investigation was carried out by the author, with the help of Dr. Hanau and Dr. Paetzmann.

harvest of 1911, the cost of fodder and other items increased. In 1912–1913, agriculture's gross receipts remained fairly steady; and in 1913–1914, they declined fairly sharply. This decline did, indeed, coincide with a falling off in industrial prosperity, but it is to be attributed to a drop in prices due to the extraordinarily abundant production of animal and vegetable products.

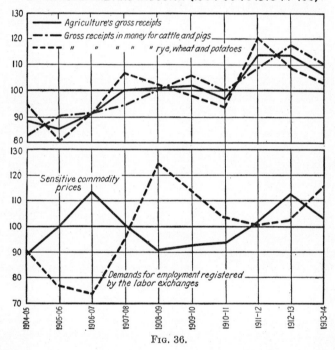

TIME SERIES ILLUSTRATING CYCLICAL FLUCTUATIONS IN AGRICULTURE AND INDUSTRY (1904-05 TO 1913-14=100)

Fig. 36.

Thus, an intimate connection between the cyclical fluctuations in German industry and agriculture can no longer be traced, though these two great branches of economic activity are, of course, still in many respects interdependent.

Agriculture's Demand for Industrial Products.

The reactions caused by variations in agriculture's gross receipts on agriculture's demand for industrial prod-

ucts may be represented in the following manner:[1] The
gross receipts of German agriculture amounted to

In the business year	Billions of marks[1]
1924–1925	12.39
1925–1926	13.03
1926–1927	12.55

[1] Figures calculated by Dr. Paetzmann, on the basis of an inquiry by
districts carried out with the assistance of the Reichstag Commission for
Economic Investigation.

In order to attain the object of our investigation, we
must now consider the manner in which these receipts
(or gross profits) were expended.[2]

The Expenditure of Agriculture's Takings.

For this purpose, we must distinguish several stages in
expenditure, some of which really correspond to the process
of exchange in a money economy, while others are more in
the nature of arithmetical ciphers, employed only for bookkeeping purposes. In order to illustrate the relationships
and procession question, we shall take the gross receipts
for 1925 to 1926 and estimate roughly the manner in which
these receipts returned to the national economy.

Stage 1 in Expenditure.

In the first stage of expenditure, agriculture's gross
receipts must be divided into costs of production and net
receipts. Costs of production are understood as comprising
payment made for the collaboration of other business
branches (industry, commerce, and the like) in enabling
agriculture to produce profitably—that is, expenditure
on artificial manure, machinery, building, insurance, and,
also, in respect of taxation[3] on business. Thus, this
heading covers expenditure on material objects. If we
deduct costs of production from gross receipts, the remain-

[1] This material has already been published by the author in *V.z.K.*, vol.
3, No. IA, pp. 45 *ff.*
[2] Material already published by the author in *V.z.K.*, vol. 3, No. IA.
[3] This last item cannot at present be fully estimated.

STAGES IN THE EXPENDITURE OF AGRICULTURAL TAKINGS REPRESENTED
IN TABULAR FORM, 1925-1926

(Figures in billions of marks)

Stage 1	Stage 2	Stage 3

Gross receipts 13 — Net receipts 10

Cost of production..... 3 —— Foreign products[5]........ ¾

Industrial products (producers' goods)........... 2

Supplement to distributive trades................. ¼

Insurance, business taxes, etc.....................

Interest to capitalists[1].......... ¾

Wages[2] ....

Payments for services[3].......... } 7½

Payments for property rights[4].

Entrepreneurs' profits.......... } 1¾

Net occupational receipts 9¼

Savings and consumption expenditure of capitalists.......... ¾

Self-maintenance. 4

Industrial products (consumers' goods) 2

Supplement to distributive trades.......... ¾

Taxes,[6] schools, doctors, miscellaneous......... 2

Farmers' savings.. ½

Stage 3: Indirect demand for industrial products set up by expenditure of total money takings (less cost of self-maintenance). This demand is additional to the direct consumption of industrial products (4,000,000,000), but its value cannot be estimated.

[1] Interest payable to creditors.
[2] Wages to laborers and employees.
[3] Payment due to the independent farmer in respect of his own labor.
[4] Interest on farmer's own capital including rent, that is utilization of his own house property.
[5] Including home-produced bran used as fodder.
[6] Including business taxes (on land, buildings, and turnover); these latter belong, properly speaking, to costs of production and represent a corresponding reduction in the net national income.

der constitutes agriculture's net receipts. These include, in the first place, the sums due as interest to agriculture's creditors, who by providing capital have taken a part in bringing about agricultural production. In so far as the capital in question is family capital, inherited capital, etc., payments for its use made by agricultural undertakings have, obviously, to be included among the national net takings of agriculture; fundamentally, however, we are also justified in including other interest payments due from agriculture under the same head.

It seems advisable, however, to group the following items together as agriculture's "net occupational receipts":

1. Wages received by farm laborers and agricultural employees.

2. Payment due to the independent farmer in respect of his own labor (payment for services). This item has no separate concrete existence and can, at most, be treated only as an arithmetically separate item, for it comes to the farmer intermingled with the interest on his own capital and his profits as entrepreneur, in the form of a surplus and partly in kind rather than in money.

3. Interest on the farmer's own capital (payment for property rights). This item, which, like the last, has no separate concrete existence, includes the rent of the dwelling accommodation used by the farmer, in so far as such rent is not already covered by the item "sums due as interest to creditors." It is possible at most to make an estimate for this item only for the prewar period, when a rate of interest could be quoted as customary and when possible bases for estimating the property value of the agricultural industry existed. At present, it is quite impossible to fix the value for this item.

4. What remains is entrepreneur's profits. Enough has already been said above to show the impossibility of making a separate estimate for this item.

Stage 2 in Expenditure.

The question how these items in the first stage of expenditure fit into the national business process as a whole brings us, in accordance with the classification which we have adopted, to the second stage. Costs of production cover expenditure, in the first place, on the purchase of fodder, cattle, and seeds from abroad and of bran at home, to an amount of seven-tenths billion marks and of industrial producers' goods to an amount of two billions.[1] This amount is, however, calculated on the basis of the prices paid to the manufacturer, so that we are obliged to add supplements for commerce and transport. As such supplements are insignificant in the case of the building trade, we may estimate them at no more than a quarter billion. Costs of production also include the item "insurance";

---

[1] *V.z.K.*, vol. 3, No. IA, pp. 43,44 (Dr. Jacobs' calculations).

expenditure under this head goes, for the most part (in so far as insurance means fire insurance), to the building trade, except for money which remains in the hands of the insurers. On the other hand, allowance is already made for harvest insurance in calculating gross receipts, for allowance is made for losses on the harvest in estimating its total yield. Thus, in calculating the national costs of agricultural production, we need include really only the proportion of premiums which remains in the hands of the insurers. The sums thus involved lie inside the limits of approximation and may, therefore, be omitted from our table.

We must now consider the destination of the net receipts of the nation's agriculture.

As far as the utilization of the capitalist's receipts from agriculture (interest due to creditors) is concerned, we can, of course, say only in general terms that they are partly spent and partly saved. The net occupational income of agriculture is distributed as follows:

1. Self-support in food stuffs, estimated at four billions; the fodder consumed in agriculture is already allowed for in calculated gross receipts.

2. Consumption of industrial consumers' goods, estimated two billions on the basis of industrial manufacturers' prices. To this sum we add supplements for commerce and transport amounting to three-quarters of a billion, so that the consumption of industrial consumers' goods is estimated on the basis of retail prices at two and three-quarters billions.

3. Consumption of consumers' goods from abroad. This item is small and lies inside the limits of approximation.

4. In the absence of trustworthy information, we may, for the sake of illustration, put down a half billion for savings.

5. Taxes, in so far as these are not business taxes and already included under other items of expenditure, together with expenditure on schooling, medical attendance, and the like, absorb the residue of two billions.

Stage 3 in Expenditure.

Thus, at the second stage of expenditure, there is a direct demand for industrial products to the amount of four billion marks (two billions each for consumers' and producers' goods, respectively). In the third stage, however, a further demand for industrial products is set up by expenditure under the remaining heads. It is immediately obvious that a proportion of the capitalist's receipts, which are partly saved and partly spent, will be translated into a demand for industrial products. The savings of the farmers themselves, which, in the analysis above, have not been taken into account, owing to the absence of any sufficient basis for their calculation, will—after passing through the hands of the banks or being reinvested in the farm—reappear in the form, more particularly, of demand for producers' goods. Outlay in respect of taxes, schooling, and medical attendance flows into industry in so far as the state, the schoolmaster, the doctor and so on, require industrial products. Even out of the direct demand for industrial products, however (which we have estimated at four billions, a further indirect demand is developed, since industry itself requires industrial products and does not consume in the form of food stuffs the whole of the four billions which it has charged the farmer. We must, therefore, set down a portion of the nine billions remaining of agriculture's gross receipts (after subtraction of the four billions spent on self-support) as representing an indirect demand for industrial products, additional to the direct demand amounting to four billions. No estimate can be given for this portion, however.

Conclusions.

In estimating the extent to which a change in the amount of agriculture's takings reacts on industrial sales, one must bear in mind that some of the items of expenditure tabulated above are far less variable than others. Fluctuations in receipts will have little effect on the following items in the second stage of expenditure: foreign products (fodder, cattle), insurance, self-support, capitalist's receipts (including the savings and expenditure of the capitalist, since his receipts remain essentially unaffected by the amount of the farmer's takings). Thus, the items primarily affected by a fluctuation in agriculture's takings are industrial products and the supplements to the distributive trades, which together account for five billions. Of this sum, the proportion representing demand for consumers' goods may be regarded as comparatively invariable, since the goods in question are, with few exceptions, goods which are absolutely essential to the maintenance of life. A fall in takings of a half billion, such as we have observed to have taken place between 1925–1926 and 1926–1927, would hardly involve a drop of more than, say, 5 per cent in the consumption of industrial consumers' goods; since we have estimated this consumption to represent an outlay of 2,750,000,000, the decline involved would thus not exceed one-eighth billion. By far the greatest part of the effects of a drop in takings will fall, generally speaking, on the demand for producers' goods; and of the effective demand for such goods, that for buildings and machinery is more liable to reduction than that for artificial manure, though the position, in this respect, is not absolutely invariable.

If we assume that the total value of the net takings of German industry amounts to about 25,000,000,000 (see above, p. 36) and together with imports of raw materials and semifinished goods about 30,000,000,000 then a fall of one-half billion in agriculture's receipts will react on industry to the extent of about $1\frac{2}{3}$ per cent; a percentage which represents just under a quarter million employed persons. Supposing the effects of the decline in agriculture's receipts to be limited to the industries on which they mainly fall, that is, the industries producing producers' goods, the net receipts of which, together with the imports of raw materials, amount to, say, 15,000,000,000 (in practice, of course, the effects could never fall so exclusively on one branch), then the reaction will amount to $3\frac{1}{3}$ per cent. Bearing in mind that the decline in demand for producers' goods will react particularly on building materials and machinery, we may conclude that these industries will experience a noticeable drop in orders.

The reflections embodied in the last few sentences are, of course, not based on any thorough examination of the facts; they are put forward only with a view to indicating the direction in which the investigations of the Institute for Business Cycle Research are being pursued.

CHAPTER XVII

THE RHYTHM OF FOREIGN TRADE

The Cyclical Sensitiveness of Imports and Exports.

Soltau has shown, in the course of an inquiry into cyclical
fluctuations in foreign trade, that imports into England,
France, and particularly Germany were more liable to
cyclical fluctuations in the period 1881 to 1913 than

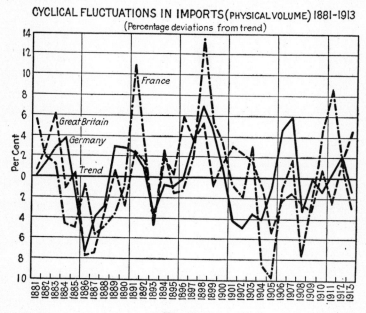

CYCLICAL FLUCTUATIONS IN IMPORTS (PHYSICAL VOLUME) 1881-1913
(Percentage deviations from trend)

FIG. 37a.

exports.[1] Whereas imports quite plainly reflect depression,
revival, prosperity, and recession, exports show scarcely
any reaction to cyclical fluctuations except during a crisis.[2]

[1] See *V.z.K.*, vol. 1, 2d, suppl.

[2] And only then provided that sales also become stagnant abroad. As
the crisis experienced in Germany at the end of 1925 was of a purely local—
and not an international—character, it was accompanied only by a seasonal
decline and not by a cyclical recession in exports.

In the postwar period, a similar phenomenon can be observed (see Figures 37a, b, and c).

The results bear on the fact that in industrial countries the movement of raw-material imports is, to a large extent,

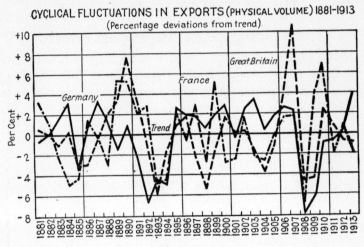

CYCLICAL FLUCTUATIONS IN EXPORTS (PHYSICAL VOLUME) 1881-1913
(Percentage deviations from trend)

Fig. 37b.

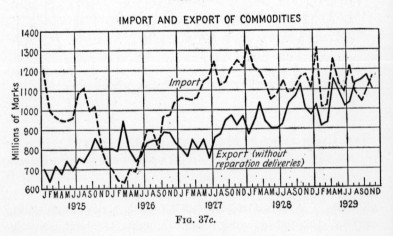

IMPORT AND EXPORT OF COMMODITIES

Fig. 37c.

determined by the general cyclical situation of business at home, while exports of finished articles, on the contrary, are determined by the situation abroad. As, however, the foreign market as a whole is infinitely greater than the domestic, and as its total volume is, therefore, less liable to variation, separate fluctuations make less impression on export trade. The proportion of exports to total world trade has remained practically stable during recent years, and exports have thus, in accordance with the development of the world market, been tending slightly to rise.

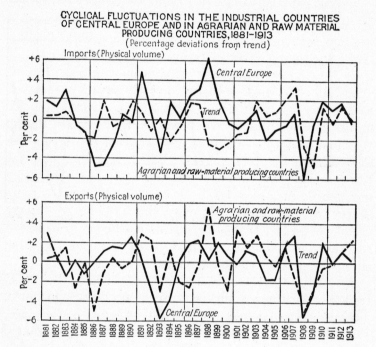

CYCLICAL FLUCTUATIONS IN THE INDUSTRIAL COUNTRIES
OF CENTRAL EUROPE AND IN AGRARIAN AND RAW MATERIAL
PRODUCING COUNTRIES, 1881-1913
(Percentage deviations from trend)

Fig. 38.

The Three Types of Movement in Export Trade.

An inquiry into the relationship between foreign trade and industry brings to light three types of movement in export figures:[1]

1. Exports move in almost entire independence of the fluctuations of the trade cycle in Germany, following the general course of movement of world exports, in its broad outlines. Exports of finished textile goods may *inter alia* be

[1] Such an inquiry was conducted by the author, with the assistance, particularly, of Dr. v. d. Gablentz; the results are published in *V.z.K.*, vol. 2, Part 4, pp. 35-37.

classified as conforming to this type of movement. If we examine closely the curves in question, we find that the single characteristic breach in continuity of direction which occurs in the earlier months of each year is of a seasonal character.

2. A sharp contrast to this group of exports is afforded by the group which stands in the closest relationship— whether negative or positive—to domestic cyclical fluctuations, fluctuating either inversely or parallel thereto.

a. The engineering industry may be quoted as an example of an industry whose exports have for some time moved parallel to the fluctuations of the trade cycle. In this industry, sales at home and abroad have, in any case during the three years just prior to 1927, moved in roughly the same direction. It remains to be investigated how far this parallel fluctuation is peculiar to the three years mentioned, and how far it is to be attributed to more deeply rooted causes. It may, in fact, be of foreign origin—in so far, that is to say, as machinery is exported to countries in which the trade cycle assumes the same character as it does in Germany.

b. Conversely, there are a number of products the export trade in which moves inversely to the trade cycle at home. These include bar iron (figured and unfigured), raw paper, and leather. This group comprises, generally speaking, all the basic materials exchanged on the world market which are more or less representative wholesale commodities and are not produced with a view to any specific body of consumers. The nature of these commodities is such that when business is stagnant at home they easily find new markets abroad—even though at comparatively unfavorable prices—and, conversely, an extension of the domestic market will immediately involve a reduction in the quantity of exports, as better prices will be obtainable at home. The effects of a comparative lack of definite connection with any particular group of consumers are extremely clear if we compare the fluctuations in the leather-export trade with those in the export of manufactured leather

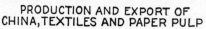

PRODUCTION AND EXPORT OF
CHINA, TEXTILES AND PAPER PULP

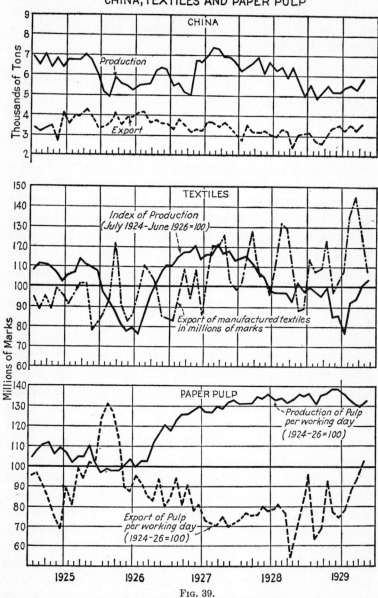

FIG. 39.

articles. In the case of the latter, a domestic depression or crisis spells reduced production without involving any corresponding increase in exports, while leather exports increase in proportion to the shrinkage of the home market.

3. The manner in which exports fluctuate does not, of course, depend entirely on the extent to which production is destined for a particular group of consumers. This is particularly evident if one considers those groups of exports which represent a mixed type of fluctuation. In the case of cutlery and china, for example the state of the home market is observed to exercise an influence almost solely in the second half of the crisis and at the beginning of the depression, while the remaining phases of the trade cycle make no further impression upon export trade in these commodities. Obviously, this means, in the case of such relatively simple products, representing the final stage in industrial transformation, that when a crisis occurs, the producers succeed in avoiding stagnation by disposing of their stocks abroad. Once this has been done, exports again decline, even though the home market has not yet opened up again. Production then shrinks in proportion. The cyclical revival, which means a revival in domestic sales, has no effect on export trade.

We have, however, seen that, in contrast to the above group, exports in most of the main basic material industries are maintained at a high level as long as business is stagnant at home and decline again when the domestic situation improves. In such cases, the dominant consideration is to maintain the level of production; this, in turn, is connected with the fact that, as a rule, the great raw-material industries are intensively capitalized and so dominated by overhead costs.

Classification According to Size.

It is, of course, possible to give only a very rough estimate of the magnitude of the exporting industries belonging to the various types described.[1] For this purpose, we may

----

[1] *V.z.K.*, vol. 4, p. 32.

begin by considering the proportion of exports to total production in the various groups of industries.[1]

Mainly Dependent on Exports (that is, exporting over 50 per cent of total production).—Only a few groups of industries producing consumers' goods fall within this category in Germany; these are the toy, musical-instrument, and glass-manufacturing industries and sections of the fine pottery, iron- and metal-goods, and carved-goods industries. These are all industries whose products possess a high specific value and, therefore, involve low transportation costs; a large proportion are industries based on small factories or home work, producing quality articles. According to the industrial census figures, they employ about 700,000 workers and employees, of whom about 350,000 work for export trade. (These figures do not include workers employed in the iron- and metal-goods industry, which is classified in the next group.)

Most of the main groups of German industries depend on the export trade to an extent of from 10 to 50 per cent. The only exceptions are industries producing goods of low specific value or handmade articles for the domestic wholesale trade—the furniture trade and most groups in the building-materials industry and the ready-made clothing trade.

Largely Dependent on Exports (that is, exporting from 20 to 50 per cent of total production).—The important groups in this category are the chemical, iron, engineering, and electrotechnical industries and the silk branch of the textile industry. In the case of these industries, the export level depends, of course, largely on the cyclical trade situation.

Slightly Dependent on Export (that is, exporting from 10 to 20 per cent of total production).—This category includes the textile industry as a whole (excluding silk), a few relatively small groups of industries producing producers' goods (manufacture of boxes and barrels, and

[1] See *V.z.K.*, vol. 4, pp. 32 *ff.*, where the material is assembled by Dr. v. d. Gablentz.

the coopering trade), and the cement section of the building-material industry.

Most of the production for export is comparatively little affected by the trade cycle at home. This applies particularly to the production of consumers' goods in the first two of the above three groups. Exports fluctuate parallel to the trade cycle in only a few special cases.

Inverse fluctuation as between the domestic trade cycle and exports is noticeable mainly in the case of industries producing producers' goods and from 10 to 30 per cent of whose total production is for export. In these industries, foreign sales serve primarily—as explained above—to keep production going and, thus, to smooth out the extreme fluctuations of the trade cycle. This category includes, in particular, the heavy-iron industry, coal mining, and the paper and leather industries, employing altogether about 1,500,000 persons. Let us suppose that in case of a crisis and depression about 10 per cent of the total production of these industries can be diverted at a month's notice from the home to the foreign market (this can hardly be called an exaggerated estimate); this would mean that these industries possess, in virtue of their ability to switch over from one market to another, a kind of reserve against the trade cycle which makes it possible for them in case of a crisis to relieve the labor market to the extent of, say, 150,000 persons.

CHAPTER XVIII

CREDIT CYCLES

On the basis of our experience before the World War, and, again, in the last three years, it appears possible to distinguish four cyclical stages of credit, which slip naturally into the framework of the general sequence of cyclical phases (see Chap. IV).

Phases in Credit Phenomena.

1. During the *depression*, finance capital accumulates in the banks. It is true that the amount credited on loan to the deposit account of their clients declines and that the amount of credit obtained by the banks for themselves is also reduced. On the other hand, "genuine" deposits increase. The offer of short-term credit becomes more and more pressing. As the demand for such credits remains feeble, it is found to be easier to place sums on long-term credit, which is in greater demand owing to the lower interest rates. More money is, therefore, placed on loan or in mortgages. By the end of the depression, a considerable increase has taken place (*a*) in the amount of long-term indebtedness and (*b*) in the amount of cash in hand and short-time reserves maintained by business in the form of bank deposits.

2. During the *revival*, the demand for fixed-interest-bearing securities gradually slackens, while investment in dividend-bearing securities increases. Business uses the short-notice bank deposits which it has accumulated during the depression in order to cope with the growing volume of trade, while the increase of such deposits begins to slacken. As the revival proceeds, there is a growing demand for short-term bank credits. The note circulation increases,

and it becomes more and more necessary to fall back on the banks of issue for business credits.

3. The *high-tension* phase is marked by increasing difficulty in obtaining either long-term or short-term credits. It is difficult to place new share issues, and

CYCLICAL PHASES IN CREDIT PHENOMENA

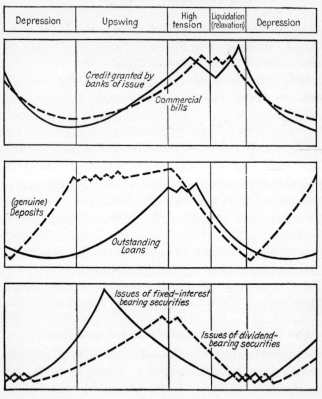

Depression	Upswing	High tension	Liquidation (relaxation)	Depression

Fig. 40.

short-term bank credits are harder to obtain. On the other hand, credits granted by the banks of issue as "supplementary credit" at first increase rapidly. Another feature is, however, quite peculiarly characteristic of this phase: as business is increasingly thrown back on its own resources, and particularly on its current takings, a kind of independent system of financing, an involuntary financial self-sufficiency of the commodity trade, develops independently of the banks. The outward expression of this development is a decline in deposits concurrent with increasing turnover. As the phase proceeds, the difficulty of disposing of stocks leads to the granting of credits to distributors, who, in turn, are obliged to demand such credit by the tightening of the money market; this leads to an unusual growth in the number of bill drawings, which, in any case, increases considerably in consequence of the greater activity of the entrepreneurs.

4. When an excessive straining of credit compels the banks of issue to exercise a restraining influence and the financial self-sufficiency of business, maintained out of its own resources or by granting credit to distributors, reaches a certain point, the upward movement is interrupted by a *crisis*. The credits granted by the banks of issue, which had already begun to be restricted toward the end of the high-tension phase, are heavily reduced—though usually after a last brief rally (see Chap. XI). Simultaneously, or, rather, as a general rule, just beforehand, the number of bill drawings suddenly drops. Similarly, deposits now decline sharply, followed by outstanding advances. Issues of both dividend- and fixed-interest-bearing securities oscillate about the lowest point of the trough.

Genuine Deposits and Miscellaneous Creditors.

As regards the relationship between deposits and advances, the above description[1] differs from that drawn up by Hahn.[2] Hahn makes no distinction between genuine deposits and other liabilities, especially as he proceeds on the assumption that the curves representing deposits and advances must move parallel to each other. In this assumption he is wrong, however; for even if it is correct to say that every debtor implies the corresponding existence

[1] Published for the first time by the author, with the help of Dr. Herrmann, in *V.z.K.*

[2] A., HAHN, Zur Frage des volkswirtschaftlichen Erkenntnisinhalts der Bankbilanzen, *V.z.K.*, vol. 1, suppl. 4, pp. 49 *ff*.

of a creditor, this statement applies only to the national economic system as a whole and then only if foreign relations are left out of account. But in the debit and credit relationships between banks and other undertakings, in the course of the trade cycle, displacements of decisive importance may easily occur; indeed, such displacements may even be regarded as a distinguishing feature of cyclical fluctuations. During the depression, the banks usually become more heavily indebted to the rest of the business world, while during the revival, the indebtedness of business to the banks increases.

The Banks and the Trade Cycle.

The monetary or credit school of business-cycle theorists —upholders of the quantity theory in a new disguise— explain the relationship between credit movements and variations in business activity by asserting that cyclical fluctuations are caused by variations in the volume of credit determined by banking policy.[1] This assertion is borne out by experience only to a very limited extent. The part played by the banks in regard to business in general is similar—if a parallel may be suggested—to that of the publisher in regard to the world of authors; for just as the publisher is in a position to impede or facilitate the production of books, so are the banks in a position to influence the production of goods and business activity in general. Their powers and importance are, however, subject to similar restrictions. Even when they appear to be most powerful, that is, at the peak of the trade cycle, when business in general is most heavily in their debt, so that their ability to damp down the fires of business

---

[1] See the works of Hahn, particularly "Aufgaben und Grenzen der Währungspolitik," Kiel Lectures, 1927, Jena, 1928; also, Grundprinzipien der monetären Konjunkturtheorie, *Schriften des Vereins für Sozialpolitik* 173, vol. 2, 1928. See, also, R. G. Hawtrey, "Currency and Credit," 2d ed., London, 1923; J. R. Bellerby, "Control of Credit," London, 1923; Röpke, Kredit und Konjunktur, *Jahrbücher für Nationalökonomie und Statistik*, vol. 124, 1926; J. M. Keynes, "A Tract on Monetary Reform," London, 1923.

activity by the manipulation of credit is relatively considerable, credit policy is still subject to certain restrictions.
As we have seen above, one of the most important characteristics of the high-tension phase consists in the ability of
many business undertakings during that phase to free
themselves—though, of course, only up to a certain point—
from the bonds of bank credit by employing drafts and
commercial acceptances more extensively and similar
devices adopted for the purpose of attaining financial
self-sufficiency. The banks are, however, condemned to a
position of almost complete impotence during a recession
and a depression, for during these phases finance capital
is accumulating in consequence of the tendency to liquidation which marks such periods, and deposits are flowing
into the banks, which are as powerless as they are unwilling
to stop them. The low rate of interest, which, after all,
is a consequence of the process of liquidation and is practically independent of banking policy, provides a new
stimulus to the entrepreneur—but, as we shall shortly
see, in a manner quite different from that which the theorists of the credit school appear to imagine, judging from
the present character of their discussions. In point of
fact, the more deep-lying connections between credit and
the business cycle, and, particularly, between fluctuations
in the rate of interest and production, have not yet been
properly cleared up. The deductive method (as exempli-
fied in the quantity theory) can help us only to a very
limited extent to improve our knowledge in this respect;
while inductive investigation on the subject in question has
not yet been carried far enough. There is no other way of
accounting for the manner in which the theoretical school
contradicts itself on this as on other points.

Deductive Conclusions Concerning Prices and Interest.

Most writers have adopted Wicksell's theory of the
interconnection between prices and interest, a theory of
which we already find hints in Ricardo. According to
Wicksell, the prospects of profit arising from the difference

between "real interest"[1] and bank interest in the period
of depression stimulates the entrepreneur to fresh activity.
The effects of such activity are felt first in the producers'
goods markets. Mises tries to account for trade revival
by similar arguments,[2] which may be stated roughly as
follows: If the rate of interest is low in proportion to the
"fund available for consumers' goods," the entrepreneur
tends to consider that it would be to his advantage to
turn to "roundabout production," that is, to say, to
produce producers' goods instead of consumers' goods,
with the result that the demand for labor and producers'
goods increases, the prices of these two items rise, the
prices of consumers' goods follow suit (owing to the rise
in wages caused by the increased demand for labor), and,
finally, interest rates gradually move upward, also, until
they again reach the level of the "natural interest on
capital."

This is one of a number of cases where darkness rather
than light is thrown by "theory" on the established facts;
for it is sheer metaphysics to say that money rates must
correspond to the "natural interest on capital." How is
such a rate to be determined? And how are we helped by
the assertion that there is a point at which the rate of
interest is lower in proportion to the "fund available for
means of subsistence"? By what concrete equations can
the relationship between these two factors be expressed?
In answering such questions, the mystical ideology of the
quantity theory—so remarkably like the pathology of
"humors" of the Middle Ages—is absolutely useless to

[1] By this he means the rate of interest "which would be determined by
supply and demand if real capital were loaned in kind, without the intervention of money" (Wicksell, "Geldzins und Güterpreise," Jena, 1898).
Elsewhere, he says: "The rate of interest representing an exact coincidence
between *the demand for capital on loan and the supply of saved resources,* and
thus corresponding more or less to the profit-earning prospects of new
capital supplies, would be the normal or natural (real) rate" (Wicksell,
"Vorlesungen über Nationalökonomie," vol. 2, p. 220, Jena, 1922).

[2] MISES, L. VON: "Theorie des Geldes und der Umlaufsmittel," 2d ed.,
pp. 347–375; Munich, 1924; "Geldwertstabilizierung und Konjunkturpolitik," Jena, 1928.

us. Even the other authors who enlarge on the same subject are quite unable to substantiate the assertion that, in a depression, a low market rate of interest stimulates the entrepreneur to new activity and primarily to the production of producers' goods. Our unhappy "theorists" remain rooted to the bed rock of material experience; for they cannot turn their eyes away from the ascertained fact that when the corner of a depression is turned and a revival begins, the price and volume movements of the producers' goods industries lead the way toward recovery. How this comes about, however, is more than they can say. A series of abstract reflections, on a question like this, does not supply the place of definite proof.

The Problem Expressed in Concrete Terms.

What we really need is to be shown what is the real nature of the economic possibilities offered to the entrepreneur by a low rate of interest and where those possibilities present themselves. That is to say, we want to know how it is that in spite of the generally low and declining prices during a depression, the entrepreneur is emboldened to borrow money in order to extend his business activity. The mere fact of a low rate of interest is not in itself sufficient to account for such optimism. To fall back, as is usually done, on the "psychology" of business men is equivalent to giving up all hope of political economy as an independent branch of organized scientific study.

It is, moreover, not necessary to throw up the sponge in this manner. The argument can quite well be pursued in concrete economic terms. This is, indeed, a case where deduction breaks down and induction must come to the rescue.

The first thing which the available material tells us is that a revival begins in the various branches of business where prices and sales prospects get out of the grip of the depression. This takes place at two points: (*a*) in production for export and (*b*) where there exist long-term contracts, specific customs as regards sales, and similar economic safeguards.

Money Rates and Foreign Sales.

Foreign sales are, as we have already seen (see p. 177), only slightly affected by cyclical fluctuations at home, because the wave movement of the trade cycle is so distributed over the various fields of economic activity throughout the world that the total volume of world trade remains more or less unaffected. Even though the fortunes of the principal industrial countries as regards the trade cycle have become more and more closely linked together, they still present, in this respect, a dynamic contrast to the agrarian countries, which continue to be able to absorb products even when trade is stagnant in the industrial countries (see, in this connection, Chap. XXV). When, therefore, domestic sales are at a standstill during a process of general liquidation, industry is still able to find new outlets abroad. Thus, the increase in exports appears in the light of a first symptom of revival by which the surface of the depression is first broken. This fact, however, is not a sufficient foundation on which to base any conclusion as to whether it is the low rate of interest which is responsible for keeping going the production of raw materials for the export trade or for reviving such production. We can at least say that one of the determining causes for this trade movement is to be found in price relationships—in the fact, that is to say, that prices abroad are more favorable than those at home.

Money Rates and House Building.

The position of certain raw-material industries under the influence of export trade is similar to that of productive industries which find some support for their efforts to dispose of produce in long-term contracts, and so forth. It is highly significant that the building trade—not, as many representatives of the theoretical school imagine, the industrial, but the house-building trade—is very active during a depression, although during a revival it may even suffer a decline. This is, no doubt, to be viewed in connection with the fact that the building industry's final product—the use of dwelling accomodation—is paid for by house rent, which is a fairly constant item in national expenditure. The building industry is, therefore, in a favorable position where credit is cheap and the price of raw materials low, while, conversely, dear credit and high raw-material prices make its position more difficult. Whether the cyclical revival of this industry is influenced more by low prices or by low rates of interest of raw material remains, of course, to be demonstrated; and this is a problem which the theoretical school has evidently overlooked.

Free and Tied Markets.

To summarize: Even if it is true that the revival from a depression usually begins in the production of raw materials, this is probably far more closely connected with price conditions than with low money rates, if we view industry as a whole. Nor is it correct to say that the way in a revival must "naturally" be led by those industries which produce producers' goods, as is indicated, for example, by the fact that an industry producing consumers' goods, like the publishing trade, is very actively productive during a depression. Publishing is economically akin to house building in this, that just as rents are fixed for years ahead, so the price of a book is not, as a rule, modified during the life of a single edition. Publishing, moreover, like house building, is in a position to profit by low costs of production.[1] It is quite possible that further investigation might bring to light the fact that other more important industries producing consumers' goods are in a similar position.

Many representatives of the theoretical school evidently imagine that if the production of consumers' goods is to be revived, it is first necessary to create the productive resources for the purpose. The entrepreneur, however, appears not to be of the same opinion, for his attention is

[1] See WAGEMANN, Konjunkturfragen des Druckgewerbes, *Zeitschrift für Deutschlands Buchdrucker und verwandte Gewerbe*, September, 1928.

fixed not on national economic problems but on the possibility of securing a profit for himself personally.   There
is no inherent reason why the productive apparatus should
not during a depression be sufficiently equipped to meet an
increased demand for consumers' goods when it was
perfectly well able to do so a short time previously, during
the preceding period of prosperity.   As we have seen, the
way toward a revival is, in fact, led by an upward movement
in the production of producers' goods; but the immediate
cause of this does not lie in the necessity of increasing the
quantity of producers' goods in order to secure increased
output; indeed, even raw materials are actually exported
during a depression.   The cause is to be sought rather in
the connection between the markets in which the trade
cycle has full play and other economic spheres where the
perpetual fluctuations of supply and demand are prevented
from exercising their full effect on prices by certain customs
and practices (price fixing, long-term contracts, and the
like) the origin of which is, perhaps, to be traced back to
the epoch before the advent of modern capitalism (see Chap.
XXV).

Secondary Significance of Money Rates.

These observations, which, of course, are not put forward
as a theory of the business cycle, but with a view simply to
throwing light on a certain particular relationship, bring
us back to the question of the significance in business affairs
of credit fluctuations.   I have, I think, succeeded in making
it appear probable that the rate of interest plays a somewhat
secondary part in the cyclical process.   Such responsibility
as can be attributed to it for the up-and-down movement is,
however, independent of the banks in so far as its variations
have their origin in the general fluctuations in the state of
business.   The banks can by no means be said to have no
influence on the tempo and extent not only of the trade
cycle, in general, but also of cyclical fluctuations in the
several branches of business activity.   They are able, in a
number of ways, to shape credit policy, through their

determination as to whom and on what terms credits are to be granted and the extent to which they will consent to grant supplementary credits. In the main, however, business proceeds unfettered by credit policy. Variations in the total volume of credit are determined far more by industry than by the banks.

Foreign Capital and the Trade Cycle.

Apart from this, credit policy in Germany is now, as it was before the World War, essentially based on domestic

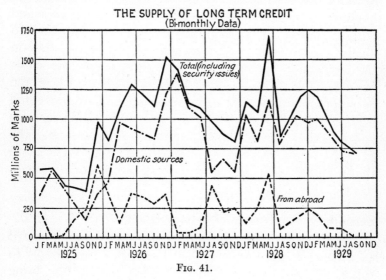

THE SUPPLY OF LONG TERM CREDIT
(Bi-monthly Data)

Fig. 41.

factors. The importance of foreign capital for the development of the trade cycle in Germany has lately been much overestimated.[1] This is, in my opinion, plainly demonstrated by the diagram reproduced above—at any rate, as regards long-term capital.[2] It is true that the revival

[1] See, for example, HAHN, "Aufgaben und Grenzen der Währungspolitik"; also, WEBER, ADOLF, "Allgemeine Volkswirtschaftslehre," pp. 387, 388, Munich and Leipzig, 1928; "Hat Schacht recht"? 1927.

[2] It appears to me to be well worthwhile to follow Plenge in distinguishing between long and short capital. Similarly, I would suggest using the terms "long" and "short" credit, instead of the clumsier "long-" and "short-term" credit (see Plenge, Kapital und Zins, *Weltwirtschaftliches Archiv*, vol. 24, pp. 299 *ff.*, 1926).

in the second half of 1924 was due essentially to the Dawes loan. Since then, however, the inflow of foreign long capital has proceeded more or less independently of domestic cyclical fluctuations. As viewed from Germany, it appears, so to speak, as an accidental factor. The depression and the beginning of a recovery in 1926 and, subsequently, the development of high tension in the second half of 1927 are all clearly reproduced in the German long-credits curve, while the foreign curve is quite featureless. In the first half of 1928, however, foreign capital seems to have exercised a stronger influence.

Balance of Trade and Balance of Capital.

The part played by short-term credits must, of course, also be considered. These are, in my opinion, dependent primarily on the balance of trade the state of which is determined predominantly by domestic business conditions.

It should be realized that the balance of payments is composed of three main items:[1] the balance of trade, the balance of services, and the balance of capital. If, for the sake of simplification, we agree to eliminate the relatively insignificant balance of services (freights, insurance premiums, etc.), we are left with the balance of trade and the balance of capital as the two main items (using the term "balance of capital" as comprising all payments arising out of the movement of capital—long- and short-term credits, interest payments, loan redemptions, etc.). These two items are closely interrelated, from the fact that the balance of payments as such always comes out even in the long run.

The lead is, indeed, sometimes taken by the balance of capital. This phenomenon is, however, frequently due to disturbances in the organic process of the trade cycle. It occurred, for instance, in the second half of 1923, when the disorganization of the currency was at its worst and the flight of capital from Germany and the unloading of German

---

[1] See papers published by the author (a) in *Deutsche Wirtschaftszeitung*, July 14, Aug. 12 and 19, 1925, and (b) in *V.z.K.*, 2, 1, p. 10.

securities abroad made the balance of capital so unfavorable that imports were strangled and exports necessarily swollen. We have already pointed out that the situation also was affected from outside in 1924, when the Dawes loan prepared the way for a revival.

In general, however, the international ebb and flow of capital is dominated rather by the balance of trade—particularly in respect of short credits. As far as Germany is concerned, an increasingly "unfavorable" balance of trade has, for decades past, been an indication of a cyclical trade revival, while an increasingly "favorable" balance has spelled crisis and depression. It is true that these relationships are extraordinarily involved, for they are exposed to the influence of movements set up by the gravitational forces in world business (Chap. XXV), as expressed, for instance, in differences between money rates at home and abroad. The stock market, moreover, as well as the commodity market influences the situation. More thorough investigation on this question is, therefore, urgently required.

We must be careful not to confuse with the problem of the relationship between cyclical fluctuations and the shifts of the balance of payments the other question as to the structure and operation of the balance of payments itself. Herein lies, too, the question—today so weighty for Germany—how a country with an "unfavorable" balance of trade can bear the burden of paying off debts to foreign countries. This brings us to the difficult problem of the relations between structural and cyclical variations.

Bibliography

Reference may be made here, from among the very extensive literature on monetary and credit business-cycle theory, to the following recent titles:

HAWTREY, R. G.: "Currency and Credit," 2d ed., London, 1923.

KEYNES, J. M.: *A Tract on Monetary Reform*, London, 1923.

HAHN, ALBERT: "Volkswirtschaftliche Theorie des Bankkredits," 2d ed., Tübingen, 1924; "Aufgaben und Grenzen der Währungspolitik," Jena, 1928; Konjunkturlose Wirtschaft, *Wirtschaftsdienst*, 1925.

RÖPKE, WILHELM: Kredit und Konjunktur, *Jahrbücher für Nationalökonomie und Statistik*, 1926; Auslandskredite und Konjunktur, *Schriften des Vereins für Sozialpolitik*, vol. 173, Part II, pp. 213 *ff*., 1928.

Foster and Catchings: "Money and Profits," New York, 1925. Here too, mention should be made of:

Fisher, Irving: "The Purchasing Power of Money," New York, 1911.

Wicksell, K.: "Geldzins und Güterpreise," Jena, 1898; "Vorlesungen über Nationalökonomie," Vol. 2, pp. 238 *ff.*, Jena, 1922.

Sombart, Werner: Die Störungen im deutschen Wirtschaftsleben während der Jahre 1900–1907, *Schriften des Vereins für Sozialpolitik*, vol. 113, p. 121, Leipzig, 1904; "Moderne Kapitalismus," vol. 3, Part 2, pp. 563 *ff.*

Stucken, R.: "Theorie der Konjunkturschwankungen," Jena, 1926.

Mises, L. von: "Theorie des Geldes und der Umlaufsmittel," 2d ed., pp. 347–375, Munich and Leipzig, 1924.

Mitchell, Wesley C.: "Business Cycles," New York, 1927.

Among the critical works on monetary theory are especially to be mentioned:

Schumpeter: Kreditkontrolle, *Archiv. für Sozialwissenschaft und Sozialpolitik*, vol. 54, 1925.

Heinrich: "Grundlagen einer universalistischen Krisenlehre," Jena, 1927.

Löwe, A.: Über den Einfluss monetärer Faktoren auf den Konjunkturzyklus, *Schriften des Vereins für Sozialpolitik*, 173, 2, pp. 355 *ff.*, 1928.

Burchardt, Entwicklungsgeschichte der monetären Konjunkturtheorie, *Weltwirtschaftliches Archiv*, July, 1928.

CHAPTER XIX

PRICES AND TURNOVER IN THE BUSINESS CYCLE

Do Prices Indicate or Regulate Business Fluctuations?

Down to the first years of the twentieth century, it was the accepted view that the business cycle was expressed primarily in price movements. Cyclical fluctuations and price movements were regarded almost as synonymous terms. Prices were looked upon as representing the principal thermometer of the state of trade (Rodbertus). In those days, price movements did, indeed, reflect with remarkable accuracy the state of business; they were, accordingly, of decisive significance to the economist and the business man, for the purpose of following the business process. Right down to the present day, many economists have gone on tending to define the business cycle as the fluctuation of market conditions or the market situation, in general;[1] that is to say, their attention is concentrated particularly on prices or the factors which determine prices. As, however, the business cycle in practice affects all parts of the economic system, it may be doubted whether market fluctuations, and particularly price movements, should be given special prominence.

How far, if at all, can the business man rely on price movements for guidance at the present day? At the time when Adam Smith published his great work on "The Wealth of Nations," in which he developed the theory that a wonderful harmony as between production and demand is effected by prices, this view may have been well founded. Production by hand on a small scale was then

---

[1] For example, Sombart (with some justification, as far as he is concerned, since he employs this definition in the course of his study of early capitalism, "Der moderne Kapitalismus," 2d ed., vol. 2, Part 1, pp. 208 ff., 1917). Many others, however, do so in regard to present-day conditions—Mombert, Röpke, Heller, for example.

the rule and was adapted to demand in a simple manner, for the market could be easily surveyed, the division of labor among the various parts of the national business organism was in its infancy, and the process of production was free from complication. As the division of labor became more perfect, as technical processes evolved, as the periods on which production is based lengthened, and as the way from producer to consumer grew longer and markets more multiform, prices necessarily tended more and more to lose their importance as the regulator of business. The period of crises, the occurrence of which is in itself a proof that business is not properly regulated, began.

Nevertheless, down to the World War, prices did provide some sort of index of the state of business. Down to 1914, the index of industrial raw-material and semifinished-goods prices reflected the employment level fairly well. The diagram on page 92 shows with complete clearness the simultaneity of the wave motion in the commodity and labor markets.

Price Fixing.

The relationship between these two factors has since altered considerably, to the extent that the process of price fixing has progressed. In branches of business where prices have been fixed, the simultaneity of price and wage movements has necessarily disappeared, just as has that between fluctuations in prices and the employment level. This development is very clearly discernible in, for instance, the case of coal and iron. The intimate interconnection between prices and the business cycle is, thus, being more and more broken up; indeed, the two are reaching such a state of mutual opposition that the German papers are justified in contrasting, as they occasionally do, physical-volume fluctuations with price fluctuations within the business cycle. How large a section of the market as a whole is at present immobilized by price regulation cannot easily be estimated; but it is already possible to argue whether it represents more or less than half of the total industrial turnover. So many prices have, in any case, acquired the characteristics of rigidity involved in elaborate

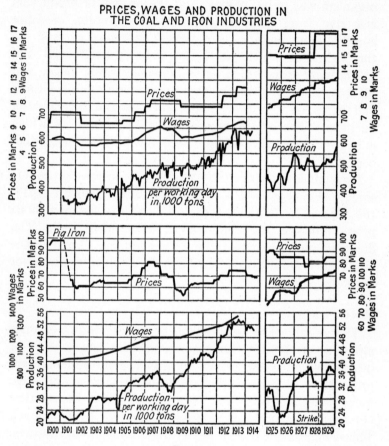

Fig. 42.

Observations.—*Coal:* prices per ton of Rhine-Westphalian coal at the pit head. *Wages:* actual earnings per shift in the coal-mining industry of the district covered by the Dortmund District Mines Office (prewar, quarterly; postwar, monthly). *Pig iron:* prices per ton of No. 3 foundry pig iron at the foundry. *Wages:* prewar—average yearly wages of worker insured with the iron and steel trades Societies—postwar—hourly wage (according to scale) of fully trained metal workers (monthly; the scale is fitted to an average wage of 66.8 pfennig in 1913).

tariff listing that it is quite difficult to discover price series suitable for compiling the index of sensitive commodity prices. In Germany, this index at present covers 10 such series (some of which certainly represent very important sections of the market) as against the 400 (some of them representing only very small sections of the market) from which the wholesale price index is calculated.

The Interplay of Price and Wage Curves.

The diagram reproduced below—Picture of a Price Storm, it might almost be called—gives some idea of the complicated interplay of price and wage curves. The industrial price curves have already been shown in the diagram reproduced on page 159. In the latter diagram, the strictly inverse fluctuation is noteworthy as between industrial raw-material and semifinished-goods prices, including sensitive commodity prices, on the one hand, and retail prices, on the other, during the revival from the middle of 1926 to the middle of 1927. The sensitive commodity prices and, to some extent, the prices of other raw materials and semifinished goods are, for this period, in strongly marked positive correlation to the employment level; while the correlation between the prices of industrial finished goods (especially consumers' goods) and the employment level is negative. Only at a later period do the prices of finished goods follow those of raw materials. During the prewar period, a similar sequence, though at a shorter interval, must certainly have been noticeable; unfortunately, however, we are not in possession of equivalent data for the comparison of the relevant time series during this period.

Price and Physical Volume Fluctuations.

A point in regard to which an essential distinction must be drawn between the present and the past is the relationship between price and physical-volume fluctuations. The difference in trend between the course of turnover and prices is another question; for the fact that the trend of the index figure of prices of industrial materials from 1924 to 1927 slanted downward, while the trade in commodities in general and turnover as a whole advanced steeply is a sign of important organic changes in the post-stabilization period. At the same time, however, a considerable degree of inverse cyclical fluctuation as between physical-volume turnover and prices is also noticeable at the present day.

A comparison of series, showing the rise in physical-volume turnover simultaneously with declining prices for clothing and, also, for furniture and domestic equipment is quite suggestive. Such a comparison indicates the negative tensions which preceded the revival of 1927.

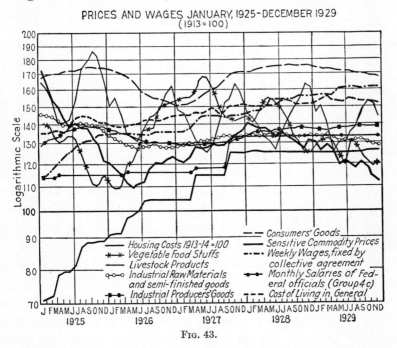

FIG. 43.

The deeper implications of the interrelation of price and physical-volume fluctuations have as yet been little investigated.

Let us proceed on the assumption that, from the point of view of the theory of prices, four factors combine to form the price[1]—two of them relating to supply and two to demand:

[1] See WAGEMANN, Theorie des Geldwerts und der Währung, "Allgemeine Geldlehre," vol. 1, p. 123.

Supply:
  1. Quantity of goods (storage plus production).
  2. Demand for money (expenditure of money, costs of production).
Demand:
  1. Demand for goods.
  2. Supply of money (finance capital and income).

Dynamically considered, commodity prices may be classified according to the degree of their dependence on fluctuations in these four factors. We may, in particular, distinguish between prices which are mainly affected by fluctuations on the demand side and on the supply side, respectively. The prices of goods in relatively constant demand are dominated in a particularly high degree by fluctuations in supplies; the demand for such goods varies little.

Durable and Ephemeral Goods.

Different degrees of variability in demand appear to arise not so much from varying degrees of urgency in human needs (contrary to a theory upheld in the textbooks from very early times) but essentially from another factor—a factor underlying the ancient and well-known distinction between "commodities for use" and "commodities for consumption." As producers' no less than consumers' goods are, in either case, concerned, it might be preferable to speak of *durable* and *ephemeral* goods.[1] Ephemeral goods are those of which the economic subject is constantly renewing his supplies; durable goods, on the other hand, are renewed only from time to time, and their renewal can be easily postponed. The former category includes most food stuffs, beverages, tobacco, and the like; while the latter includes furniture, miscellaneous domestic equipment—such as glass and china—and, above all, articles of clothing. Housing accomodation is, in the fullest sense, a durable commodity. The inclusion of any particular commodity in either of these groups is, however, not necessarily definitive, and the line of demarcation

[1] TRANSLATOR'S NOTE.—The German terms *Vorratsgüter* and *Verzehrgüter* have been rendered freely in the spirit of the context.

between the two groups is, indeed, indefinite. We observe the increasing tendency of textiles to lose the character of durable goods as time goes on; whereas, in the old days, articles of clothing were handed down from one generation to another, and whereas in peasant families this practice still survives, as far as urban consumers are concerned such commodities have been gradually losing their character

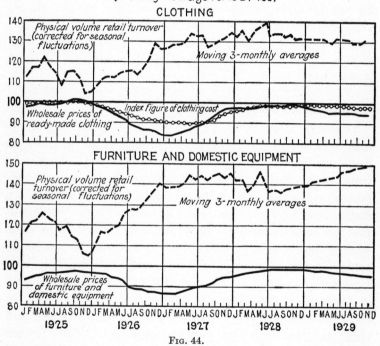

RETAIL TURNOVER AND PRICES FROM JANUARY, 1925
(Monthly Average for 1924=100)

Fig. 44.

as durable goods. So far has this tendency progressed in America, that it is no longer uncommon not to have one's clothes or shoes repaired.[1]

[1] A noteworthy distinction must be drawn between men's and women's clothing. Men's clothing is, at the present day, a durable commodity to a far greater extent than women's, and this difference is very clearly evident in the curves of cyclical fluctuations in turnover for the two categories. Even in Germany, women's clothing has become subject to constant renewal, and the turnover therein is, therefore, much more regular than in men's.

The fact that ephemeral goods (that is, food, drink, and tobacco, in particular) are affected only to a relatively slight extent by fluctuations in demand is evidence not only of the comparatively constant character of retail turnover in such commodities but, also, of a remarkable degree of lack of sensitiveness in their prices with regard to fluctuations in income. As we have seen above, in the case of the price of hogs, this lack of sensitiveness goes so far that in working out forecasts for short periods one can leave the demand factor entirely out of account. During the World War, of course, conditions in the food markets were turned wholly upside down, as the overwhelming shortage of all commodities obliged the population to cease renewing its supplies of durable goods, with the result that fluctuations in income reacted more considerably on ephemeral goods.[1]

The Predominance of Demand in the Case of Industrial Products.

Under normal conditions, however, it is durable, not ephemeral, goods of which the prices are dominated by fluctuations in demand. As the majority of industrial products (whether producers' or consumers' goods) fall within the former category (in contrast to agricultural produce), the prices of industrial products are far more liable to the effects of variation in demand than are those of the products of agriculture. We can, therefore, understand industrial price movements only on the basis of a very thorough investigation into the nature and variation of the demand for industrial products—an investigation to which our examination of the dynamic relationship between industry and agriculture and of the position of export trade in the business cycle furnishes an introduction.

[1] The manner in which food-stuff prices were brought into intimate relationship with the state of demand and income, with the result that price fluctuations and price relationships assumed peculiar characteristics, is described in the author's article on Die Lebensmittelteuerung und ihre Gesetzmässigkeiten, *Schmollers Jahrbuch*, 1919.

It might at first glance appear as if our conclusion that industrial prices (in a free market) are dominated to a large extent by variations in demand is in contradiction with the old theory of the classical economists that the prices of goods the supply of which can be increased at will (and which are products of industry) are determined by costs of production. The contradiction is, however, apparent rather than real, for the old theory of costs of production is based on a static, not on a dynamic, view. From the static viewpoint, it is quite correct to regard the price of industrial products as dependent on costs of production and, therefore, on the conditions under which production takes place. In reality, this axiom amounts only to an abstract assertion of the results shown by the books of a given concern. From the static viewpoint, moreover, it can be reversed and the assertion advanced that prices are determined by income, since costs of production, as the exchange equation shows, are, in the final analysis, income (see Chap. II).

Business-cycle theory utilizes the knowledge of such static relationships simply as a point of departure. Viewed dynamically, the interplay of supply and demand factors in determining prices assumes a quite different appearance. In recent years, the cyclical changes which have affected business in Germany have brought to light the system of relationships described below.

Prices in the Trade Cycle.

When a revival sets in, the physical-volume turnover of goods in elastic demand increases (1) in order to satisfy the growing current demand of consumers and (2) in order to replenish traders' stocks, unduly depleted during the liquidation period. Retail prices do not, however, rise immediately, notwithstanding the increasing demand due to expanding receipts; on the contrary, they tend to decline as long as they are calculated on the basis of the falling wholesale prices of the preceding period of depression.

When the stage of full prosperity is reached and the upward movement of the employment level, together with receipts and demand, comes to a stop or even turns into a downward movement, the prices of finished goods (both wholesale and retail) nevertheless go on rising, since calculations are now based on rising raw-material prices and rising wages. Thus, while during the revival phase the "scissors" formed by turnover and prices opened in favor of physical-volume turnover, now in the full-prosperity phase they open in favor of prices. When the tension between turnover and prices reaches a certain point—in other words, when the demand for consumers' goods is definitely left behind by the rise in prices—the latter turns into a decline in consequence of the fall in physical-volume sales. Retail trade is obliged to check its current renewal of stocks, and wholesale prices of finished goods and raw materials began to fall in consequence. Indeed, retail trade is forced to reduce, if not to unload, its reserve stocks, with the result that retail prices begin to weaken.

During the revival and full-prosperity phases, retail prices are, in the main, determined by costs of production. It is, however, open to question whether the really determining factor during the phase of recession is the shrinkage in receipts. The fact that it is possible for prices to get ahead of income can be explained only by taking into account the part played by working capital, because the continued expansion of prices during this period is, to an increasing extent, rendered possible by credits granted to distributors. The breakdown in prices which occurs in the recession phase thus takes place in immediate relationship with the tensional situation in regard to credit, mainly by reason of the breakdown of the financial self-sufficiency of business. But it is, on the whole, difficult to decide whether the decline in gross income underlies the fall in prices as the really determining cause.

Bibliography

AEREBOE, FR.: "Allgemeine landwirtschaftliche Betriebslehre," 6th ed., 1923; "Die Beurteilung von Landgütern und Grundstücken," Berlin, 1924; "Agrarpolitik," Berlin, 1928.

SERING, M.: "Das Sinken der Getreidepreise und die Konkurrenz des Auslandes," Berlin, 1894.

SKALWEIT, A.: "Agrarpolitik," 2d ed., Berlin and Leipzig, 1923.

VON BECKERATH: "Kräfte, Ziele und Gestaltungen," 2d ed., Jena, 1924.

EULENBURG, F. (ed.): Neue Grundlagen der Handelspolitik, Schriften des Vereins für Sozialpolitik, vol. 171, 1925, 1926.

HARMS, B.: "Die Zukunft der deutschen Handelspolitik," vol. 1, 1925; (ed.): "Strukturwandlungen der deutschen Volkswirtschaft," 2 vols., Berlin, 1928.

HIRSCH, J.: Der moderne Handel, "Grundriss der Staatswissenschaft," vol. 5, 2d ed., Tübingen, 1925.

LEDERER: Monopole und Konjunktur, V.z.K., vol. 2, suppl. 2.

SCHNEIDER, H. J.: Zur Analyse des Eisenmarkts, V.z.K., special issue.

SOLTAU: Statistische Untersuchungen über die Entwicklung und die Konjunkturschwankungen des Aussenhandels, V.z.K., vol. 1, suppl. 2.

TEUBERT, WERNER: Der Güterverkehr und seine Veränderungen in der Nachkriegszeit, V.z.K., Special issue 5.

VERSHOFEN, W.: "Die Statistik der Wirtschaftsverbände," Bamberg, 1924.

WIEDENFELD: "Gewerbepolitik," Berlin 1927.

WILBRANDT, R.: Kapitalismus und Konsumenten, "Grundriss der Staatswissenschaft," vol. 9, No. 2.

LEHMANN, M.: Various essays in Betriebsw. Rundschau, 1926.

LIEFMANN, R.: "Kartelle, Konzerne und Trusts," 7th ed., 1926.

NICKLISCH, H.: "Wirtschaftliche Betriebslehre," 6th ed., Stuttgart, 1922.

OBST, G.: "Das Buch des Kaufmanns," 1928.

SCHMALENBACH: "Dynamische Bilanz," 4th ed., Leipzig, 1926; "Grundlagen der Selbstkostenberechnung und Preispolitik," 3d ed., 1927.

BONN, M. J.: "Befreiungspolitik oder Beleihungspolitik," Berlin, 1928.

VAN DORP, E.: Die Bestimmungsgründe der intervalutarischen Kurse, Weltwirtschaftliches Archiv, vol. 15, 1919.

EUCKEN, W.: "Kritische Betrachtungen zum deutschen Geldproblem," Jena, 1923.

GOSCHEN: "The Theory of Foreign Exchanges," 1861.

PALYI, M.: Der Zahlungsbilanzausgleich bei einseitigen Wertübertragungen, Archiv für Sozialwissenschaft und Sozialpolitik, vol. 56, 1926.

SCHMIDT, F.: "Internationaler Zahlungsverkehr und Wechselkurse," 1919.

WEBER, ADOLF: "Allgemeine Volkswirtschaftslehre," p. 387, 388, Munich and Leipzig, 1928; "Hat Schacht Recht?" Munich, 1927.

BERRIDGE, WINSLOW, and FLINN: "Purchasing Power of the Consumer," New York, 1925.

GÜNTHER, A.: "Sozialpolitik," Part I, Berlin, 1922.

HERKNER, "Die Arbeiterfrage," 8th ed., 1922.

JASTROW, I.: Die Arbeitsnachweise als Umschlagstelle des Arbeitsmarktes, Schriften des Vereins für Sozialpolitik, vol. 109; Arbeitsmarkt und Arbeitsnachweise, "Sozialpolitik und Verwaltungswissenschaft," vol. 1.

ZWIEDINECK-SÜDENHORST, O. VON: Arbeitsbedarf und Lohnpolitik der modernen kapitalistischen Industrien, "Grundriss der Staatswissenschaft," vol. 1, No. 3; Die Lohnpreisbildung, ibid., vol. 4.

GERLOFF and MEISEL: "Handbuch der Finanzwissenschaft."

LOTZ, W.: "Finanzwissenschaft," Tübingen, 1917.

MANN, F. K.: Steuerüberwälzung, "Handbuch der Staatswissenschaft," 4th ed.

PLENGE, J.: "Von der Diskontpolitik zur Herrschaft über den Geldmarkt," Berlin, 1913; Kapital und Geld, *Weltwirt. Archiv*, vol. 24.

PRION, W.: Das Wechseldiskontgeschäft, *Schmollers Forsch.*, 1907; Geldmarktlage und Reichsbankpolitik, *V.z.K.*, vol. 1, suppl. 4.

SECTION VI

THE MOVEMENT OF BUSINESS CONSIDERED AS A WHOLE

CHAPTER XX

THE DIAGNOSIS AND FORECASTING OF CYCLICAL CONDITIONS

The Notion of Diagnosis and Forecasting.

The comparison of sectional movements with the help of the business barometer and the highly subtle methods of analysis which its use permits enable us to diagnose the cyclical business situation which shows us the state and configuration of the various economic time series at a particular moment. Cyclical situation and cyclical tension are thus brought to light, and these together constitute the phases into which we divide the business cycle as a whole.

In the final analysis, our diagnosis is based on the idea of typical movement forms. Our object is always to classify the situation at any given time in one of the numerous movement categories which recur in the alternation of the phases and which we know from experience. An absolutely new phenomenon, therefore, cannot be positively diagnosed. Consequently, as our diagnosis is based on movement types which, as follows from the mere notion of movement, are related to each other in time, every diagnosis contains within itself, either exposed or concealed, a projection of the future course of events.

Just as many people are afraid of a doctor's verdict, so, to a remarkable extent, do people display a terror of business forecasting—a terror so overpowering that even serious politicians and investigators deny its possibility. They try to misrepresent its significance—for instance, by likening it to second sight or prophecy—or even to the astrologer's horoscope or to soothsaying. In reality, business forecasting is an affair of reason and discrimination, soberly conscious of its limitations and with no pretensions whatsoever to infallibility. It should be borne in mind that the very idea of business implies forecasting, for business means planning—planning how to meet requirements, what supplies to lay in. Every plan is based on some view in regard to the future and, therefore, includes the notion of forecasting. Planning, of course, takes various forms. Planning by the state takes the form, for instance, of budget estimates; the business man does not, generally speaking, give his plans a form[1] so definite and concrete, but their importance for his activities is all the greater; for whereas the non-realization of the budget estimates involves, at most, a conflict with the auditing authority, faulty planning by an undertaking involves it in loss, if not in bankruptcy.

National business forecasting is an operation essentially identical in character with the plans and provisions of the individual business man; the only difference is that the former utilizes the universality and exactitude of the ideas and observations of economic science.

The Organic-biological Principle in Forecasting.

The diagnoses and forecasts of the Institute for Business Cycle Research are based primarily on the organic-biological principle and, particularly, on the hypothesis that cyclical fluctuation is always and essentially endogenous (see above, pp. 11 *ff.*). This hypothesis has so far been proved convenient and useful by experimental tests—that is to say, by the actual forecasting which has been based on it. A forecast cannot, of course, determine the conditions under which the business cycle is to proceed on its course, but it

---

[1] Recently, business has also been tending to adopt the "budget" system. Undertakings draw up a business program at the beginning of the business year which embodies the lines on which it is proposed to manage the concern during the year in question.

can, to some extent, elucidate them. The institute's diagnoses and forecasts have, thus, up to the present, been made subject to the entire exclusion of extraneous factors, such as the English coal strike of 1926 or the inflow of foreign loans in 1927. Political developments like the Locarno agreement have *a fortiori* been left entirely out of account. As these forecasts have been abundantly substantiated by subsequent events, even apart from any reservations, we may safely conclude that the autonomous character of the business process in Germany is, under existing conditions, so definite that any extraneous influence may be regarded as of secondary importance. The erroneous character of the theory that the revival in the middle of 1926 was mainly motivated by the English coal crisis[1] has been demonstrated by the fact that when that crisis was terminated, the upward movement of German business continued steadily and without interruption. Even the views which have more recently been put forward as to the determining influence of foreign credits do not altogether fit the facts.

The institute's diagnoses and forecasts in principle cover all the four basic forms of economic movement.

Structural Forecasting.

In the case of isolated variations, it would seem, at first sight, that forecasting of any kind must be out of the question, since previous experience forms a fundamentally inadequate basis in such a case. It is, indeed, true that cyclical diagnosis and forecasting, with which the foregoing paragraphs deal, apply only in the case of periodical economic fluctuations. Nevertheless, it is, perhaps, legitimate to speak of "structural forecasting"; even discontinuous, isolated variations can, at times, be fitted into the scheme of national business calculation—in so far, that is to say, as they "cast their shadows before them." Forecasting in this sphere may, it is true, easily overstep the

---

[1] This theory was, it will be remembered, held at the time by practically everybody.

limits of sober reasoning and trespass on the domain of clairvoyance, intuition, or prophecy. As instances of such predictions may be quoted Turgot's prophetic words, uttered in 1750: "Colonies are like fruits, which cling to the tree only until they become ripe; once ripe, they do what Carthage did and what America will one day do"; or those of Goethe, who in 1820, when the United States controlled no more than a narrow fringe of territory on the Atlantic seaboard, expressed the opinion that "One fine day, the Isthmus of Panama will be pierced by a canal, and it will be the United States which will carry out this feat."[1]

Trend Forecasting.

The forecasting of continuous isolated variations, that is to say, of the basic course of development or trend, is of a different nature. As we have seen above, the idea of a trend, or basic direction of movement, is, in a certain sense, fictitious (see Chap. III). Trend may, indeed, change its direction at any moment, and it can never be affirmed with certainty that its future course will be the same as in the past. It is nevertheless possible to make correct estimates of the future course of development on the basis of the form or tendency of movement in the past. Thus, all sorts of prognostications, of great practical value, can be made as to the development of the population. Such estimates can, for instance, be made as to the number and age distribution of the population of Germany over the next few years.[2]

Closely akin to trend forecasting are the predictions which can be made in regard to long-wave cyclical fluctuations—supposing that such fluctuations do really represent a rhythmically recurring phenomenon.

The species of forecasting which is, strictly speaking, proper to business-cycle theory is primarily that dealing with comparatively brief periodical fluctuations.

---

[1] Schultze, E., Die Möglichkeit wirtschaftlicher Prophezeiungen, *publication* 38 of the Federation of German Industries, pp. 9 *f.*, June, 1928.

[2] *V.z.K.*, vol. 3, No. 1A, pp. 31 *ff.*

Seasonal Forecasting.

The easiest and surest forecasts are those which deal with seasonal fluctuations. The business world itself usually understands such fluctuations so thoroughly without external aid that it generally allows for them in its plans for the future. It is true that the business man often relies far too much on tradition and routine; he would certainly effect by no means inconsiderable economies if in laying in his stocks for coming seasons he would have recourse to more adequate statistical data (see pp. 58 *ff.*).[1]

Business-cycle Forecasting.

The problem of business-cycle forecasting is much more difficult though, within certain limits, not insoluble. Results can be secured in three quite different ways.

Examinations of the Plans of Individual Undertakings.

The first of these is to examine the plans and views of individual businesses and undertakings. The simplest way of doing this appears to be to maintain a constant system of questioning the firms themselves. This is already done on a large scale by associations, chambers of commerce, and banks. The Institute for Business Cycle Research had made such investigations in connection with the Leipzig fair. Attempts have been made in both Germany and America to condense into tables and diagrams the information thus brought to light. The method as a whole is, however, confronted by an immediate and decisive obstacle, in that a really rapid and comprehensive survey is simply out of the question.

Indirect methods of investigation are accordingly adopted for the purpose of obtaining a closer insight into the plans and opinions of the business world. In the first place, the statistics of orders booked shows us at what points and to what extent production is being affected by purchases. The statistics for the engineering industry are a

---

[1] The weekly reports of the Institute for Business Cycle Research include seasonal forecasting among their essential objects.

particularly rich mine of information, for they are subdivided in such a manner as to show what branches of
industry intend to expand their manufacturing potentiali-
ties. Similar information can be gleaned from the statistics
of raw-material imports. Less directly, statistics of borrowings indicate whether firms are contemplating an
extension of their activities. Conclusions can thus be
drawn not only concerning the state of business activity at
any given moment but also concerning the probable
development of such activity in the near future, since
borrowings, raw-material imports, and orders produce
their effects only after a certain time has elapsed.

This method of ascertaining the plans and expectations
of the business community, however, is subject to sharp
limitations. As regards both subject matter and time,
its forecasting possibilities are very limited; in regard
to subject matter, inasmuch as it usually enables us to
draw conclusions only in regard to the employment level
and turnover development; and in regard to time, because,
as far as my own experience goes, it permits forecasting
only for, at most, say, from $1\frac{1}{2}$ to less than 3 months ahead.
But it yields trustworthy results if fairly adequate statistics
are available, especially as it often throws considerable
light on business plans over and above that derived from
the information communicated directly. One may almost
go so far as to say that, when resting on this basis, and
provided that the interaction of the various factors in the
business process is not disturbed by some altogether
extraordinary political or natural event, such as the outbreak of a war, forecasting is what is meant by the familiar
English saying: "Prophesy only if you know!"

Barometric Diagnosis.

The scope of the forecasts made by this method would
be far greater if the business man could, at all times,
carry out his plans and intentions unhampered. This,
as we know, is not the case. It lies in the fundamental
nature of our economic system that obstacles continually

arise to hinder their fulfilment. After all, the wave movement of the business cycle is nothing but the interaction of the tendencies of business to move forward and the contrary tendencies which check its progress and which, to some extent, are generated by its own efforts to advance; so that every expansion of business assumes the appearance of a reaction following on a preceding contraction, and every contraction, that of a reaction following on an expansion. It is the task of barometric diagnosis to ascertain the nature, direction, scale, and duration of these reactions. Such diagnoses offer forecasting possibilities in a twofold respect: (*a*) The reactions may be considered in a purely symptomatological light, and (*b*) they may be considered in the light of a theory of causation or, better, of functional relationship.

Symptomatology.

When the Institute for Business Cycle Research first took up its work, the first task which it had to perform was to construct a comprehensive system of symptomatology. This involved, at the outset, an attempt to form a clear, general idea of the interplay of economic forces; for the crisis theories which had hitherto been applied in dealing with the subject matter of business-cycle research were far too much concentrated on the effort to force the facts of business fluctuations into the framework of a deductive logic. This is as though a doctor were to try to find a pathogenic agent before he had formed a proper notion of the disease itself by a study of the symptoms.[1] To look for the causes of a phenomenon before acquiring a fairly adequate knowledge of its external manifestations is an absurdity; how can one search for causes before one has a grasp of the subject itself?

Functional Theory.

The principle that business-cycle theory should start by examining the symptoms does not, of course, involve

---

[1] See the author's introduction to *V.z.K.*, vol. 1, No. 1.

abandoning any idea of classifying the facts according to some system. It would be irrational to shut one's eyes to the theoretical ideas evolved in the course of building up the static system placed at our disposal at the present day by economic science and practical business observation.[1]

To start building up a study of dynamics, or, in other words, of movement, on a basis of ideas and theorems, without any adequate and serviceable empirical material, is to build it up from the beginning on false foundations. The first essential is to observe the movement symptoms without bias. If in doing so one begins by relying on a static method of classification—which is, of course, not the same thing as basing one's observations from the beginning on a particular theory of business cycles, for business-cycle theory must always be of a purely dynamic character—one will certainly soon be obliged to revise one's concepts in accordance with the requirements of dynamics.

An adequate study of symptoms enables us to form essential conclusions for the purpose of diagnosis and, therefore, of forecasting; for just as an experienced doctor can, without knowing the underlying causes of a malady, draw conclusions from the general state of the patient as to its future course, so is it also possible, from observing the regular succession of typical movement phenomena, to draw by analogy conclusions as to the future development of the business situation—and in very many if not most, cases with considerable success. A certain verdict is, however, impossible, (a) because one movement never follows the identical course of another, (b) because in plotting our curves we are bound to rely, in the first instance, on the static system of classification, and that system cannot be entirely adequate for the purpose of a dynamic study, and (c), above all, because the manner in which movements succeed each other changes with any

---

[1] There is no need here to discuss the question of the manner in which this system has been constructed. It is certainly itself based primarily on empirical observation—that is, on a study of symptoms—and that study might, in this case, have been based on some other theoretical system.

alteration in the business organism. In the case of relatively short periods, however, transformations in the
business organism are usually of comparatively slight
importance.

We shall, therefore, go on trying to discover the "pathogenic agents responsible for the business cycle" (though
this phrase must not, of course, be understood as implying
that cyclical fluctuations represent a diseased condition in
the economic body).

As regards the discovery of the cause of fluctuations,
however, business-cycle theory is still in its infancy. The
earlier crisis theories have, notwithstanding the energetic
efforts of their upholders, contributed extremely little
toward such a discovery. If one examines them closely,
one finds that, in any case, as a general rule, they completely
fail to get on to the track of the ultimate causes of economic
fluctuations. This does not matter much to modern
business-cycle theory, seeing that its object is not to discover the ultimate causes but to show their effects, however
the causes themselves may be conceived. It aims at seeing
through the interconnection and interlacing of the different
movements, at first on purely symptomatological lines,
but in the last resort from the point of view of the natural
laws which determine them. It does not by any means
always end by attributing a primary determinant character
to any particular sectional movement. For its purposes,
it is more important to succeed in establishing an internal
functional interrelationship between movements in general.
My meaning may be illustrated by an example. A study
of business symptoms tells us, for instance, that when home
trade is stagnant, the balance of foreign trade tends to
record a certain activity, while, at the same time, the
money and capital markets are quite easy and unemployment is acute. If the above configuration of cyclical
phenomena is recognized as depending on an internal
interconnection, their functional relationship is established.
Those who are trying to discover causes will want to take
a step further and to select one or other of these phenomena

as primarily determinant or to refer the whole complex of interrelated phenomena back to some quite separate underlying cause. This further step is, however, usually extremely hazardous. For the present, we may consider that we have made considerable progress when we have succeeded in thoroughly elucidating the complex of functional relationships.

Bibliography

The following titles are selected from the literature on the forecasting problem, literature today so extensive as to exceed one's capacity to keep track of it all.

AFTALION, ALBERT: "Cours de statistique," pp. 248 *ff.*, Paris, 1928; Le problème des prévisions économiques aux États-Unis, *Revue d'économie politique*, vol. 41, 1927.

BABSON, R. W.: "Business Barometers," 17th ed., 1925.

BRESCIANI-TURONI, C.: Considerazioni sui barometri economici, *Giornale degli economisti*, 1928.

BULLOCK, C. J., W. M. PERSONS, and W. L. CRUM: The Construction and Interpretation of the Harvard Index of Business Conditions, *Review of Economic Statistics*, April, 1927.

DAY, EDMUND E.: The Role of Statistics in Business Forecasting, *Journal of the American Statistical Association*, No. 3, vol. 23, 1928.

DELBANCO, G. A.: Konjunktur—Konjunkturprognose, *Conrads Jahrbücher*, 3d ser., vol. 68, 1926.

FISHER, I.: Our Unstable Dollar and the so-called "Business Cycle," *Journal of the American Statistical Association*, vol. 20, 1925.

GINESTET, P.: "Les indices du mouvement général des affaires," Paris, 1925. Publication 111 de l'institut d'étude et de documentation économiques et sociales, University of Bordeaux.

GOWIN, E. B.: "Forecasting Business Conditions," 1923.

HARDY, CHARLES O., and G. V. COX: "Forecasting Business Conditions," New York, 1927.

JORDAN, D. F.: "Business forecasting," 1921; "Practical Business Forecasting," 1927.

KONDRATIEV, N. D.: Das Problem der Prognose, *Annalen der Betriebswirtschaft*, vol. 1, 1927.

LACOMBE, EDOUARD: La prévision en matière de crises économiques, "Bibliothèque générale d'économie politique," Paris, 1925.

MITCHELL, W. C.: "Business Cycles," 2d ed., 1927; "Generating Economic Cycles," New York, 1923.

PERSONS, W. M. (ed.): *The Problem of Business Forecasting*, 1924.

SILBERLING, NORMAN Y.: A New Method of Presenting a General Business Index and Forecast, *Journal of the American Statistical Association*, suppl. vol. 23, 1928.

SNOW, E. C.: Trade Forecasting and Prices, *Journal of the Royal Statistical Society*, vol. 86, 1923.

SNYDER, C.: "Business Cycles and Business Measurements," New York, 1927.

VANCE, RAY: "Business Investment Forecasting," 2d ed., 1925.

VANDERBLUE, HOMER B.: "Problems in Business Economics," New York and Chicago, 1924.

WALLACE, W.: "Business Forecasting and Its Practical Application," London, 1927.

WORKING, H.: Bank Deposits As a Forecaster of the General Wholesale Price Level, *Review of Economic Statistics*, vol. 8, 1926.

CHAPTER XXI

EMPLOYMENT AS AN INDEX OF THE CYCLICAL MOVEMENT

We select the employment level as the most important subject of business-cycle investigation, for the particular reason that we consider it to constitute the best general index of the course of the national business cycle, as far as present-day conditions in Germany are concerned.

Statistics of the Labor Market.

The statistics of the German labor market provide us with a fairly considerable mass of material on which to estimate the employment level.

The object of labor-market statistics is to determine the number of persons actively employed in the economic system (employment statistics) and of the amount of additional human labor power for the time being unutilized and available for economic purposes (unemployment statistics). These figures are determined on the basis of returns regularly compiled for specific periods by official departments, corporations, and private organizations. The persons responsible for compiling the statistics aim at determining the employment level for each trade and district, taking into account, where possible, the hours actually worked.

1. Unemployment statistics are compiled by the Federal Labor Exchange and the Unemployment Insurance Department. They consist of:

    a. Statistics of persons receiving benefit under the unemployment-insurance scheme and from the fund for the assistance of those suffering from prolonged unemployment:

        Days selected as typical: the fifteenth and the last day in each month; subject subclassification: male, female, benefits received for less than 13 weeks, 13 to 26 weeks, over 26 weeks; district subclassification: figures for the fifteenth of each month. according to districts covered by local exhanges, and for the last day of each month, according to municipalities with 10,000 or more inhabitants.

b. Statistics of persons seeking employment:

Day selected as typical: the last day of the month; subject subclassification: occupational groups; district subclassification: districts covered by provincial labor offices. The statistics show the number of persons seeking employment, the number of situations vacant, and the number of applicants suited in each month. The inverse fluctuation as between the number of persons seeking employment and the number of situations vacant is very suggestive for the purpose of estimating the situation in the labor market; the relationship between the figures for these two items gives us the pressure-of-applications figure, that is, the number of persons seeking employment per one hundred vacant situations. This figure is, accordingly, a sensitive index of fluctuations in the labor market.

c. Statistics of short-time workers receiving benefit:

Week selected as typical: the calendar week preceding the first of the month. Returns are published only by the separate provincial labor offices.

2. Employment statistics are supplied by the membership returns of the Social Insurance System. These include:

a. Monthly membership figures for the sickness insurance funds, subdivided according to sex, provincial labor offices, class of fund.

b. The annual returns of the accident insurance system, subdivided according to separate occupational groups (these returns can be used only for investigations into past years).

3. The statistics of the trade union federations are intermediate between the above two groups.

Week selected as typical: the last complete calendar week in each month; subclassification: occupational groups, unemployed members, members working short time as a percentage of total membership.

4. The industrial reports (labor statistics) compiled by the Institute for Business Cycle Research on the basis of information concerning about 2,500 typical establishments may also serve as a representative survey of labor-market statistics. The following items of these reports are of special significance:

a. The relationship established for the various industries between the number of workers which the industry can employ if the total plant is fully utilized (capacity) and the number of workers actually employed in the period under review.

b. The relationship established for the various branches of industry between the number of worker-hours which can be worked if the total plant is fully utilized (capacity) and the number of worker hours actually worked in the period under review (hours taken into account for the calculation of wages).

Notwithstanding certain defects, the labor-market statistics reflect the movements of the trade cycle, particularly as regards industry, better than any other statistics available.

The Limits within Which Cyclical Fluctuations Move.

Let us now attempt to measure, from the employment figures, the limits within which the up and down movements of the trade cycle take place.

UNEMPLOYED INDUSTRIAL WORKERS IN GERMANY 1906–1914[1]
(In thousands)

End of month	1906	1907	1908	1909	1910	1911	1912	1913	1914
January.............	....	131	232	349	225	233	269	307	467
February...........	....	123	216	341	199	197	241	278	367
March..............	....	100	200	291	156	170	148	221	278
April...............	....	100	224	241	156	161	158	221	278
May................	....	108	224	233	173	143	176	240	278
June..............	88	108	232	233	173	143	158	259	248
July...............	59	108	216	208	164	143	167	278	288
August............	52	108	216	191	147	161	158	269	
September.........	74	108	216	175	156	152	139	259	
October...........	81	123	232	166	138	134	158	269	
November.........	81	131	256	166	138	152	167	298	
December.........	118	207	352	216	181	215	260	461	
Total number of workers in industry[2] in the same years....	7,372	7,679	7,999	8,319	8,639	8,959	9,279	9,599	

[1] Calculated by relating the percentage rate of unemployed trade union members to the total number of industrial workers. The latter figure was obtained for 1907 from the occupational census and for 1913 by using the factory inspectors' statistics; the figures for the intervening years are interpolated.
[2] Including mining.

This table tells us that during the months of deepest business depression, from 4 to 5 per cent of the total number of industrial workers were thrown out of work; at the end of 1908, this amounted to 350,000 out of a total of 8,000,000 (or 4.4 per cent), and at the end of 1913, 460,000 out of 9,500,000 (4.7 per cent). This does not mean that 4 to 5 per cent represents the extent of the cyclical fluctuation in national business, for the unemployment figures include many workers out of work owing entirely to the seasonal nature of their occupation. It must also be borne in mind that extraindustrial unemployment is always less severe. My personal opinion is that before the World War the amount of unemployment caused by cyclical fluctuations did not exceed 2 to 3 per cent. During the hard times which followed the inflation period,[1] unemployment temporarily rose to an abnormal level. At the end of 1923, far more than one-third, and at the beginning of 1926, approximately one-third, of the total number of industrial workers were unemployed (taking short-time workers into account). In relation to the total number of employed persons, the proportion was at one time higher than 10 per cent.

The fluctuations in national business turnover as a whole (by which the movement of the business cycle would be most comprehensively expressed) are not adequately represented by these figures. In the first place, as has already been pointed out, the industrial unemployment figures do not reflect the extraindustrial movement, which takes a quite different course and is, in some respects, far smoother; and, secondly, they give us only a very inadequate idea of the variations in wage income, not to speak of entrepreneur's income.

Employment and Wage Income.

Wage income depends not only on employment but also on the level of wage rates. This raises the question of the relationship existing between employment and wages. The whole of the struggle which goes on around wages is dominated by an outstanding antithesis. The worker's argument is briefly as follows: High wages = high purchasing power for the masses = high turnover = high employment level and entrepreneur's activity = high takings for the entrepreneur. The employer's chain of reasoning is, conversely, as follows: Low wages = low costs of production = low prices = large sales = abundant employ-

[1] During the inflation period, the unemployment rate was almost exclusively a function of the exchange value of the dollar.

ment possibilities. Viewed from a purely static standpoint, the antithesis immediately dissolves, for when the circular flow of business has completed its circuit, costs of production work out equal to the sum total of all receipts. The only question which really arises is, therefore, one of distribution—namely, the question of the respective shares of the employer and the worker in the social product.

Viewed dynamically, however, the question assumes a different aspect. Our perception lights immediately upon the fact that employment and wages are moving, on the whole, in the same direction but that wage income fluctuates still more considerably than employment; for during the revival and even during the high-tension phase, wages increase simultaneously with the rise in the number of employed workers, while during the recession and depression phases, employment and wages both decrease. An examination of the prewar figures brings these facts clearly to light. During the postwar period, wage rates ceased, to some extent, to fluctuate in sympathy with the trade cycle, just as in the case of prices. Wages, like prices, have been fixed on the basis of regular scales, with the result that they can be varied only slowly and with difficulty. It is true that notwithstanding wage scales, the earnings of labor are still, to some extent, exposed to the effects of the trade cycle. When business activity is increasing, labor's earnings are increased by overtime; while the employer is more inclined to pay wages above the listed rates, particularly for skilled labor (owing to the lack of specialized workers). Conversely, during recession and depression, hours are reduced and wages under the listed rates tend to be paid. A certain tendency of the listed wage rates themselves to move in sympathy with the trade cycle has also become noticeable.

The relationship existing between wage and price movements may be considered from two standpoints: (1) with special reference to the position of wage income as a constituent part of purchasing power and (2) with reference to the part played by wages in costs of production. The greater sensitiveness of prices is in itself evidence which might lead us to suppose that during a phase of full prosperity, wages lag behind prices, though, with the material available, no entirely satisfactory statistical proof of this can be offered. It is similarly probable that during a depression, wages will be high in proportion to prices.

This, of course, does not tell us anything decisive about the relationship between wage rates and entrepreneur's profits. This is a problem which can be solved only by analyzing the situation in particular undertakings (compare Chap. XV).

Factors Affecting the Employment Level.

In reckoning up the various factors by which the employment level is determined, we may begin by assuming that within any national business system, the demand for labor power depends on:

1. Output, that is:
   a. The number of persons engaged in gainful activity.
   b. Productive efficiency.
2. Sales, that is:
   a. Exports.
   b. The domestic market for
      (1) Personal services and dwelling accommodation.
      (2) Consumers' goods.
      (3) Producers' goods.

1. Employment and Output.

a. An increase in the number of persons available for gainful activity represents in itself an increase in unemployment, and a reduction in the number so available represents in itself a decrease in unemployment. It may be estimated that by the middle of 1925 there were about 32,000,000 persons available for gainful activity in Germany, as compared with 27,500,000 in 1913 (present German territory), so that the number increased during the interval by 4,500,000.

b. Similarly, unemployment rises when productive efficiency increases and falls when it decreases. The fact that in the middle of 1925 the number of unemployed was estimated to have fallen to a half million, although sales had not increased in proportion to the growth in the number of persons gainfully employed, could be explained only by reference to the following changes in the productivity of the national economic system.[1] It was clear that the intensity of the work done per head of population in comparison with the prewar period must have declined, owing to the fact that elements of lower working capacity had been brought into the labor market (disabled exsoldiers and persons who had previously lived on investment income). It appeared probable that shorter hours of work had had a similar effect. The reduced output was, however, due primarily to a weakening of the national productive apparatus as a whole, to the loss of particularly fertile provinces and the lessened economic efficiency of agricultural and industrial establishments; above all, to the purely economic structural disturbances (deranged price relationships, reduction in the amount of mobile working capital). At the same time, the technical productive apparatus as a whole had been considerably improved, and the national business organism further strengthened. The prewar level of productive efficiency had probably been more or less attained, not, of course, in the case of agriculture, but certainly in many branches of industry; indeed, in some cases, the prewar level had been far surpassed. Productive efficiency is a factor which it is very difficult to express in figures. As, however, it alters relatively slowly, we may, in studying cyclical fluctuations over comparatively short periods, leave it out of account, as we do changes in population.

2. Sales.

Cyclical fluctuations in the employment level are, therefore, dominated mainly by the sales situation. The importance of the different items in sales varies widely,

[1] See Von Zwiedineck-Südenhorst, Beiträge zur Erklärung der strukturellen Arbeitslosigkeit, *V.z.K.*, vol. 2, suppl. 1, pp. 15 *ff.*, 1927.

however, in this respect. The total value of the national production in 1913 (about 50,000,000,000 marks—see p. 35) was made up of the following items, expressed in rough percentage figures (these being quite adequate for our present purpose):

	Per cent
Exports (including the supplements charged by commerce)..	15
Personal services and dwelling accomodation...........	20
Agricultural production (including the supplements charged by commerce).............................	25
Producers' goods (including the supplements charged by commerce).......................................	20
Consumers' goods (including the supplements charged by commerce)......................................	20
Total...	100

As the demand for personal services and dwelling accommodation is subject only to slight cyclical fluctuations, as the employment level in agriculture is practically unaffected by the trade cycle, and as exports are, directly at least, also relatively slightly subject to cyclical fluctuations (see pp. 177 *ff.*), the interest of the trade-cycle investigator must necessarily be concentrated mainly on domestic sales of industrial products, though only on such sales as are dependent on an elastic demand. Within the total national turnover, therefore, scarcely more than one-third of the total sales will be affected by the trade cycle. This point has been dealt with in some detail in Section V. Fluctuations of as much as 30 per cent in these variable sales, thus, do not affect the national employment level as a whole by more than about 10 per cent.

CHAPTER XXII

STABILIZATION OF BUSINESS AND ELIMINATION OF ITS CYCLES[1]

The fluctuations in the employment level, and in the loss of income which they cause, are relatively slight in relation to the total values created by the whole economic process; but the actual unemployment figures, running at times into hundreds of thousands and even into millions, give rise to an extraordinary amount of suffering and hardship. Consequently, the elimination of these fluctuations would seem to be one of the paramount problems within the entire field of economic policy.

Arguments against Stabilizing Trade.

The efforts directed to this end have, of course, touched the sensibilities of some "theorists"—sensibilities of the kind that constantly reveal themselves as obstacles to technical and cultural progress. Just as modern means of transport still incur the reproaches of romantic admirers of the stage-coach and the sailing ship, so do we find "theorists" who see in the struggle against crises and unemployment a kind of iconoclasm, an attempt to rob the capitalist paradise of its God. They appear to overlook the fact that it makes a considerable difference whether a reasonable and properly distributed tax of a few per cent is laid on income or similar burdens are imposed by a crisis, reacting blindly on the community in the manner of a war or a levy of ransom. Two main arguments are brought forward against a trade-stabilization policy:

1. It is urged that if crises and periods of depression were effectively eliminated, a very important factor in

[1] See the author's paper entitled Konjunkturlose Wirtschaft und Konjunkturstabilisierung, *Deutsche Wirtschaftszeitung*, 16, 1928.

economic selection would be lost; for a depression is necessary from time to time in order to weed out rotting or unfit undertakings. A similar argument is, it will be remembered, very popular among antivaccinationists and other critics of the struggle against disease, in their anxiety lest the human race should degenerate in consequence of an excess of well-being. But even admitting the desirability of giving the greatest possible play to the selective principle, we cannot help concluding that in a competitive business system it ceases to have any common sense, if it turns out to mean that excellently organized undertakings, disposing of a wealth of skill and energy and with highly developed technical capacities for production, are to collapse in a business crisis, simply owing, for instance, to some lack of foresight on the part of commercial management—just as war ceases to be a "refreshing bath of steel" when the fighting no longer takes place man against man but is waged with mines and poison gas.

2. The second, and more serious, argument is to the effect that business stabilization would eliminate not only the slump, not only crisis and depression, but also the boom, with all its beneficial effects. A boom (it is argued) and the rise in prices which it involves favors the producer, whether he is an employer or a worker, against officials and persons living on investment income; it is like a tax levied on the whole population in favor of production. It creates new possibilities and leads to the foundation of new undertakings and thus brings progress in its train. The possibilities of profit which suddenly open up in a trade revival are an immense source of stimulation to the business man, while an economy from which the trade cycle had been eliminated must encourage bureaucracy and stereotyped routine. This view is based on the observed fact that the mighty development of capitalist economy in the last century took place in a series of great thrusts forward, each followed by a reaction; it was based on a series of upward movements of the trade cycle, which were followed but not fully smoothed out by depressions, so that each fresh

revival started from a higher level than the preceding one. The answer to these arguments may be expressed somewhat as follows: It was not the increased profits reaped during booms, nor the gains brought in by lucky speculation, which led to economic progress; on the contrary, they impeded it, as experience during the inflation period has shown in a quantity of cases. Activity and output can develop more freely when property is secure and income steady—a simple truth which has, for a long time past, been transformed into practice, in the organization, for instance, of the pursuit of scientific knowledge.

Above all, however, it must be remembered that cyclical fluctuations arise from the fact that the various sectional movements in the business system fail to coincide chronologically (whatever may be the deeper-lying causes of the trade cycle). This leads to a defective distribution of goods and forces in time, which, in turn, gives an irrational twist to the business process—in much the same way as does a defective distribution of goods and forces in space. Centuries of experience have taught business by means of commerce and the transportation of goods, through postal and railroad, service, and as a result of choices of geographical situation and of sales policy—to tackle the question of distribution from the space point of view, on more or less the right lines; though, as a matter of fact, the ideal solution for the postwar period is still by no means found, as is shown by the differences, frequently of astonishing proportions, in prices between one district and another— for frequent and considerable local differences in prices indicate that a proper spatial distribution of goods and forces has not yet been achieved. Still less, however, have those responsible for business management succeeded —notwithstanding all their efforts—in establishing a satisfactory distribution in time. The clearest proof of this is afforded by the fluctuations in prices and, where prices are fixed, in physical-volume movements, which, at times, occur from one month—even from one week— to another.

Yet, after all, it is largely a waste of time to argue on such points, for all efforts to eliminate cyclical fluctuations have so far proved vain, and the extent to which business is dependent on nature (harvests, seasons, weather, and the like) makes it appear improbable that such efforts could, in any case, achieve success. Even in the United States, where business activity has, for the last few years, been maintained at a fairly steady and constant level, closer investigation shows that trade stabilization has not become even remotely possible.[1]

Trade Stabilization in America.

The wholesale price index fluctuates in the United States at least as greatly as in the prewar period. Even the physical-volume movement, as reflected in the Brookmire Business Index or Babson's "physical-volume-of-business" chart shows no striking tendency to approach a state of rest. The stock market is equally unstabilized. It is true that interest rates are definitely steadier than before the World War; more important still, the turnover curve is smoother than it used to be.

These phenomena are evidently attributable to the fact that the various branches of business now follow deviating lines of cyclical fluctuation. Since 1924, the crests and troughs of the wave have not become more frequent in the several branches of business; instead, a certain equilibrium has been achieved from the fact that a wave-crest situation in some branches is balanced by a simultaneous wave-trough situation in others. Thus, in 1925 and 1926, the industries producing producers' goods, led by the building trade, enjoyed great prosperity, while during the same period, the industries producing consumers' goods, particularly the textile, boot and shoe, leather and food-stuffs industries, were, for the most part, in a depressed state, and agriculture was hit by bad harvests. On the other hand, in 1924, while many industries suffered a setback,

[1] The ensuing argument has already been developed by the author in *V.z.K.*, vol. 2, No. 4.

this was quickly compensated by the unusually favorable balance with which agriculture was left.   In many quarters, it is supposed that the course of events in 1928 is likely to turn out similarly; that is to say, while about the beginning of the year a number of signs were apparent, indicating an impending unfavorable situation for American industry, favorable symptoms were also noticeable in the shape of heavy bookings of orders for agricultural machinery and fertilizers and considerable purchasing activity among the country customers of the mail-order houses.

The question arises whether this compensatory tendency among the cyclical fluctuations in the various branches of business is accidental or deeper-lying causes for it can be discovered.

It is possible that the movement of business in America is due to the interaction of structural and cyclical factors.[1]

The rapid expansion of the building trade, and of producers'-goods industries in general, was very likely a case of reconstruction in the truest sense of the word and, therefore, a structural phenomenon, making its appearance in the midst of the cyclical depression by which a number of the remaining industries were affected in 1925 to 1926. Only after several more years have elapsed shall we know whether this explanation to which objections have been raised in some quarters in Germany is really the right one; for not till then shall we be able to form a clear idea of the trade cycle's rhythm in the postwar period.   In any case, the period during which we have been able to observe something resembling trade stabilization—a term to be used only with the greatest caution, as we have seen—has been far too short to permit us already to begin talking of a fundamental alteration in the phase length and extent of cyclical fluctuations in the United States.

It is in itself quite conceivable that in comparison with the prewar period the general or average trade cycle, resultant of various kinds of sectional fluctuation, will

[1] See *V.z.K.*, vol. 2, No. 4, p. 11.

remain less violent from other quite different causes. Two factors appear to support this conclusion.

1. The size of the American market and the multiform nature of American production, it may be said, bring the United States fairly near to the ideal of a closed business state with a huge market. Any general statement of the way that the tendencies toward a smoothing out of cyclical fluctuations increase in proportion to the expansion of the market applies, in particular, to the American business system as a whole.

2. The second, and perhaps the decisive, factor in balancing out the sectional fluctuations is to be found in the immense capital wealth of the country. The United States has become the great creditor country of the world, with the largest gold reserves, the largest amount of national industrial capital, and the highest proportion of savings. This capital wealth not only makes possible a credit policy conceived on the most generous lines but also, and above all, signifies the liberation of business from the fetters imposed elsewhere by dearth of capital. In such a case, the state of business is not only dominated primarily by fluctuations in the supply of capital, it is also simultaneously influenced more considerably by many other factors. As all these factors, which include consumption, foreign sales, and dependence on raw-material imports, do not exert a uniform pull in one particular direction but constitute a most complex tangle of conflicting forces, a certain balance is produced by this fact alone.

The situation in the United States may be stated in these words. Trade stabilization has been achieved during recent years only in a very limited sense, and in any case only for a period of some 3 years, so that this experience alone is as yet insufficient to justify us in drawing very extensive conclusions; especially as the less violent general shaping of the trade cycle results from a balancing of different movements in the various branches of business. It is quite possible that the intervention of structural factors has also contributed to this balancing process. Two factors, however—leaving out of account the possible effects of a deliberate policy in regard to the trade cycle—appear to favor the likelihood that a comparative absence of any violent cyclical fluctuations may be reckoned on for the future: namely, the size of the American market and the immense capital wealth of the country. The present balance is established by the interplay of very heterogeneous forces; this means that if, in consequence of some—scarcely probable—accident, the bulk of these forces bore down on either side, cyclical fluctuations of very great dimensions might result.

The influence of credit policy will be dealt with in the next chapter.

What many people regard as a victory won by a far-sighted trade-cycle policy is probably nothing but a change in the rhythm of the trade cycle, for just as in Europe during the course of the nineteenth century the duration of the full cycle was reduced from 10 to 11 years to 7 to 8 years, so it is possible that the waves of the trade cycle are now gradually becoming flattened out throughout the world and that their periodicity is changing at the same time.

Recently, in any case, such an alteration appears to have been taking shape in Germany. After the stabilization, until about the autumn of 1926—throughout a period of about 3 years—the separate phases lasted for some 7 or 8 months (with the exception of the crisis, which is usually over more quickly), following one after another in a succession of abrupt jerks. Now, many signs indicate that in this, as in other respects, we are gradually getting back to prewar conditions. This would mean that, in the next few years, we may count on a lengthening of the duration of the trade cycle and on a flattening out of its fluctuations.

Bibliography

HAHN, A.: Konjunkturlose Wirtschaft? *Wirtschaftsdienst*, No. 16, 1925.

SCHUMPETER, JOSEF: Kreditkontrolle, *Archiv für Sozialwissenschaft und Sozialpolitik*, vol. 54, 1925.

BELLERBY, J. R.: "Control of Credit," London, 1924; "Monetary Stability," London, 1925.

LAYTON and others (ed.): "Is Unemployment Inevitable?" London, 1925.

KEYNES, J. M.: "A Tract on Monetary Reform," London, 1923.

EDIE (ed.): "Stabilization of Business," New York, 1924.

MITCHELL, WESLEY C. (ed.): "Business Cycles and Unemployment," New York, 1923.

PERSONS, W. M., FOSTER, and others (ed.): "The Problem of Business Forecasting," New York, 1924.

BEVERIDGE, W. A.: Employment and the Business Cycle, *Harvard Review of Economic Statistics*, January, 1922; "Cycles of Unemployment," Boston, 1923.

WAGEMANN, ERNST: Konjunkturlose Wirtschaft und Konjunkturstabilisierung, *Deutsche Wirtschaftszeitung*, No. 16, 1928.

CHAPTER XXIII

THE RESOURCES OF ECONOMIC POLICY

The Variety of Resources.

Two sorts of measures lie within practical reach when we propose to make trade-cycle fluctuations less violent: (a) public or national and (b) private or commercial.

The state may intervene in two fundamentally different ways. It may either exercise directly the economic powers entrusted to it or bring indirect influence to bear by imposing a trade-cycle policy on private business through legislative or administrative measures.

The indirect methods, which specifically consist in the effectuation of wage and price policies, and, particularly, of the discount policy, are usually regarded as calculated to smooth out the business cycle. Yet there can be little doubt that discount policy represents nothing more than a palliative. Down to the present, at all events, it has been powerless to prevent business crises. It must, of course, be taken into account that in Europe discount policy has been used far more to protect the exchange value of the currency than for regulating the business cycle. In the United States, the Federal Reserve Board has, it will be remembered, relied extensively on credit policy for the purpose of general business regulation and in doing so has, to some extent, opened up new ground (a) by partially restricting credit and (b) by direct intervention, influencing supply and demand on the credit markets through the purchase or sale of government securities or acceptances. The purchase of other sorts of securities and even of commodities has been proposed. These measures are known in the United States as "open-market operations"; they are linked up with discount policy and, also, with a system of directly influencing the demand for credit through the

Federal Reserve Banks themselves, including direct supervision and control of the business operations of the member banks, development of the information services of the Reserve Banks, and, above all, with special study of the trade cycle for the purpose of following the current development of business life.

Fundamentally new, however, are the measures adopted in the United States to make a given credit policy work. Such methods have, of course, for a long time past been employed by other central banks as well, but on a different scale and for a quite different purpose—that of strengthening the currency. The methods usually employed in the United States constitute something essentially distinct, for they amount to the use in the grand manner by the state of its own economic power in pursuit of a trade-cycle policy. They are, therefore, entitled to be ranked on the same level as the other two sets of measures in this category of economic policy, which in recent years have been increasingly perfected, especially in Germany: that is, unemployment insurance and the organized planning of industry. It is significant that three new and powerful systems within the field of economic policy are developing, from apparently quite different motives. This is certainly not the place to attempt to indicate, even in outline, the greatest sociological range of these efforts, which may constitute the beginnings of an entirely new economy. In the following pages, an attempt will be made simply to outline the way in which these measures have hitherto been employed and the results they have produced.

THE APPLICATION OF CREDIT POLICY

Reserve System Measures.

After the crisis of 1920, efforts very soon began to be made in the United States to ensure that business life should never again suffer a similar shock. The way was laid open for an effective credit policy in America by the fact that the Federal Reserve System, with about 10,000 member banks,[1] comprises about one-third of all the banks

[1] Slightly over 8,500 on Dec. 31, 1929.—TRANS.

of America, with about two-thirds of the total finance capital administrated by all the banks (excluding savings and private banks).[1]

As soon as the most difficult problem—that of neutralizing or sterilizing the vast quantities of gold which had poured into the United States after the World War—had been solved, a deliberate attempt was made to measure the volume of credit throughout the country in scale with the volume of business. Whereas the old credit policy had aimed primarily at ensuring that the discount rate should definitely follow the market—raising it when the demand for credits from the banks of issue increased and lowering it when the demands on the banks slackened— the modern heads of American banking set out deliberately to achieve the stabilization of business.

A rough means of estimating the volume of credit is afforded by the observed fact that the total amount of credits granted by the American banks during the last 50 years has increased annually by about 6 to 7 per cent. It has been constantly emphasized that the efforts of those responsible for American banking policy have been directed solely to regulating the total volume of credit and never toward making their policy depend on a particular credit situation, in other words toward taking special account of the movement in particular markets.[2]

The new credit policy dates, in the main, from the spring of 1922, when steps began to be taken to have a special committee set up for the uniform regulation of buying and selling of government securities; this committee—the Federal Reserve Board's Open-market Investment Committee—was officially appointed in 1923.

The policy of intervention can be very clearly traced in the succeeding years. Where a falling tendency in prices appears to be of sufficient duration to threaten business

---

[1] See BURGESS, "The Reserve Banks and the Money Market," 1922.

[2] A change of policy appears to have been introduced quite recently in this respect, judging from the efforts made to check speculation on the New York Stock Exchange.

prosperity, government bonds are bought on the open market—as, for example, in the periods January to May, 1922; December, 1923, to September, 1924; April, 1926, and, again, in 1927. Conversely, where offers on the money market are so abundant that an unhealthy rise in prices and in speculation sets in, considerable quantities of government securities are sold; or, in other terms, the market conditions are tightened. So it was from June, 1922, to July, 1923; November, 1924, to March, 1925; August, 1926, to September, 1926; and since the beginning of 1928. The manipulation of credit policy has been conducted, as we have already mentioned, in close relationship with discount policy. In many cases the purchase of government securities has been accompanied by a lowering of discount rates, and, conversely, the selling of bonds increased the indebtedness of the member banks to the Reserve Banks, so that money rates rise and the discount rate is increased.

Furthermore, credit policy has been manipulated not only with a view to the general business situation but also for the purpose of smoothing out seasonal fluctuations (such as by the purchase of government securities on settlement day and the like). Such measures, moreover, afforded a useful step toward compensating the effects of the inflow of gold, which continued without interruption until the autumn of 1927; by buying gold and at the same time selling government securities, it was possible to put a brake on the expansion of credit (such operations were conducted in April, May, and June, 1927).

Results.

Opinions are very much divided as to the extent to which the credit policy of the Federal Reserve System has attained its objects. The developments which took place in 1927 are sufficient to make it appear extremely doubtful whether the policy of the Reserve System is really in a position to prevent a cyclical business decline. In that year, although, in consequence of a decline in business activity, the discount rate was lowered and considerable quantities of government securities were taken off the markets, the demand for credits by business fell away steadily. Whereas the total volume of credits granted by the Federal Reserve Banks increased in the course of the year, the flow of credits to the productive spheres of business steadily diminished. General interest was aroused when, in February, 1928, the Federal Reserve Board found itself obliged to admit that the credit policy which it had pursued during the last few months had by no means yielded the results expected.[1] It was openly admitted that the greater part of the credits which had been so freely granted had flowed into the stock market for purposes of speculation. Subsequent developments have also shown, moreover, that the change in credit policy which took effect from the beginning of 1928 has completely failed to realize the expectations based upon it. Notwithstanding its earnestness and persistency, the effort made, through the tightening of the money market, to check the extraordinary rise in stock prices which was setting in failed to put a brake on speculation. Despite heavy sales of government securities, frequent increases of the discount rate, and a substantial exportation of gold, which must certainly have favored the credit-restriction policy of the banks, stock prices continued to rise. It is thus clearly indicated that credit policy, as an instrument of economic policy, must remain ineffective until it is able to steer the flow of credit in a particular direction as well as increase or diminish its volume. In the United States, as a matter of fact, a depressed state of business in various branches of industry has itself served to thwart the policy of the banks, inasmuch as the free capital for which production did not offer sufficiently attractive possibilities of reinvestment was rushed into speculation and almost entirely neutralized the effects of the tightening policy.

UNEMPLOYMENT INSURANCE

Unemployment insurance is akin to credit manipulation from the point of view of economic policy, in so far as it

[1] See *Federal Reserve Bulletin*, 2, 1928.

also draws economic power at specific times out of business in order to restore the same power to business at some other time in the future. In Germany, contributions are levied from employers and workers, to an amount which varies according to the state of business, to be restored to the workers to a smaller or greater extent, according to the extent of the unemployment.

In a period of prosperity, the funds of the unemployment insurance system increase, while in a period of business decline and increasing unemployment, they are again reduced. The fluctuations in income caused by the trade cycle are thus, in a measure, smoothed out. The amounts involved in the unemployment insurance system are in themselves very considerable. At the present rate of contribution, amounting to 3 per cent on the earnings of 17,000,000 insured persons, a sum of 750,000,000 marks is collected annually; a limit is, however, set to the possible accumulation (if the emergency reserve reaches the sum of 135,000,000 marks, contributions are reduced), and for a long time to come the amounts accumulated will be constantly melting away again, even in periods of prosperity, owing to the amount of permanent unemployment existing. At present, unemployment insurance in Germany is conducted with a view to social rather than trade-cycle policy.

BUSINESS PLANNING

The business planning of public authority could well assume considerable importance, in the first instance, from the point of view of business-cycle policy.

The Prewar Period.

During the prewar period, practically nothing had been done in this direction. It may even be asserted that the free market did much more to compensate cyclical fluctuations. According to the investigations carried out some time ago by Bramstedt, municipal expenditure on construction work, and the like, in the years 1895 to 1912 followed the fluctuations of the trade cycle fairly closely. Similarly, the expenditure of the German railways for such purposes in 1890 to 1913 moved almost exactly parallel to the trade cycle. Thus, the public corporations and utilities have regularly increased their expenditure on works during prosperous periods and reduced it in times of depression. This policy, which was due to fluctuating receipts, increased the severity of the cyclical fluctuations and, therefore, at the same time, of the economic tension involved by those fluctuations. In consequence, the municipal authorities were regularly taken unawares

EXPENDITURE OF THE GERMAN RAILWAYS, FINANCIAL YEARS 1887-1913
(In units of standard deviation)

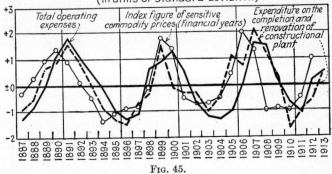

FIG. 45.

by the unemployment caused by each industrial crisis and so could make headway against it only by organizing emergency relief work (excavation, road making, stone breaking, mat weaving, woodwork, copying, and similar activity). Under the pressure of the rapidly rising tide of unemployment, the number of towns in which relief work was organized would quickly increase and decline no less quickly as soon as unemployment became less acute. As soon as the state of industry revived, the unemployment problem would disappear from the agenda of discussions on social policy, until the state and the municipalities, again taken unawares, were compelled to resort to the same inadequate measures of relief-work organization. In the prewar period, in any case, although the problem of shifting the incidence of unemployment had already been considered, no attempt was made to organize preventive measures—indeed, no such attempt could have been made, seeing that the indispensable basis, in the shape of an efficient business service, was entirely lacking.

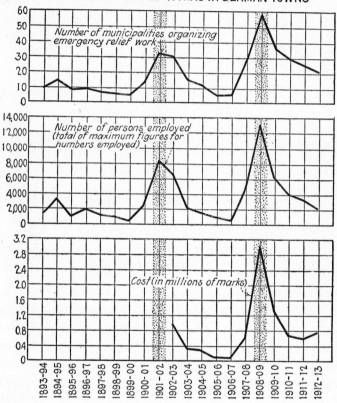

Fig. 46.

House Building by Private Enterprise.

On the other hand, private enterprise in the house-building trade has pursued a business policy running counter to the general movement of the trade cycle. During the revival and high-tension phases, it holds back, and during the depression phase it regularly expands its building activities, as is proved by the statistics of building permits in German towns in 1895 to 1912.

Thus, house building more or less automatically smooths out cyclical fluctuations in a certain degree, while the business plans of public authorities, owing to the fact that their building orders have fluctuated parallel to the course of the trade cycle in industry, have hitherto accentuated the trade cycle rather than softened its effects.

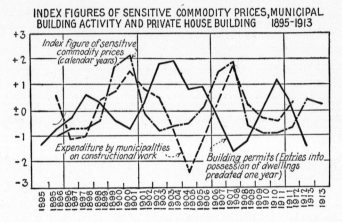

INDEX FIGURES OF SENSITIVE COMMODITY PRICES, MUNICIPAL BUILDING ACTIVITY AND PRIVATE HOUSE BUILDING   1895-1913

FIG. 47.

The Postwar Period.

It is, therefore, rightly urged that the public corporations should, as far as possible, postpone construction operations during the revival and high-tension phases until a period of depression again sets in. This policy is, of course, subject to certain limitations; but in 1926 a deliberate policy of ordering on the part of the German Federal Government, the states, and the municipalities was successfully used to counteract the effects of the depression in that year.

Quantitative Measurement of Efficiency.

If we wish to form a quantitative notion of the efficiency of a well-directed policy of planning in counteracting the effects of the trade cycle, we must proceed on the assumption, derived from our experience in the last few years, that a crisis involves a loss in wages of, say, 3,000,000,000 marks (the actual loss reduced to a yearly basis) to the whole body of workers hit by unemployment. If this deficiency is to be covered by supplementary orders for the execution of large-scale operations on public or quasipublic account, it will be necessary, supposing the crisis to have been preceded by two years of advancing prosperity, to postpone in each of those two years 1,500,000,000 marks' worth of public works (in behalf of the Nation, the states, and the municipalities)—that is, about 25 per cent of the total, which, at present probably represents an expenditure of roughly 6,500,000,000.[1] It is unlikely that postponement on a scale so large would be possible. It is however, clear that if orders for the execution of such tasks could be held back to the extent even of 5 to 10 per cent during periods of increasing prosperity, a useful reserve would be accumulated against cyclical fluctuations.

The Problem of Financing.

A difficult problem of financing is, of course, involved. In theory, two methods are possible: Building funds can either be accumulated during the revival and prosperity phases, to be expended during the depression, or else, in times of prosperity, the actual expenditure on building can be restricted (either by cutting down the relevant items in the budget estimates or by refraining from borrowing), funds being raised only when the depression arrives, either by borrowing or by taxation.

Where funds are accumulated in times of prosperity, this does not mean that finance capital is withdrawn from business, seeing that the funds in question are always invested at interest. They thus encourage business development and, consequently, may altogether fail to put a brake on the trade cycle. If they are withdrawn in time of depression, there is a risk that their withdrawal may

---

[1] It should, of course, be borne in mind that this estimate includes other costs (interest, imports) which reduce the amount payable to German wage earners.

accentuate the tendency toward liquidation and, in consequence, stimulate the recession process.   The significance of the capital sums involved, from the point of view of trade-cycle policy, is, of course, unaffected in so far as they again become available for public purposes in time of depression and as they may serve to revive business when it is depressed and its initiative capacity temporarily crippled.

If the alternative method, of refraining from expenditure on building without accumulating reserves, be adopted, such abstinence serves, no less than the accumulation of reserves, to increase the possibilities of development for business in general.   In time of depression, however, the effects are different; for at this juncture, either taxation must be increased—which is, in practice, out of the question when business is stagnant—or money must be borrowed. The latter course, however, means increasing the tension on the money and capital market and signifies, therefore, a lessening of the chances offered to particular sections of the business community by low prices and interest rates.

The validity of all the above deductions is problematical; they do not tell us how, in fact, business is affected by systematic planning of the public business and the financing measures which it involves.   It must assuredly be of decisive importance, however, that planning of this sort must be associated most closely with a reasonable credit policy.

PRIVATE BUSINESS FORECASTING

In our existing economic system, the center of gravity of trade-cycle policy must lie not with the state but with the individual undertakings, which, as the cells of the business organism, bear the brunt of trade fluctuations.

Instead, therefore, of trying to influence the undertakings only by means of a general character, it is, also, possible to approach them individually.   For this purpose, however, the active collaboration of the undertakings themselves is necessary. A collective trade-cycle policy, even though based on the best of national forecasting services, cannot take the place of a trade-cycle policy pursued by individual businesses; for although the general movement of business as a whole is nothing but the resultant of the economic fate of all the individual businesses, the business experience of the individual undertaking never entirely coincides with the movement of the national trade cycle. The truth is rather that the business curves of private undertakings are either only approximately parallel to the national business curve or that the respective fluctuations follow one another at a certain interval, if, indeed, they do not move inversely or deviate totally from each other.

So far, nothing much has been done, generally speaking, toward a systematic study of these relationships in Germany. Rationalization, which, in recent years, has made such progress, has been mainly concentrated on technique and works organization, on such points as normalization, standardization, the use of conveyors, increased use of machinery, or the rational application and employment of labor power. But rationalization should not stop short at technique and organization. It should, in particular, also cover the trade-cycle policy of undertakings. It is true that exact methods of calculation have nowhere made greater progress or been brought to a state of greater precision than in the commercial departments of undertakings; but leaving aside the technique and practice of commerce, more particularly bookkeeping and calculation, the approach to the market from the point of view of trade-cycle policy has in Germany scarcely progressed beyond the stage of intuition and improvization. Yet a proper approach to the market implies a correct chronological coordination of the separate activities of an undertaking within the framework of the business process as a whole and should rest on a systematic scientific basis. Such a basis could be provided by a private business forecasting service in conjunction with an efficient national forecasting service and a detailed sectional survey.

In the United States, a good deal has been done in this direction; for the heavy losses suffered by industry during the severe crisis of 1920 to 1921 helped considerably to encourage the extension, in breadth and in depth, of methods based on the scientific study of business cycles.

The methods principally employed in the United States by private business forecasting services are based, in part, on those elaborated in the public business services and, in part, on a special study of the results of research carried out by the individual business undertakings. Some of the more important firms, which even before the World War disposed of a useful mass of statistical material collected by themselves, still rely, to some extent, on the principle of a general index, enabling them particularly to follow the direction and course of development of national business as a whole. Other firms have gone further and have compiled barometers of a wide variety for their own respective branches. These firms have either employed the methods of business-cycle forecasting, based, for instance, on the principle of consecutive fluctuation (see *The Barometer* of the Simonds Saw and Steel Company of Fitchburg, Mass.), or else they have practiced a kind of trend forecasting, in conjunction, for the most part, with the so-called "budgeting system." The adoption of or special preference for either or both of these two methods depends essentially on the particular nature of the individual business. The object may be either to obtain a basis for calculating buying possibilities, sales, and prices in advance with some degree of certitude or, in conjunction therewith, to obtain some firm ground on which to build plans for extending plant or buildings.

Bibliography

BARBER: "Budgeting to Business Control," New York, 1925.

BERNET, F.: "Konjunkturforschung und Wirtschaftsrationalisierung."

BRAMSTEDT, PAUL: "Das Problem der Beschaffung von Arbeit durch Staat und Gemeinde," Kiel, 1909.

FEILEN, J. F.: Kreditplanwirtschaft? *Deutsche Arbeit*, 1928.

HIRSCH, JULIUS: "Das amerikanische Wirtschaftswunder," Berlin, 1926.

LUKAS: "Arbeitslosenversicherung und produktive Arbeitslosenfürsorge," 1926.

MAHLBERG: Konjunkturbeeinflussung durch Kalkulation und Kreditpolitik, *Zeitschrift für handelswissenschaftliche Forschungen*, No. 5, 1925; Statistik im Betriebe, *Grundriss der Betriebswirtschaftslehre*, vol. 2, Leipzig, 1927.

MOMBERT, P.: Konjunkturbeobachtung und Konjunkturpolitik, *Grundriss der Betriebswirtschaftslehre*, vol. 2, Leipzig, 1927.

MÜLLER, ALFRED: "Oekonomische Theorie der Konjunkturpolitik," Leipzig, 1926.

PALYI, M.: Wirkungslose Konjunkturpolitik in Amerika, *Der Deutsche Volkswirt*, August, 1928.

PRION, W.: "Kreditpolitik," Berlin, 1925.

SALIN, EDGAR: "Staatliche Kreditpolitik."

SCHUMPETER: Die goldene Bremse an der Kreditmaschine, "Die Kreditwirtschaft," vol. 1, Leipzig, 1927.

SPIETHOFF, A.: Kreditpolitik, "Die Kreditwirtschaft," vol. 2, Leipzig, 1927.

VANDERBLUE, HOMER B.: "Problems in Business Economics," New York, 1925.

WALB: Absatzstockungen und Preispolitik, *Betriebswirtschaftl. Rundschau*, 1924.

WILBRANDT, R.: "Der Volkswirt als Berater der Volkswirtschaft," Stuttgart, 1928.

SECTION VII

CAUSATION OF THE BUSINESS CYCLE

CHAPTER XXIV

THE SEVERAL THEORIES OF CAUSES

Just as from the astronomer's point of view, the question of the origin of the heavenly bodies is one which lies on the border line and does not constitute the proper subject of his science, so from the point of view of business-cycle theory, the question of the causes of economic fluctuations lies outside the bounds of its special subject matter. In the following pages, therefore, this question is dealt with in summary outline only.

The object of such a study of causation is not, of course, to investigate the forces which produce the circular flow of business or the motives underlying business activity but merely to inquire into the nature of the forces which *disturb* the circular flow of business or "the national economic balance." These causes can be sought in various strata of the economic substructure—and even right outside it. Theories of crises and business cycles can, indeed, be classified according to the distance from the "subject matter"—that is, the cyclical fluctuations—at which the theorists do their burrowing for the "causes."

1. The first main group of business-cycle theories is characterized by the fact that the cause is sought in the subject matter itself. These theories locate the origin of business cycles in some maladjustment arising out of the circular flow of business. We can see at a glance from our tabular or diagrammatical representations of the circular flow of business (see Chap. II) what scope there

is for elaborating causation theories of this kind. The possible theories may be classified in four main groups:

a. Disturbances in the relationship between the commodity and financial sides. Currency and credit theories of business-cycle causation (propagated by Hawtrey, Hahn, Keynes).

b. Disturbances in relations inside the elements on the financial side For example: maladjustment between income and prices (part of Hobson and Lederer's theory).

c. Disturbances in balance between the elements on the commodity side. For example: maladjustment between the respective production of consumers' and producers' goods (to some extent, Tugan-Baranowski and Spiethoff) or between organic and inorganic production (Sombart).

d. Disturbances in the relationship between specific elements on the financial side and specific elements on the commodity side. For example: maladjustment between capital accumulation and the production of producers' goods (Cassel).

Compound types of business-cycle and crisis theories can be formed by taking more than one of the above possibilities into account.[1] Indeed, most of the theories maintained in these days are of a compound character, especially as many of them wander off into other strata of the economic system in search of the causes of the causes themselves. All the theories in the group above are obliged to do this, because—inasmuch as they claim to reveal causal relationships—they involve a vicious circle,

---

[1] The business-cycle and crisis theories derived from the doctrine of marginal utility (such as those of Wicksell and Mises) are of this kind, although, in appearance, they do not deal with the relations between the concrete economic elements themselves, in so far as their upholders maintain that fluctuations occur when the market rate of interest does not correspond to the "natural rate of interest on capital" or that price variations occur because the "intrinsic value" or "marginal utility" imposes them. Although no concrete reality can be conceived as corresponding to these notions of "intrinsic value" or "natural rate of interest on capital," they are intended, nevertheless, to represent some sort of synthesis of concrete phenomena (such as supply and demand). Thus, Wicksell maintains that the natural rate of interest on capital "would be fixed by supply and demand if real capital, without any interposition of money," were loaned, while Mises ("Theorie des Geldes und der Umlaufsmittel," p. 369) defines the rate of interest on capital as determined "by the yield of the last economically justified extension of production and the first extension not so justified." It would, of course, take as long to discover a gage of this extension of production as to find the philosopher's stone.

as Löwe has acutely observed.[1] Thus, for instance, when Cassel argues that

. . . depression itself creates the low rate of interest which ultimately spells its own end, just as prosperity causes the rate of interest to rise to a level at which it becomes intolerable and must, therefore, cause the collapse of the very prosperity which involved such a rise,

Löwe is able to retort by asking: "Whence arises the depression which creates the low rate of interest?" Löwe's reply to his own question is:

Apparently from the high rate of interest during the preceding period of prosperity; but this period of prosperity itself owed its existence to the low rate of interest during the previous depression.

Cassel's intention is, of course, only to demonstrate a functional relationship; in any case, all the theories in this first group point only to functional connections. They are quite inadequate as explanations of the origin of trade fluctuations.

2. A second group consists of crisis theories which look for the causes not in the relations of the elements in the circular flow of business with each other but in the economic structure in which they are contained. These theories embody, as far as I can see, two main lines of possible argument:

a. Sudden or gradual transformations of the structural elements lead to disturbances in the circular flow of business. The number of such transformations is limited only by the number of structural elements existing or coming into existence. Some authors regard technique (progress in regard to which leads to the foundation of new or the extension of old undertakings, which operates, Liefmann thinks, through the agency of the individual's efforts to secure profits) as the most important of these elements. Others (such as Pohle) locate the origin of the trade cycle in increasing population.

---

[1] LÖWE, ADOLF: Wie ist Konjunkturtheorie überhaupt möglich? *Weltwirtschaftliches Archiv*, vol. 24, pp. 177 *ff.*

b. The origin might be located not in the time factor of structural transformations but in the space factor of structural contrasts as between various coexistent economic systems. So far as I know, this possibility is not represented in the existing literature. Rosa Luxemburg explains the possibility of accumulation and, therefore, of capitalism by reference to the "advance into non-capitalist spheres," such possibilities of expansion constituting a kind of safety valve against pressure which would otherwise become intolerable. As against this theory, however, it might be shown that it is the very fact of one particular economic organism's being linked up with economic bodies of a different character which leads to cyclical fluctuations.

3. Before we go more deeply into the hypothesis above, so as to make our scheme of possible crisis theories complete, we must mention the third main group of causation theories. The theories in this group look for the roots of economic fluctuations outside the economic subsoil itself. In this case, again, two main lines of possible argument exist:

a. A cosmic rhythm is regarded as responsible for the rhythm of economic fluctuation. Jevons attributes the responsibility to variations in sun-spot activity, which affect the harvests, and Moore to the 8-year cycle of the planet Venus.

b. We move still farther away from the object which we are trying to explain if we assume a psychological fluctuation in the entrepreneur, not in itself explicable (Pigou, Schumpeter, Spiethoff), or, possibly, in the consumer as well (Aftalion's theory is compatible with this latter assumption). Such theories, however, in my opinion lead us outside the bounds of science into the realm of metaphysics or offer us instead of an idea an empty word; for, if we may adapt a well-known saying of F. T. Vischer, in business the psychological element is self-evident.[1]

---

[1] Liefmann justly objects to the "psychological crisis theories" that all economic activity is psychological in character.

Bibliography

ADAMS, A. B.: "Economics of Business Cycles," 1925.

ANGELL, J. W.: "The Theory of International Prices," 1926.

CASSEL, G.: "Theoretische Sozialökonomie," 4th ed., Leipzig, 1927.

CLARK, J. M.: "The Economics of Overhead Costs," 1924.

DIETZEL, H.: Ernten, "Handbuch der Staatswissenschaft," 3d ed.

FISHER, I.: "The Rate of Interest," 1907.

HANSEN, A. H.: "Business Cycle Theories," New York, 1927; "Cycles of Prosperity and Depression," 1921.

HALM: Das Zinsproblem am Geld- und Kapitalmarkte, *Jahrbuch für Nationalökonomie und Statistik*, 1926.

HELLER, WOLFGANG: "Theoretische Volkswirtschaftslehre," vol. 1, 1927.

HEXTER, M. B.: "Social Consequences of Business Cycles," 1925.

HILFERDING, R.: "Finanzkapital," Wien, 1923.

HOBSON, J. A.: "Economics of Unemployment," 1922; "The Industrial System," 1909.

KUZNETS, SIMON S.: "Cyclical Fluctuations," 1926.

LAVINGTON: "The Trade Cycle," 1922.

LEDERER, E.: Konjunktur und Krisen, *Grundriss der Staatswissenschaft*, vol. 5.

LESCURE, J.: Krisenlehre, *Die Wirtschaftstheorie der Gegenwart*, vol. 4.

LEXIS: "Allgemeine Volkswirtschaftslehre."

CHAPTER XXV

GRAVITATION IN THE WORLD ECONOMIC ORDER

The Four Basic Structural Forms in the World Economic Order.

Sombart holds that a precapitalist, an early-capitalist, a mature-capitalist, and a late-capitalist era follow each other, in just this order. Following the same line of thought, we may classify the characteristic basic structures underlying the various economic systems of the world as follows:

1. The non-capitalist.
2. The neocapitalist.
3. The semicapitalist.
4. The mature capitalist.

Group 4 includes such countries as Great Britain and Germany; group 2, the South-American countries and Australia; and group 3, China and India. The United States and Japan have passed into the fourth group from the second and third, respectively. The first group includes peoples living in a state of nature—so far as economics are concerned—and whose relations with other economic units are practically non-existent. They are of interest in this connection only in so far as they represent portions of the earth's surface which have not yet been brought within the economic orbit, that is, only as potential economic factors (such as parts of Africa).

The four groups of countries may be divided from each other on purely formal lines according to the interrelationship of the productive factors. The characteristic feature of a fully-capitalist area consists in the fact that the quantity of capital and labor power per unit of territory is large; that of a neocapitalist area, in the fact that the quantity of each is small. In a semicapitalist area, there is little capital but a great deal of labor power per unit of territory; while in a non-capitalist area, capitalist possession of natural resources is non-existent. It is difficult to give a concrete classification of existing countries on these lines, because the line of demarcation is not hard and fast, and because, in many cases, the statistical

	Population per square kilometer	Consumption of machinery		Foreign-trade turnover per capita, marks	Imports	Exports
		Per capita, marks	Per sq. kilometer, marks		Of finished articles as percentage of total	
1. Mature-capitalism:						
a. Europe (excluding Russia and Turkey).....	85	20	1,706	376	28	61
b. United States	15	125	1,845	326	21	33
c. Japan.......	162	6	997	131		
2. Semicapitalism:						
a. Russia in Europe......	20	5	97	24	37	5
b. Asia (excluding Japan and Asiatic Russia)......	40	0.5	20	35	54	9
3. Neo-capitalism:						
a. Central and South America.....	4.4	6	27	222	67	2
b. Australia....	0.8	47	36	981	81	8
c. South Africa	6.1	1.3	81	387	76	
4. Non-capitalist countries: (Asiatic Russia, Belgian Congo, French West Africa, Sudan, Tripolitania)...	2.1					

These countries represent	Population, millions	Area, millions of square kilometers
Mature capitalism......................	544	23
Semicapitalism..........................	1,018	30
Neocapitalism...........................	106	30
Non-capitalism..........................	58	27
Total................................	1,726	110

As the total population of the world is reckoned at 1,844,000,000, and the total area of inhabited or inhabitable land at 136,000,000 square kilometers, the above survey accounts for practically the whole economic area of the earth.

material available for determining the amount of capital wealth is very inadequate.

The survey reproduced above shows, however, that the differences between the main economic groups are very clearly marked if we classify them (1) according to density of population and (2) according to capital wealth. For the purpose of estimating the latter, the following items have been taken into account: (a) money value of machinery consumption per head and per unit of territory and (b) foreign trade, which, in many respects, may be taken as indicating the intensity of economic life in a country and the amount of which is in this case shown (1) by turnover per capita of population and (2) by the proportion of imports and exports of finished articles to the total volume of imports and exports. These figures do not, of course, provide anything like a perfect representation of capital wealth; but the main results of the calculation, notwithstanding their defects, may be shown as constituting a first attempt, capable of being pushed much further.

Economic Systems and Their Cyclical Characteristics.

The differences between the bases on which the economy of the various respective areas is built up, as shown in the different relationships between the productive factors, largely determine the character (a) of the economic activity and (b) of the economic fluctuations in each case.[1]

[1] See WAGEMANN, "Die Wirtschaftsverfassung der Republik Chile," Munich and Leipzig, 1913; Konjunktur und Weltwirtschaft, *Weltwirtschaft*, No. 4, April, 1927.

Let us take just a few examples, based on a comparison between neocapitalist and mature-capitalist countries. In the former, the scarcity of population and capital makes production always assume an "extensive" form. The "new" countries, consequently, for the most part, export raw materials and import finished articles. Foreign trade is inversely constituted in mature-capitalist countries, where imports consist mainly of raw materials and exports of finished articles.

Furthermore, scarcity of capital in the new countries leads to high interest rates, while "extensive" production leads to high premiums for the covering of risks. These two factors together make the prices of industrial products of domestic manufacture relatively high, and the profits of the entrepreneur high but extremely variable. Consequently, an alteration in interest rates affects production and prices only to a very slight extent. Interest rates have, therefore, scarcely any regulating influence—a phenomenon also experienced in Germany during the inflation and after stabilization.

To take yet another example: The scarcity of capital in neo- and semicapitalist countries explains the marked predominance of a natural economy, the slight development of the division of labor throughout the economic system, and the economic paradox of the frequent coexistence of a fully developed urban market economy with foreign connections and a clumsy, undeveloped system of domestic exchange or barter. In such countries, therefore, agricultural prices frequently have little relationship with prices in general. This is brought very plainly to light in the fact that even an inflationary fluctuation in the exchange value of the currency has only a very slight effect on agricultural prices. It has been observed that the price of bricks in the Argentine remained stable at a time when the national currency unit, the peso, sank to a mere fraction of its former value. The same may be said of potato prices in Chile, which remained constant from the twenties to the nineties of the last century, notwithstanding a considerable fall in the value of the currency. Similar cases are reported from China.

Reactions in neo- and semicapitalist countries appear to be comparatively feeble, perhaps, in the last analysis, in consequence of very imperfect methods of business budgeting, which, in turn, are due to the "extensive" character of business in such countries, arising out of a scarcity of capital and, in some cases, of population.

Gravitational Forces in World Economy.

The structural differences between the various national economic systems are expressed not merely in a varying intensity of economic reactions, and, consequently, of economic fluctuations; they must probably also be counted as among the motive forces of business, among the causes of economic fluctuations. In any case, the following deductive argument suggests itself. The fundamental differences in relationship between the productive factors (land, capital, and labor) involve, as it were, a steep incline between the various structural groups in world economy. On the one hand, population tends to move away from the densely inhabited fully or semicapitalist areas to the neo- or non-capitalist countries, as is shown by international migration. On the other hand, there is a distinct tendency to export capital from the mature capitalist to the neo- or semi-capitalist communities—a tendency indicated by the considerable differences between rates of interest in the two groups.

These tendencies may be expected to produce very different effects in the different phases of the trade cycle. In periods of depression, that is, in periods when supplies of labor power and finance capital are lying fallow, mature-capitalist countries will tend to try to export population and capital. Where, at such a time business, in the neo- and semicapitalist countries is mainly prosperous—as may very well be the case, in view of their quite different economic structure—business fluctuations will thus, to some extent, be compensated. But even if depression prevails throughout the whole economic universe, finance capital and labor power could still, owing to the gravitational forces generated by the incline between the various structural groups, flow to the neo- and non-capitalist countries, where possibilities of expansion always exist. A revival might, thus, be set in motion in the latter countries which would make them more capable of absorbing industrial products and would give the mature-capitalist countries an initial impetus toward an escape from their depressed situation. If a state of full prosperity were reached, the upward movement would be brought to a standstill, if for no other reason, because the increasing demand for money and resources would level the incline in world economy.

It is far from my intention to put forward these reflections as in themselves constituting a theory, or even a theorem, of crises. For the present, I submit them only in a tentative way but with the feeling that they do seem to fill a gap in our tabulation of possible causation theories. They may, perhaps, represent a useful way of approaching the question, destined to set in motion a number of valuable inductive investigations. It should, of course, not be assumed for a moment that the gravitational forces in world economy exert themselves in the mechanical fashion outlined above; for the various economic systems always influence each other, so far as our experience shows, only in accordance with the organic-biological principle, economic movement being regulated by its own inherent laws.

Only when the economic structure of the world could develop into an organic unit, only, in other words, when business could be made uniform at all its stages, would these gravitational forces cease to exist. At present, they exist even to some extent within the various economic units, owing particularly to differences in the respective levels of development reached by agriculture and industry. Indeed, the great national economic systems are constantly undergoing a process of fresh upheaval which may in the end endanger their coherent organic character; for, on the one hand, trusts, cartels, and amalgamations, along with systems of price and wage regulation, and, on the other, the large-scale business activities of the public authorities must be regarded as representing if not new conceptions at any rate forms belonging to another stage of economic organization. It will be one of the great tasks of the next few generations to adjust the issue as between an unfettered régime of mature capitalism and systematic economic planning, which may, perhaps, itself drive out capitalism.

The mutual interpenetration of these two different and incompatible economic orders raises numerous problems for business-cycle theory. What, for instance, is the effect of price and wage regulation over large areas of the business world on the cyclical fluctuation of economic elements not yet brought within control? Are those fluctuations increased or diminished by the narrowing down of the sphere within which capitalism has free play? Is the enforced steadiness of prices in particular areas of the business world also transferred, as experts in economic policy seem to think, to other branches of business and to physical-volume movements as well? Or may we not say that the phenomena which make their appearance in this connection are similar rather to those noticeable during the inflation period, when the progressive habit of reckoning in terms of gold, by which the realm of the paper mark was continually further restricted, simply accentuated the fluctuations in the exchange value of the currency, seeing that the limits within which the frenzied creation of inflated currency could operate were constantly reduced? And, if we may pursue a line of reflection closely related to the foregoing, is it not possible that the increasing practice of price and wage regulation may bring other factors to the foreground which until now have played a comparatively secondary part? May not the rate of interest, which, as we have seen above, is only a minor factor in the business cycle, become much more powerful than the rigid scale of prices, and may not the influence of banking policy consequently increase to an extent at present impossible to foresee?

The new theory which deals with the movement, and particularly the rhythm, of business must grow and develop precisely through research work grappling with these and a thousand other problems now germinating in the soil of economics. It will do so, however, only if all the several methods of scientific approach to the subject are brought into closer and more intimate collaboration, and, above all, only if and to the extent that the empirical and inductive methods, at present treated in a manner so stepmotherly by economic "theory," come into their own. Only then will the economic sciences once again assume the position which they were able to obtain a century ago, in the great days of the classical economists. The latter owed their success to no lifeless doctrinaire spirit, such as their successors have succeeded in distilling from their dissection of the corpse of classical economy, but to the intimate sympathy for the great tasks of their time by which they were inspired. The economic sciences can themselves become instinct with life only by rendering active service to a living and growing economic order.

APPENDIX

SOME SIGNIFICANT STATISTICAL SERIES

TABLE I.—ECONOMIC SERIES (ANNUAL), 1850-1913

Year	Rediscount rate, Bank of Prussia (later Reichsbank), % per annum	Wholesale price index (industrial raw materials) (1913 = 100)	Miners' wages in Ruhr Valley,[1] marks per man per annum	Soft coal consumption,[2] kilos per capita	Pig-iron consumption,[2] kilos per capita	Total foreign trade,[2] marks per capita
1850	4.00	.....	313	168	.....	35.7
1851	4.00	68.5	380	174	10.50	36.3
1852	4.00	68.6	352	191	11.20	37.5
1853	4.25	84.4	343	208	12.60	44.1
1854	4.36	98.2	408	213	15.00	55.5
1855	4.08	91.4	459	150	17.50	57.3
1856	4.93	92.3	532	290	21.00	60.9
1857	5.76	93.1	525	277	24.50	63.9
1858	4.29	79.1	517	321	25.50	60.3
1859	4.20	78.6	449	291	20.50	56.7
1860	4.00	78.5	462	331	18.50	87.1
1861	4.00	77.3	428	375	19.41	65.4
1862	4.00	82.9	487	412	22.50	65.1
1863	4.08	90.5	515	446	25.35	62.6
1864	5.31	95.5	572	496	26.45	63.9
1865	4.96	84.6	659	553	30.60	66.5
1866	6.21	85.8	606	537	30.80	88.4
1867	4.00	80.5	639	582	31.53	96.7
1868	4.00	77.5	701	621	32.51	123.2
1869	4.24	78.2	772	637	37.36	125.4
1870	4.90	78.1	739	619	37.65	105.7
1871	4.16	79.7	763	718	46.53	134.3
1872	4.29	109.3	799	728	59.61	145.6
1873	4.95	123.8	1,044	818	66.87	162.6
1874	4.35	100.3	898	803	52.33	146.9
1875	4.71	86.7	896	825	53.80	145.5
1876	4.16	81.0	785	828	48.77	152.9
1877	4.42	75.8	654	801	48.13	155.4
1878	4.34	69.7	683	819	50.12	152.1
1879	3.70	70.4	543	860	48.94	152.2
1880	4.24	80.2	653	938	60.88	130.6
1881	4.42	73.9	677	962	64.94	135.3
1882	4.54	74.0	733	1,031	77.91	142.0
1883	4.05	71.5	736	1,087	77.35	144.5
1884	4.00	68.0	753	1,107	79.71	142.3
1885	4.12	65.6	744	1,121	79.47	127.5
1886	3.28	63.2	772	1,116	72.64	128.5
1887	3.41	64.1	796	1,153	83.71	135.6
1888	3.32	68.1	863	1,240	92.35	142.2
1889	3.68	76.4	941	1,289	96.53	150.1
1890	4.52	86.8	1,067	1,320	99.91	155.4
1891	3.78	76.7	1,086	1,385	94.96	155.0
1892	3.20	69.9	976	1,324	98.98	146.2
1893	4.07	68.2	946	1,351	98.89	144.8
1894	3.12	66.3	961	1,393	103.69	142.3
1895	3.14	64.9	968	1,416	104.39	146.9
1896	3.66	67.1	1,035	1,502	123.45	156.9
1897	3.81	69.1	1,128	1,576	133.33	160.9
1898	4.27	72.0	1,175	1,614	135.53	173.0
1899	5.04	81.8	1,255	1,693	153.87	183.0
1900	5.33	96.7	1,332	1,802	161.83	191.9
1901	4.10	81.9	1,224	1,744	137.02	179.0
1902	3.32	77.6	1,131	1,687	140.47	183.1
1903	3.84	78.4	1,205	1,803	164.22	194.6
1904	4.22	77.8	1,208	1,847	166.33	203.8
1905	3.82	79.0	1,186	1,861	173.84	219.3
1906	5.15	87.8	1,402	2,065	197.80	243.0
1907	6.03	97.0	1,562	2,196	208.90	257.9
1908	4.76	86.6	1,494	2,185	185.30	230.7
1909	3.93	83.0	1,350	2,152	191.60	245.8
1910	4.35	84.6	1,382	2,157	218.50	261.6
1911	4.40	85.1	1,446	2,199	226.90	277.9
1912	4.95	96.7	1,629	2,321	252.70	303.0
1913	5.89	100.0	1,755	2,470	276.60	318.4

[1] Dortmund Mining District.
[2] Within the German Customs Union.

265

TABLE II.—ECONOMIC SERIES, 1900 TO 1913 (MONTHLY)

Period	Movement of the three markets				Prices and production of coal and pig iron				
	Discount rate in Berlin, per cent per annum	Fixed-interest securities (six 4 per cent bonds)	Index of stock prices (1913 = 100)	Index of variable commodity prices (1913 = 100)	Price of Westphalian coal at colliery, marks per ton	Coal miner's wage (average per shift), marks*	Soft-coal production, thousands of tons per working day	Price of pig iron at smelter, marks per ton	Pig-iron production, thousands of tons per calendar day
1900 January	4.42	99.6	84.0	89.2	9.38				21.5
February	4.21	99.4	85.7	91.3	10.25	4.11			22.5
March	5.21	99.1	85.3	92.1	10.25				22.7
April	4.43	99.1	85.1	91.6	10.25				22.9
May	4.56	98.4	83.0	91.1	10.25	4.17			23.3
June	4.86	98.1	80.0	90.8	10.25				23.0
July	4.06	98.0	76.9	90.4	10.25				22.7
August	4.03	97.9	76.9	89.4	10.25	4.24			23.6
September	4.41	97.9	75.5	89.2	10.25				23.9
October	4.03	98.1	75.9	88.5	10.25				24.0
November	4.16	98.1	78.3	86.7	10.25	4.21			23.7
December	4.49	97.7	77.2	84.5	10.25				23.3
1901 January	3.57	98.3	76.6	81.6	10.25	4.13	367.0		22.4
February	3.22	98.7	77.5	80.5	10.25		353.8		22.3
March	3.79	98.5	78.7	78.5	10.25		354.1		21.7
April	3.37	98.7	77.4	77.7	10.25	4.09	351.9		21.7
May	3.19	99.0	76.3	77.9	10.25		356.0		21.8
June	3.20	98.7	74.0	77.7	10.25		336.4		21.1
July	2.81	98.6	70.5	75.5	10.25		349.3		21.0
August	2.26	98.9	70.9	75.2	10.25	4.07	345.2	66.00	20.8
September	2.68	98.1	69.5	74.1	10.25		349.6	66.00	20.8
October	2.83	98.0	68.7	73.5	10.25		351.6	61.00	20.8
November	2.84	98.7	70.1	73.1	10.25	3.98	358.3	61.00	20.9
December	2.96	99.1	71.6	71.7	10.25		358.8	60.50	20.7
1902 January	2.11	100.1	73.3	70.4	10.25		334.9	59.00	21.2
February	1.85	100.7	75.6	72.7	10.25	3.88	340.9	59.00	21.3
March	1.79	100.6	74.4	73.0	10.25		340.9	61.00	22.0
April	1.65	100.5	73.1	73.4	9.38		336.6	61.00	22.4
May	1.98	100.5	73.6	74.8	9.38	3.78	342.0	61.00	22.9
June	2.17	100.8	74.3	74.8	9.38		344.5	61.00	23.2
July	1.59	100.5	72.8	74.8	9.38		342.1	61.00	22.3
August	1.73	100.8	72.6	74.0	9.38	3.81	349.7	61.00	23.8
September	2.14	100.8	73.0	73.8	9.38		354.4	61.00	24.0
October	2.73	100.9	72.3	73.7	9.38		372.6	61.00	24.0
November	3.11	100.7	72.1	72.8	9.38	3.81	382.2	61.00	24.4
December	3.38	100.6	72.7	73.2	9.38		374.4	61.00	24.3
1903 January	2.26	101.3	74.1	74.2	9.38		379.4	61.00	25.6
February	1.90	101.5	75.7	75.9	9.38	3.81	372.8	62.00	26.6
March	2.69	101.7	76.5	79.3	9.38		365:0	62.50	27.6
April	2.61	102.0	76.1	78.7	9.38		370.6	64.00	27.8
May	3.09	101.7	75.4	77.4	9.38	3.84	377.8	64.00	28.1
June	3.29	101.5	74.3	76.3	9.38		353.2	64.00	28.0
July	2.96	101.4	74.7	76.1	9.38		384.4	64.50	27.9
August	3.30	101.1	75.6	76.0	9.38	3.91	387.3	65.00	28.3
September	3.68	101.0	76.1	75.5	9.38		390.2	65.50	28.3
October	3.32	101.3	78.6	75.7	9.38		396.9	64.50	28.0
November	3.46	101.4	80.8	75.0	9.38	3.94	414.0	65.00	28.1
December	3.54	101.3	82.4	75.9	9.38		397.4	65.50	27.4
1904 January	2.58	101.6	81.8	76.7	9.38	3.96	398.8	64.00	26.8
February	2.77	100.7	79.1	77.0	9.38		388.7	64.00	26.9
March	3.44	101.1	81.2	77.7	9.38		394.1	64.00	27.4
April	2.83	101.3	82.3	78.4	9.38	3.96	391.4	64.00	27.8
May	3.10	100.9	82.7	78.0	9.38		395.6	64.00	28.0
June	2.98	101.2	82.9	77.3	9.38		369.6	64.00	27.9

* Quarterly average of actual shifts of entire pay roll in Dortmund coal-mine district.

TABLE II.—ECONOMIC SERIES, 1900 TO 1913 (MONTHLY).—(*Continued*)

Period	Discount rate in Berlin, per cent per annum	Fixed-interest securities (six 4 per cent bonds)	Index of stock prices (1913 = 100)	Index of variable commodity prices (1913 = 100)	Price of Westphalian coal at colliery, marks per ton	Coal miner's wage (average per shift), marks*	Soft-coal production, thousands of tons per working day	Price of pig iron at smelter, marks per ton	Pig-iron production, thousands of tons per calendar day
1904 July	2.60	101.3	83.2	78.0	9.38	3.99	383.9	64.00	27.3
August	2.62	101.3	85.7	78.4	9.38		384.1	64.00	27.5
September	3.09	101.4	86.8	78.7	9.38		374.3	64.00	27.8
October	3.69	101.1	88.4	79.4	9.38	4.00	398.7	64.00	28.0
November	3.99	101.0	89.8	81.1	9.38		414.2	64.00	27.8
December	3.94	101.6	90.5	81.7	9.38		406.2	64.00	28.1
1905 January	2.56	101.7	90.4	82.0	9.38	3.94	292.0	64.00	24.7
February	1.93	101.7	92.6	81.4	9.38		324.8	64.00	24.0
March	2.22	101.9	93.4	81.6	9.38		445.6	64.00	28.9
April	1.91	101.8	93.9	82.0	9.53	4.01	415.8	64.00	29.8
May	2.30	101.8	92.9	82.6	9.53		418.8	64.00	30.7
June	2.34	101.7	92.7	83.6	9.53		389.3	64.00	30.6
July	2.12	101.6	94.0	84.4	9.53	4.06	412.6	64.00	30.4
August	2.23	101.6	94.8	85.6	9.53		408.3	64.00	31.2
September	2.99	101.5	95.8	86.4	9.53		414.4	64.00	31.8
October	4.00	101.2	95.6	88.5	9.53	4.07	415.2	67.00	32.5
November	4.62	101.2	93.6	90.8	9.53		428.9	67.00	32.9
December	4.99	101.2	92.4	93.4	9.53		434.8	67.50	33.2
1906 January	3.81	101.3	92.9	93.6	9.53	4.17	457.0	70.00	32.9
February	3.35	101.4	93.5	92.0	10.25		455.0	70.00	33.4
March	4.02	101.3	93.5	93.0	10.25		460.7	70.00	33.9
April	3.44	101.3	94.0	94.6	10.25	4.26	439.4	70.00	33.7
May	3.39	101.1	94.0	96.3	10.25		445.1	70.00	33.8
June	3.68	101.3	93.0	96.9	10.25		413.6	70.00	33.6
July	3.49	100.9	91.2	96.9	10.25	4.43	443.0	70.00	33.6
August	3.43	100.7	92.8	98.1	10.25		450.1	70.00	34.4
September	4.23	100.5	92.6	101.0	10.25		447.3	76.00	34.6
October	4.83	100.3	92.4	103.8	10.25	4.59	451.8	76.00	34.6
November	5.27	100.4	92.8	104.8	10.75		456.8	76.00	35.4
December	5.58	100.7	94.2	105.8	10.75		449.8	78.00	34.5
1907 January	4.90	100.2	93.1	106.4	10.75	4.70	473.0	78.00	34.3
February	4.68	100.1	91.6	106.9	10.75		463.4	81.00	34.9
March	5.40	99.7	88.2	106.5	10.88		477.7	81.00	35.5
April	4.65	99.7	87.0	106.9	11.25	4.81	458.4	81.00	35.9
May	4.44	99.3	86.2	108.2	11.25		445.1	81.00	35.3
June	4.66	98.8	84.1	107.1	11.25		458.3	81.00	34.8
July	4.44	98.2	84.3	106.2	11.25	4.94	473.6	81.00	36.3
August	4.62	97.9	82.6	101.6	11.25		468.7	78.00	36.1
September	5.08	98.0	85.3	100.3	11.25		463.4	78.00	36.4
October	4.91	97.7	85.3	96.9	11.25	4.99	470.4	78.00	36.7
November	6.61	97.3	83.2	93.8	11.25		483.8	78.00	37.1
December	7.07	97.7	83.4	89.5	11.25		491.9	78.00	35.7
1908 January	4.98	97.5	83.9	89.2	11.25	4.87	483.8	71.00	34.2
February	4.48	97.1	84.2	88.3	11.25		505.7	71.00	34.3
March	4.49	97.3	83.6	87.7	11.25		479.8	71.00	33.8
April	4.11	97.3	85.2	85.7	11.25	4.82	483.2	71.00	32.7
May	3.91	97.4	85.1	84.2	11.25		488.9	71.00	32.6
June	3.33	97.2	83.5	83.5	11.25		447.2	71.00	31.9
July	2.76	97.1	83.6	83.1	11.25	4.82	489.3	69.00	32.6
August	2.82	97.3	85.9	82.6	11.25		488.6	69.00	30.2
September	3.14	96.9	87.4	82.5	11.25		491.6	69.00	31.0
October	2.79	97.0	85.8	82.4	11.25	4.76	487.7	69.00	30.4
November	2.54	97.9	86.1	82.9	11.25		507.1	69.00	31.0
December	2.92	98.6	86.3	82.3	11.25		475.3	69.00	32.8

* Quarterly average of actual shifts of entire pay roll in Dortmund coal-mine district.

TABLE II.—ECONOMIC SERIES, 1900 TO 1913 (MONTHLY).—(Continued)

Period	Movement of the three markets				Prices and production of coal and pig iron				
	Discount rate in Berlin, per cent per annum	Fixed-interest securities (six 4 per cent bonds)	Index of stock prices (1913 = 100)	Index of variable commodity prices (1913 = 100)	Price of Westphalian coal at colliery, marks per ton	Coal miner's wage (average per shift), marks*	Soft-coal production, thousands of tons per working day	Price of pig iron at smelter, marks per ton	Pig-iron production, thousands of tons per calendar day
1909 January	2.24	99.6	86.6	81.8	11.25	4.56	480.4	60.00	33.0
February	2.17	99.9	86.9	81.7	11.25		481.3	58.50	33.9
March	2.66	99.5	85.4	81.9	11.25		478.4	58.00	34.6
April	1.98	99.6	87.6	82.3	11.25		487.7	58.00	34.9
May	2.32	99.6	88.6	84.0	10.75	4.45	489.6	57.50	35.2
June	2.91	99.5	88.3	84.3	10.75		460.5	57.50	35.6
July	2.28	99.6	89.2	84.2	10.75		491.7	56.00	35.2
August	2.13	99.5	92.0	83.9	10.75	4.48	489.0	54.50	35.5
September	3.06	99.5	93.9	85.0	10.75		490.0	55.50	35.6
October	3.83	99.0	94.4	85.7	10.75		499.0	58.50	36.3
November	4.47	99.2	95.3	85.1	10.75	4.48	507.6	59.00	37.3
December	4.34	99.3	97.4	85.8	10.75		501.1	60.00	37.6
1910 January	3.09	99.5	98.6	86.5	10.75		497.0	61.00	38.0
February	2.94	99.3	99.2	86.3	10.75	4.48	488.1	63.00	39.0
March	3.52	99.3	99.7	85.8	10.75		489.2	63.50	40.3
April	3.14	99.2	98.6	84.7	10.75		485.6	63.50	40.1
May	3.19	99.5	99.8	84.4	10.75	4.51	491.1	64.00	40.7
June	3.23	99.2	99.5	83.4	10.75		482.6	64.00	40.6
July	3.03	99.2	99.3	83.6	10.75		501.2	64.00	39.6
August	3.33	99.1	101.3	84.5	10.75	4.57	494.8	63.50	40.6
September	3.85	99.2	103.2	84.9	10.75		500.8	63.50	41.1
October	4.15	99.4	102.8	84.6	10.75		511.1	64.00	41.7
November	4.50	99.1	102.2	85.4	10.75	4.61	530.0	64.00	42.4
December	4.53	99.3	102.5	85.5	10.75		522.9	64.00	42.2
1911 January	3.50	99.3	102.2	85.9	10.75		520.3	64.00	42.6
February	3.07	99.4	103.6	86.1	10.75	4.64	486.1	64.00	42.1
March	3.34	99.1	103.7	85.9	10.75		518.9	64.00	42.7
April	2.96	99.2	102.9	85.8	10.75		532.9	64.00	42.8
May	2.84	99.1	101.7	87.0	10.75	4.66	533.6	64.00	42.3
June	3.38	98.7	101.8	87.0	10.75		493.3	64.00	42.1
July	2.46	99.1	102.4	87.8	10.75		523.5	64.00	41.6
August	3.03	98.6	101.5	89.1	10.75	4.72	514.7	64.00	41.4
September	4.16	98.2	98.1	89.8	10.75		523.6	64.00	41.7
October	4.32	98.5	97.3	90.8	10.75		526.1	66.75	43.1
November	4.51	98.4	99.8	91.3	10.75	4.75	553.6	66.75	43.8
December	4.86	98.8	102.4	92.3	10.75		559.7	67.50	44.4
1912 January	3.33	98.6	103.2	92.8	10.75		560.2	67.50	44.7
February	3.79	98.1	102.0	93.8	10.75	4.83	585.8	70.00	46.1
March	4.72	97.9	100.4	94.6	10.75		492.8	70.00	46.7
April	3.75	98.1	103.1	96.3	11.63		585.9	70.00	48.4
May	3.91	97.3	104.3	98.3	11.63	5.00	589.4	70.00	48.1
June	4.14	97.8	102.7	100.3	11.63		555.6	70.00	48.4
July	3.36	97.1	104.5	101.0	11.63		584.4	70.00	48.6
August	3.93	96.9	106.7	101.5	11.63	5.09	589.3	70.00	49.3
September	4.38	96.8	108.4	105.1	11.63		596.3	70.00	50.6
October	4.19	96.3	103.2	105.9	11.63		596.4	74.00	52.7
November	5.23	96.0	102.5	104.5	11.63	5.17	592.2	74.50	51.2
December	5.94	96.7	101.1	105.0	11.63		619.4	74.50	50.5
1913 January	4.68	96.6	103.9	104.0	11.63		636.0	74.50	52.0
February	5.15	96.2	102.7	102.4	11.63	5.28	650.4	74.50	53.4
March	5.90	96.2	101.9	101.1	11.63		642.2	74.50	52.6
April	4.56	95.8	100.0	102.4	12.38		608.5	74.50	53.0
May	5.31	95.6	99.5	103.6	12.38	5.37	570.7	74.50	53.0
June	5.53	94.5	97.3	100.4	12.38		637.2	74.50	53.7
July	4.65	94.4	99.3	98.1	12.38		637.0	74.50	53.2
August	4.88	94.3	99.9	98.8	12.37	5.42	636.3	74.50	52.9
September	5.35	95.0	100.2	99.4	12.37		629.1	74.50	53.0
October	4.71	94.4	97.9	98.3	12.37		627.5	74.50	53.3
November	4.45	94.5	98.3	96.6	12.37	5.38	638.7	74.50	53.0
December	4.57	95.0	99.0	95.2	12.37		624.0	74.50	52.0

* Quarterly average of actual shifts of entire pay roll in Dortmund coal-mine district.

TABLE III.—NUMBER OF MEN AND WOMEN GAINFULLY EMPLOYED IN THE GERMAN REICH (PRESENT AREA)

(Thousands)

Year		Men	Women	Total	Yearly increase or decline over preceding year		
					Men	Women	Total
DEVELOPMENT HERETOFORE							
Middle	1882	11,931	4,954	16,885			
	1895	13,855	5,901	19,756	+148	+ 73	+221
	1907	16,655	8,501	25,156	+233	+217	+450
	1913	18,300	9,370	27,670	+274	+145	+419
	1924	20,218	11,362	31,580	+267	+ 75	+342
	1925	20,463	11,419	31,882	+245	+ 57	+302
Beginning	1926	20,745	11,558	32,303	+282	+139	+421
	1927	21,018	11,686	32,704	+273	+128	+401
	1928	21,311	11,825	33,136	+293	+139	+432
PREDICTABLE DEVELOPMENT							
Beginning	1929	21,574	11,938	33,512	+263	+113	+376
	1930	21,836	12,045	33,881	+262	+107	+369
	1931	21,907	12,081	33,988	+ 71	+ 36	+107
	1932	21,856	12,050	33,906	− 51	− 31	− 82
	1933	21,786	11,999	33,785	− 70	− 51	−121
	1934	21,715	11,953	33,668	− 71	− 46	−117
	1935	21,806	11,963	33,769	+ 91	+ 10	+101
	1936	22,028	12,071	34,099	+222	+108	+330
	1937	22,301	12,184	34,485	+273	+113	+386
	1938	22,462	12,240	34,702	+161	+ 56	+217
	1939	22,594	12,281	34,875	+132	+ 41	+173
	1940	22,685	12,312	34,997	+ 91	+ 31	+122

TABLE IV.—CLASSIFICATION OF INDUSTRY ON THE BASIS OF THE INDUSTRIAL EMPLOYMENT CENSUS OF 1925

A. INDUSTRIES PRODUCING MEANS OF PRODUCTION

Classes of goods	Thousands of persons		Production, thousands per hour	
I. Sources of power:				
1. Coal		679		3,498
a. Bituminous[1]	574		2,748	
b. Lignite[1]	105		750	
2. Peat, petroleum		16		24
3. Electricity		85		222[2]
4. Gas		47		80
Total sources of power		827		3,824
II. Basic materials:				
1. Iron and non-ferrous metals[1]		514		3,059
a. Earths	46		179	
b. Iron, steel, and alloys[3]	388		2,599	
c. Non-ferrous metals and alloys	80		281	
2. Chemicals[5]		267		998[4]
3. Paper and manufactures of paper		554		978
a. Pulp and paper	115		735	
b. Paper manufactures	156		84	
c. Printed matter[6]	283		159	
4. Leather[7]		67		131
5. Wood and manufactures of wood[8]		137		371
6. Building materials		397		736
a. Gravel, sand, stone	126		127	
b. Lime, gypsum, cement[9]	54		242	
c. Brick and tile[10]	169		296	
d. Concrete and artificial stone[11]	48		71	
Total for basic materials		1,936		6,273
III. Construction:				
1. Building trades		1,679		459
a. Excavation, foundation, and concrete	1,058		418	
b. Building construction	421		26	
c. Tinware, gas, and water installation	106		5	
d. Electrotechnical installations	99		10	
2. Machines, vehicles, and apparatus		1,366		2,244
a. Machines and apparatus[12]	1,045		1,934	
b. Structural steel	31		47	
c. Shipbuilding	28		59	
d. Vehicles and aircraft	225		143	
e. Railroad rolling stock	37		61	
3. Electrotechnical products[13]		341		386
4. Tools and hardware		341		232
a. Forged materials	125		48	
b. Locks and hardware	90		35	
c. Tools	126		149	
5. Wheelwright's materials		104		109
6. Packing industries		49		62
7. Finishing industries[14]		34		49
Total for construction		3,914		3,541
Total for industries producing means of production		6,677		13,638

[1] Including combined factories.
[2] Net amount employed in driving machinery. No account taken of power employed in generation (about 5,500,000,000 hp.).
[3] Including the half of the factories combined with iron and metallurgical production. The other half is calculated in group A III (construction).
[4] Net amount employed in primary machine driving. The amount employed in generation for the electrochemical and electrometallurgical industries, about 250,000,000 hp., is not included.
[5] Without the industries dealing with pharmaceuticals, photochemicals, technological chemicals, essential oils, cosmetics, soap; wax, incandescent mantles; also, wthout chemical works connected with salt mines.
[6] Including the combined output of press and publishing industries.
[7] Tanning and technical leather articles; the production of harness and other leather goods is calculated in group B III.
[8] Sawmills, etc., amber industries (1,000 persons); woodworking is included in group B III.
[9] Including asphalt and chalk industries.
[10] Including total for building-materials industries.
[11] Including total of ceramic industries.
[12] Including the half of the factories combined with iron and steel industries.
[13] Not including electricotechnical installations.
[14] One half of the rubber industries; the other half is taken care of under B III.

TABLE IV.—CLASSIFICATION OF INDUSTRY ON THE BASIS OF THE INDUSTRIAL EMPLOYMENT CENSUS OF 1925.—(*Continued*)

B. INDUSTRIES PRODUCING CONSUMPTION GOODS

Classes of goods	Thousand of persons		Production, thousands per hour	
I. Necessities and luxuries:				
1. Milling and banking..........................		466		760
a. Flour...................................	91		613	
b. Baking..................................	375		147	
2. Sugar.......................................	34			100
3. Confectionary..............................	73			89
4. Meat and fish..............................		286		221
5. Butter, margarine, and cheese..............		58		109
6. Oil, vinegar, mustard......................		22		72
7. Preserves, pastry, soups...................		48		70
8. Water.....................................		10		141
9. Beverages.................................		144		262
a. Coffee.................................	9		13	
b. Beer...................................	91		215	
c. Wine and brandy.......................	31		29	
d. Mineral water, etc....................	13		5	
10. Tobacco...................................		215		24
Total of food, drink, and tobacco........		1,356		1,848
II. Clothing, etc.:				
1. Yarns and textile goods....................		743		1,094
a. Silk and rayon.........................	87		74	
b. Wool..................................	222		298	
c. Cotton...............................	318		587	
d. Linen, flax, jute.....................	116		135	
2. Clothing...................................		807		19
3. Hosiery and underclothing[15].............		207		69
4. Lace, ribbons, and twine...................		56		18
5. Furs, hats, caps, neckwear.................		157		29
6. Gloves....................................		45		4
7. Shoes.....................................		388		57
8. Cleansing.................................		187		32
a. Barbering trades.......................	117		1	
b. Laundry and cleaning trades............	70		31	
Total for clothing, etc...................		2,590		1,322
III. Household goods, social interests, and luxuries:				
1. Furniture..................................		440		367
2. Furnishings, curtains, oilcloth.............		157		95
3. Lamps, ornaments, enamelware..............		405		300
4. Porcelain, glass...........................		255		164
5. Wooden kitchenware.......................		216		116
6. Leather goods, linoleum....................		98		25
7. Hard- and soft-rubber goods		34		48
8. Watches, optical goods, binoculars.........		153		56
9. Musical and theatrical instruments.........		119		44
10. Candles, perfumery, pharmaceutical goods...		82		68
11. Photography..............................		16		
Total for household goods, social interests, and luxuries..........................		1,975		1,283
Total for industries producing consumption goods.......		5,921		4,453

[15] Not including glove-materials industries.

TABLE V.—THE ECONOMIC AREAS OF THE EARTH ACCORDING TO THE DISTINGUISHING CHARACTERISTICS OF THEIR ECONOMIC STRUCTURE

(A tentative classification)

Country	Population in 1925, millions	Area in 1925, thousands of sq. km.	Density of population 1925, sq. km.	Consumption of machinery			Imports 1925	Exports 1925	Excess of imports (−) or of exports (+) expressed as percentage of imports	Total foreign trade turnover per capita, marks	Proportion of finished goods	
				Total, millions of marks	Per capita, marks	Per sq. km., marks	Millions of marks				Percentage of imports	Percentage of exports
1	2	3	4	5	6	7	8	9	10	11	12	13

I. MATURE CAPITALISTIC STAGE

(Mature density; relatively extensive employment of machinery; per capita foreign trade substantial)

Country	2	3	4	5	6	7	8	9	10	11	12	13
Great Britain and northern Ireland	44.0	241.4	182	2,351	53.4	9,739	23,660	15,684	− 34	894	37.6	76.2
Switzerland	4.0	41.3	97	212	53.0	5,133	2,020	1,647	− 18	917	36.9	76.1
Germany	63.2	470.6	134	2,264	35.8	4,811	12,362	8,799	− 29	335	14.4	71.3
Belgian Luxemburg	8.0	33.0	242	199	24.9	6,030	3,558	2,896	− 19	807	22.0	55.9
Netherlands	7.4	34.2	216	168	22.7	4,912	4,143	3,050	− 26	972	36.3	35.5
Sweden	6.1	410.5	(15)	122	20.0	(297)	1,631	1,533	− 6	519	39.8	39.5
Denmark	3.4	43.0	79	59	17.4	1,372	1,720	1,588	− 8	973	...	10.1
Austria	6.6	83.8	79	102	15.5	1,217	1,668	1,119	− 33	422	33.1	75.6
France	40.6	551.0	74	570	14.0	1,034	8,841	9,174	+ 4	444	14.2	69.3
Norway	2.8	309.9	(9)	39	13.9	(126)	1,021	773	− 24	641	37.4	20.6
Czechoslovakia	14.0	140.4	100	191	13.6	1,360	2,195	2,345	+ 7	324	23.0	62.1

Italy	39.7	310.0	128	387	9.7	1,248	4,376	3,036	−30	187	15.5	39.9
Finland	3.5	343.6	(10)	32	9.1	(93)	582	587	+ 1	334		
Hungary	8.0	92.9	86	72	9.0	775	630	596	− 5	153	49.2	34.1
Latvia	1.8	65.8	27	15.5	8.6	236	226	145	−36	206	47.3	14.1
Irish Free State	3.0	68.9	44	24	8.0	348	1,247	879	−30	709		
Esthonia	1.1	47.6	23	6	5.5	126	108	108	± 0	196	31.6	40.8
Spain	22.0	505.2	44	90	4.1	178	1,818	1,284	−29	141	44.8	25.8
Poland	28.8	388.3	74	115	4.0	296	1,232	1,033	−16	79	44.0	22.3
Portugal	6.1	91.9	66	15	2.5	163	511	178	−65	113	8.9	5.1
Lithuania[1]	2.2	55.9	39	5	2.3	89	104	100	− 4	93	53.8	7.0
Bulgaria	5.4	103.1	52	12	2.2	116	222	172	−23	73	72.3	2.8
Greece	5.6	147.6	38	13	2.3	88	674	300	−55	174		
Jugoslavia	12.2	249.0	49	26	2.1	104	627	638	+ 2	104		
Rumania	17.2	294.2	58	28	1.6	95	611	589	− 4	70		
Europe (not including Russia, Turkey, and other small states)	356.7	5,123	85[2]	7,118	20.0	1,706[3]	75,787	58,273	−23	376	28	61
United States	115.4	7,839	15	14,465	125.3	1,845	17,369	20,239	+17	326	20.9	32.9
Canada	9.4	9,660	(1)	876	93.2	(91)	3,595	5,524	+42	1,002	61.5	40.2
Japan	62.0	382	162	381	6.1	997	4,282	3,822	−11	131		
Mature capitalistic states	543.5	23,004	42[3]	22,840	42.0	1,773[3]	101,333	87,858	−13	348	28	53

[1] Including Memel.

[2] Without Sweden, Norway, Finland.

[3] Without Sweden, Norway, Finland, Canada.

NOTE.—The data for columns 2 to 4 correspond mainly to the end of 1925 and are taken from the "Statistical Yearbook" of Germany; but wherever other data of official origin were ascertainable, use was made of them—as regards recent censuses, in particular. Average values in column 5 according to the publication of the Verein of Deutscher Maschinenbauanstalten entitled "Die Maschinenindustrie der Welt," p. 189. In columns 8 to 11, so far as possible, only special trade is considered.

TABLE V.—THE ECONOMIC AREAS OF THE EARTH ACCORDING TO THE DISTINGUISHING CHARACTERISTICS OF THEIR ECONOMIC STRUCTURE.—(Continued)

(A tentative classification)

Country	Population in 1925, millions	Area in 1925, thousands of sq. km.	Density of population 1925, sq. km.	Consumption of machinery			Imports, 1925	Exports, 1925	Excess of imports (−) or of exports (+) expressed as percentage of imports	Total foreign trade turnover per capita, marks	Proportion of finished goods	
				Total, millions of marks	Per capita, marks	Per sq. km., marks	Millions of marks				Percentage of imports	Percentage of exports
1	2	3	4	5	6	7	8	9	10	11	12	13
II. PARTLY CAPITALISTIC STAGE (Dense population; slight use of machines; insignificant per capita foreign trade)												
European Russia..........	115.5	5,803	20	561	4.9	97	1,596	1,216	− 24	24	36.6	4.6
Ceylon...................	4.5	66	68	...	...	...	551	798	+ 45	300		
British India............	321.5	4,675	69	225	0.7	48	3,318	5,767	+ 74	28	45.6	17.0
China...................	433.0	11,081	39	88	0.2	8	3,342	2,737	− 18	14		
Philippine Islands........	11.9	296	40	...	...	...	501	622	+ 24	94		
Indo-China..............	19.8	711	28	...	...	...	530	608	+ 15	57		
Dutch East Indies........	51.0	1,900	27	58	1.1	31	1,379	3,012	+ 118	86	68.8	1.6
Siam....................	9.8	518	19	6	0.6	12	303	369	+ 22	69	71.5	
British Malay states......	2.5	142	18	...	...	...	2,317	3,048	+ 32			

Asiatic Turkey	11.3	864	13	11	1.0	13	555	442	− 20	88	55.8	14.1
Persia	9.0	1,627	(6)	.....	...	..	(18.5)	(3.5)	(− 81)	2.4		
Asia (not including Russia or												
Japan	874.3	21,880	40	388	0.5	20	12,815	17,407	+ 36	35	54	9
Egypt	14.1	900	16	41	2.9	46	1,186	1,233	+ 4	172	59.1	
Morocco	5.5	415	13	7	1.3	17	239	113	− 53	64		
Algiers	6.1	575	11	17	2.8	30	657	482	− 27	187	67.5	7.3
Tunis	2.1	125	17	4	1.9	32	218	170	− 22	185		
Partly capitalistic states	1,017.6	29,698	34	1,018	1.0	38	16,711	20,621	+ 23	37	52	8

TABLE V.—THE ECONOMIC AREAS OF THE EARTH ACCORDING TO THE DISTINGUISHING CHARACTERISTICS OF THEIR ECONOMIC STRUCTURE.—(Continued)

(A tentative classification)

Country	Population in 1925, millions	Area in 1925, thousands of sq. km.	Density of population 1925, sq. km.	Consumption of machinery			Imports, 1925	Exports, 1925	Excess of imports (−) or of exports (+) expressed as percentage of imports	Total foreign trade turn-over per capita, marks	Proportion of finished goods	
				Total, millions of marks	Per capita, marks	Per sq. km., marks	Millions of marks				Percentage of imports	Percentage of exports
1	2	3	4	5	6	7	8	9	10	11	12	13
III. INCIPIENT CAPITALISM												
(Slight density; slight use of machines; considerable per capita foreign trade)												
Argentina............	10.1	2,987	3.4	143	14.2	48	3,367	3,333	− 1	663	69.7	4.3
Chile................	3.9	752	5.2	43	11.0	57	620	948	+53	402	66.3	0.3
Peru................	5.6	1,434	3.9	35	6.3	24	313	372	+19	122	84.0	1.0
Mexico..............	14.2	1,969	7.2	88	6.2	45	860	1,502	+75	166	78.0	....
Uruguay.............	1.7	187	9.1	9	5.3	48	299	408	+36	416	55.6	....
Brazil...............	36.9	8,511	4.3	104	2.8	12	1,730	2,060	+19	103	....	....
Colombia............	6.9	1,283	5.4	18	2.6	14	354	348	− 2	102	66.8	0.4
Bolivia..............	3.0	1,590	1.9	6	2.0	4	98	172	+76	90	....	6.6
Ecuador.............	2.0	307	6.5	....	....	....	52	61	+17	57	....	....
Venezuela...........	3.0	1,020	2.9	....	....	....	246	262	+ 7	169	....	....

Paraguay..................	0.9	445	2.0	....	....	....	41	41	±0	91		
Cuba......................	3.0	115	(26.1)	63	(21.0)	(548)	1,249	1,487	+19	(912)		
Central and South American states	91.2	20,600	4.4	509	6.0	27	9,229	10,994	+19	222	67	2
Australia.................	6.0	7,704	0.8	279	46.5	36	2,811	3,074	+9	981	80.9	7.9
New Zealand..............	1.4	268	5.2	47	33.6	175	1,063	1,110	+4	1,552	70.6	1.3
Union of South Africa.....	7.5	1,226	6.1	99	13.2	81	1,281	1,621	+27	387	76.3	
Incipient capitalistic states......	106.1	29,798	3.6	934	9.3	33	14,384	16,799	+17	294	73	4

IV. NON-CAPITALISTIC STATES

(Slight density; little or no use of machines; no significant foreign trade)

Asiatic Russia.............	30.7	16,035	1.9				175	126	-28	42	75.0	8.9
Belgian Congo.............	7.2	2,356	3.1				223	180	-19	30		
French West Africa........	13.5	4,852	2.8									
Sudan....................	5.9	2,628	2.2									
Tripoli...................	0.8	1,500	0.5									
Non-capitalistic states......	58.1	27,371	2.1				(398)	(306)	-23	34	(75)	(9)

TABLE VI.—PRINCIPAL ECONOMIC SERIES, 1924 TO 1929 (MONTHLY)

Year and month	Index figure for industrial production (July, 1924, to June, 1926 = 100)	Production: Fully employed[1] to every 100 members of labor unions — All branches of industry[2]	Production: Producers'-goods industries[3]	Production: Consumers'-goods industries[4]	Foreign trade[5] Imports	Foreign trade[5] Exports[6]	Foreign trade[5] Excess	General turnover calculated from yield of turnover tax quarterly, billions of marks	Turnover: Business credits of banks of issue (Situation at end of month)	Turnover: Currency circulation	Turnover: Total bills	Turnover: Total long-term credits[7]
					Net value of commodities, millions of marks				Million of marks			
1924 Jan	65.9				562.2	431.0	131.2		1,163	2,278	1,925	
Feb	77.4				725.8	465.9	259.9	15.12	1,557	2,634	1,719	
Mar	89.3				688.6	457.0	231.6		2,007	2,824	2,440	
April	97.5				800.6	482.7	317.9	16.89	2,177	2,825	2,335	
May	77.0				886.9	515.7	371.2		2,125	2,918	2,510	
June	83.9				734.3	476.2	258.1		2,187	3,129	2,335	
July	84.1				534.5	573.1	+38.6	19.26	2,031	3,300	2,487	
Aug	82.6				437.2	588.8	+151.6		2,217	3,535	2,534	
Sept	91.6				618.5	563.1	55.4		2,488	3,708	2,767	
Oct	96.2				847.4	611.4	235.9	24.72	2,736	3,826	3,076	
Nov	103.3				1,034.2	642.4	391.8		2,884	3,956	3,034	
Dec	105.4				1,214.4	740.7	473.7		3,044	4,274	3,296	
1925 Jan	108.9	92.5	93.0	91.4	1,265.6	696.0	569.6		2,923	4,209	3,359	376.5
Feb	112.7	93.0	93.4	92.2	1,061.5	630.2	431.3	25.11	3,043	4,391	3,321	333.1
Mar	113.7	94.0	93.4	93.1	1,017.9	708.4	309.5		3,014	4,479	3,770	274.5
April	109.7	94.5	94.7	94.0	996.5	670.8	325.7		3,116	4,503	3,467	201.3
May	106.7	95.7	95.5	94.6	983.5	728.8	254.6	25.29	3,185	4,772	3,746	195.7
June	104.7	95.6	96.2	94.3	995.1	686.6	308.5		3,260	4,775	3,887	199.9
July	103.5	95.5	95.5	94.3	1,138.1	743.8	394.4		3,301	4,891	4,046	211.4
Aug	101.2	93.8	93.9	93.8	1,171.1	725.7	445.4	25.96	3,277	4,983	3,707	165.5
Sept	105.2	92.8	92.4	93.7	1,047.0	777.7	269.3		3,295	5,056	4,402	244.1
Oct	103.8	89.6	89.0	90.7	1,068.0	845.4	222.6		3,233	5,066	4,617	232.2
Nov	106.8	85.5	77.9	83.5	851.8	791.1	60.7	29.20	3,044	4,977	3,479	433.7
Dec	101.6	76.2	73.4	72.6	766.2	794.2	+28.0		3,186	5,181	3,256	495.7
1926 Jan	95.4	70.5	73.4	64.2	715.0	795.3	+80.4		2,775	4,846	3,012	446.1
Feb	95.3	69.6	73.2	61.9	662.5	782.9	+120.4	24.00	2,631	4,924	2,988	359.5
Mar	92.5	68.1	70.5	63.1	649.4	923.1	+273.8		2,464	5,050	3,153	361.8
April	89.9	71.4	74.6	64.4	719.8	779.3	+59.5		2,186	5,030	2,859	733.6
May	90.9	71.6	74.8	64.7	706.7	728.9	+22.2	26.76	2,066	5,043	2,751	538.3
June	93.4	74.2	74.2	66.9	793.7	758.4	35.3		2,130	5,169	2,904	752.0
July	94.5	72.6	74.5	68.5	927.6	820.4	107.2		1,969	5,282	2,786	712.8

Month												
Aug.	101.3	74.6	76.0	71.4	925.0	830.5	94.5	27.97	2,040	5,305	2,727	503.1
Sept.	106.2	78.1	78.1	76.7	831.1	832.5	+1.5		2,215	5,460	2,761	575.6
Oct.	111.0	81.1	81.8	79.8	996.5	874.7	121.8		2,156	5,495	3,196	541.2
Nov.	118.7	83.2	83.5	82.7	1,004.3	869.4	134.9	30.83	2,057	5,421	3,118	735.1
Dec.	120.3	84.0	85.0	81.9	1,070.8	817.6	253.2		2,374	5,800	3,273	946.6
1927 Jan.	122.0	84.7	85.4	83.1	1,091.0	792.3	298.7		1,969	5,390	3,029	485.9
Feb.	123.3	85.9	86.4	84.7	1,089.5	750.4	339.1	28.59	2,273	5,458	3,166	901.9
Mar.	122.3	88.5	88.5	87.8	1,083.0	832.2	250.8		2,515	5,573	3,830	574.6
April	124.3	89.7	89.4	90.3	1,094.0	793.2	300.7		2,593	5,657	3,374	562.4
May	121.0	91.6	91.3	91.3	1,170.9	833.1	337.8	29.87	2,958	5,679	3,654	523.6
June	121.9	92.3	92.2	92.4	1,193.7	747.1	446.7		3,005	5,765	3,693	563.8
July	126.9	93.2	93.2	93.1	1,274.6	846.5	428.1		3,162	5,871	3,728	622.5
Aug.	125.0	93.8	93.8	93.7	1,153.0	867.4	285.6	31.75	3,325	5,883	3,909	369.0
Sept.	129.3	94.6	94.7	94.2	1,168.7	932.5	236.2		3,274	6,143	4,029	369.3
Oct.	126.5	95.2	95.6	94.4	1,240.0	961.7	278.3		2,764	6,131	4,219	505.1
Nov.	127.8	94.7	95.6	93.4	1,284.8	912.5	372.4	34.82	3,395	5,990	4,197	483.1
Dec.	129.2	92.7	94.2	93.7	1,266.0	953.6	312.4		2,661	6,331	4,296	494.6
1928 Jan.	128.1	92.3	93.4	89.9	1,359.2	861.9	497.4		2,650	5,922	4,506	401.3
Feb.	124.6	92.3	93.6	89.5	1,247.0	941.9	305.0	32.19	2,927	5,964	4,964	687.4
Mar.	121.5	92.5	94.0	89.6	1,229.2	1,021.2	208.0		2,783	6,222	4,663	461.9
April	118.8	92.4	94.4	87.0	1,174.9	920.4	254.5		2,703	6,113	4,126	581.8
May	117.5	91.0	93.9	84.5	1,086.9	893.9	193.0	32.41	2,808	6,177	4,246	948.2
June	117.8	91.0	94.0	83.6	1,108.4	890.4	218.0		2,924	6,371	4,412	854.9
July	117.6	90.4	93.6	83.9	1,183.6	913.7	269.9		2,786	6,252	4,335	499.5
Aug.	116.0	89.4	93.0	84.1	1,085.5	1,025.3	60.3	34.04	2,633	6,386	4,457	337.1
Sept.	95.5	90.1	92.9	84.2	1,088.2	1,057.9	30.3		2,879	6,567	4,276	616.9
Oct.	115.2	89.9	91.7	83.7	1,162.0	1,125.0	37.0		2,569	6,388	4,742	574.9
Nov.	123.5	89.2	90.3	80.1	1,173.8	1,009.0	164.8	35.63	3,042	6,433	4,443	655.3
Dec.	117.3	87.1	89.1	78.9	1,102.6	977.5	125.1		2,071	6,653	4,487	595.4
1929 Jan.	121.0	85.8	87.8	76.8	1,317.3	1,035.0	282.3		2,368	6,135	4,552	608.2
Feb.	128.7	84.3	88.5	78.1	1,016.1	920.2	96.6	31.06	2,677	6,247	4,014	581.0
Mar.	124.1	85.2	90.2	81.8	1,021.9	930.3	91.3		3,377	6,536	4,449	494.3
April	125.6	87.5	90.6	81.8	1,254.9	1,163.6	91.3		3,431	6,304	4,656	464.4
May	121.8	87.8	91.7	82.7	1,132.5	1,097.5	35.0	32.87	3,361	6,310	4,392	372.5
June	124.0[8]	88.7	91.4	82.8	1,077.5	1,014.9	62.6		2,972	6,503	4,183	484.4
July	124.5[8]	88.7	91.0	83.1	1,014.9	1,030.6	196.7		3,011	6,350	4,607	342.8
Aug.		88.6	90.6	83.0	1,227.3	1,057.2	50.6		3,006	6,540	4,073	377.7
Sept.		88.2			1,072.6	1,136.7	++98.4		2,828	6,576	3,807	363.5
Oct.					1,038.3					6,473		

[1] Inclusive of the part-time workers calculated on a full-time basis; since June, 1929, on a more extensive basis.
[2] Without building and clothing industries and those connected with food and luxuries.
[3] Without building industries.
[4] Without clothing, food, and luxuries industries.
[5] Since, October, 1928, on a new basis of calculation.
[6] Without reparation deliveries.
[7] Domestic and foreign issues of public and private industries, mortgage credits, and municipal loans.
[8] Provisional.

TABLE VI.—PRINCIPAL ECONOMIC SERIES, 1924 TO 1929 (MONTHLY).—(Continued)

Year and month	Money rate			The markets		Prices and wages						
	Discount rate	Time money	Average yield of gold mortgage bonds (5, 6, 7, 8, 10 %)[1]	Average price of stocks	Index figure for 10 variable commodity prices	Wholesale price index				Cost-of-living index	Regulated wages per hour in the Reich	
						Total	Agricultural products	Industrial raw materials and semi-manufactured	Finished goods		Skilled Workers	Unskilled Workers
	% per annum	% per annum	% per annum	%		1913 = 100				1913–14 = 100	Pfennigs	
1924 Jan.		28.25		136.07	133.1	140.6	116.3	150.5	162.2	125.9	58.4	45.0
Feb.		22.58		150.28	143.9	136.7	113.3	145.3	158.1	119.9	58.4	44.1
Mar.		30.00		118.51	157.2	137.5	114.5	146.1	158.0	121.9	58.9	43.2
April		44.45		85.28	158.5	139.6	114.1	149.7	162.8	125.3	64.1	45.7
May		44.31		71.00	140.6	138.0	109.1	147.9	166.7	126.3	68.4	48.9
June		32.59		57.79	129.9	130.5	98.0	142.2	160.8	123.5	70.4	51.2
July		22.92		59.35	124.9	127.9	104.4	134.8	151.7	126.4	71.8	51.1
Aug.		18.81	10.27	84.66	134.0	132.8	118.5	135.2	149.8	126.7	72.2	51.4
Sept.		16.78	9.28	84.92	142.9	138.9	132.6	136.9	151.6	129.4	72.3	51.5
Oct.		14.42	9.59	80.23	143.3	141.6	141.6	135.2	151.8	134.9	73.4	52.4
Nov.		13.81	9.44	84.14	158.8	140.5	135.1	138.3	150.9	135.4	75.2	53.9
Dec.		13.61	9.02	97.48	167.7	142.5	137.9	141.1	150.0	135.6	77.8	55.2
1925 Jan.	9.20	11.28	8.76	117.14	174.2	143.5	136.7	145.1	150.7	135.6	77.8	55.5
Feb.	8.31	11.92	8.57	113.75	162.5	142.7	134.1	144.9	152.6	136.0	78.6	56.2
Mar.	8.01	11.26	8.55	108.05	154.7	141.3	129.8	144.2	154.3	136.7	80.5	57.7
April	8.00	10.13	8.69	102.74	150.1	138.6	124.3	142.0	154.9	135.5	82.4	58.8
May	8.00	10.48	8.75	95.28	143.2	139.0	127.1	139.6	156.5	136.0	84.5	60.4
June	7.97	10.68	9.07	83.85	138.7	140.9	131.5	139.7	157.2	138.3	86.6	61.9
July	7.76	10.87	9.25	80.74	140.9	142.3	134.8	141.1	157.7	143.3	87.7	63.0
Aug.	7.88	10.84	9.30	73.65	138.7	144.3	138.5	140.8	158.8	145.0	89.4	64.4
Sept.	7.68	10.59	9.22	78.05	138.1	144.4	138.5	140.4	159.8	144.9	90.4	65.1
Oct.	7.18	10.82	9.21	73.61	133.3	144.1	136.1	139.7	159.6	144.9	90.7	66.0
Nov.	7.09	10.65	9.32	67.04	129.3	141.6	133.8	138.5	159.5	143.5	92.5	66.4
Dec.	6.75	10.29	9.25	64.41	122.2	139.8	130.7	136.5	159.2	141.2	92.6	66.5

Month												
1926 Jan.	6.27	8.99	8.83	71.84	120.8	135.8	122.3	134.4	158.0	139.8	92.6	66.6
Feb.	5.46	7.43	8.32	78.94	118.1	134.3	120.9	132.7	157.1	138.8	92.7	66.6
Mar.	5.00	6.78	7.99	83.56	115.1	133.7	119.8	131.2	156.0	138.3	92.7	66.6
April	4.86	6.01	7.65	91.00	112.1	132.7	121.5	129.6	154.3	139.6	92.6	66.5
May	4.69	5.93	7.67	89.71	109.9	132.3	122.5	128.6	152.5	139.3	92.6	66.4
June	4.52	5.77	7.64	95.11	111.1	131.9	124.0	127.6	149.9	140.5	92.5	66.4
July	4.54	5.80	7.58	102.84	112.3	133.0	128.7	128.9	146.5	142.4	92.5	66.3
Aug.	4.61	5.88	7.53	112.69	117.7	133.4	131.8	128.5	145.1	142.5	93.3	66.4
Sept.	4.88	6.23	7.53	115.69	120.7	134.9	134.1	129.3	144.4	142.0	93.3	66.8
Oct.	4.84	6.34	7.52	126.94	120.2	134.3	139.7	128.3	143.9	142.6	93.4	66.9
Nov.	4.63	6.41	7.49	134.26	122.0	136.2	142.8	128.4	143.5	143.8	93.5	66.9
Dec.	4.73	7.39	7.29	133.40	122.0	137.1	143.7	128.8	142.3	144.4	93.7	66.6
1927 Jan.	4.20	6.27	7.15	152.15	124.0	137.9	140.3	129.3	141.6	144.6	94.3	67.0
Feb.	4.23	6.92	7.10	161.12	122.2	135.9	139.1	130.2	142.0	145.4	96.1	67.1
Mar.	4.59	7.28	7.14	155.95	121.3	135.6	136.0	129.3	143.0	144.4	98.6	67.2
April	4.62	7.07	7.15	164.85	123.1	135.0	135.2	131.1	144.3	146.4	99.5	67.7
May	4.90	7.63	7.20	158.08	128.2	134.8	139.3	131.2	144.0	146.5	99.5	67.7
June	5.39	8.24	7.30	144.49	127.8	137.9	139.9	132.2	146.1	147.7	99.7	69.0
July	5.90	8.45	7.33	148.79	128.0	137.9	137.8	134.0	147.1	150.0	100.6	72.7
Aug.	5.83	8.22	7.36	146.34	129.2	137.9	136.9	134.3	148.3	146.6	100.9	72.9
Sept.	5.90	8.28	7.41	140.91	129.0	139.8	138.7	134.4	150.7	147.1	101.3	72.9
Oct.	6.69	8.67	7.52	137.26	129.1	140.1	137.3	133.9	152.9	150.2	101.9	73.1
Nov.	6.76	8.80	7.65	124.50	132.7	139.6	135.2	133.8	154.6	150.6	102.1	73.9
Dec.	6.87	9.05	7.62	131.73	134.7	138.7	132.2	133.5	155.5	151.3	103.5	74.1
1928 Jan.	6.20	9.98	7.57	138.77	136.1	137.9	130.1	135.0	156.1	150.8	106.5	74.3
Feb.	6.70	7.77	7.61	135.31	139.6	138.5	131.3	135.1	156.8	150.6	106.8	75.4
Mar.	6.72	7.89	7.66	133.22	140.9	139.9	133.5	134.3	157.0	150.7	106.8	75.6
April	6.66	7.98	7.69	138.70	138.2	141.3	135.9	133.5	157.6	151.4	107.5	77.1
May	6.62	8.07	7.72	142.60	138.8	141.6	136.0	134.0	158.4	152.6	107.6	79.0
June	6.74	8.00	7.75	144.51	135.5	141.5	136.6	134.0	159.1	153.5	107.9	79.3
July	6.69	8.18	7.77	141.21	133.0	139.9	137.6	133.6	159.6	152.1	108.1	79.7
Aug.	6.65	8.42	7.81	140.62	133.8	140.3	134.2	134.3	159.5	152.7	108.2	79.9
Sept.	6.58	8.70	7.84	140.87	132.2	139.9	135.2	133.1	159.5	152.9	108.6	80.6
Oct.	6.28	8.56	7.87	139.11	129.5	138.8	134.1	131.5	160.0	153.1	108.6	80.6
Nov.	6.31	8.23	7.88	138.76	128.0	139.3	131.7	131.5	159.5	154.4	110.8	81.1
Dec.	5.81	8.89	7.90	140.48	131.2	139.6	133.9	131.6	158.8	156.5	111.1	81.2
1929 Jan.	6.31	7.57	7.92	138.63	130.3	137.1	133.7	130.9	158.2	153.5	111.1	81.3
Feb.	6.63	7.31	7.96	133.58	129.6	135.5	128.2		158.0	153.4	111.1	81.4
Mar.	7.49	7.65	8.00	132.58	126.8	135.1	125.7		157.5	154.4	111.2	81.8
April	7.50	8.08	8.11	132.92	118.4	137.8	124.7		157.3	153.6		83.4
May	7.40	9.76	8.11	127.56	120.7	138.1	132.4		157.3	153.5		83.6
June	7.18	10.00	8.15	130.47	118.8	137.2	132.6		157.2			83.7
July	7.28	9.85	8.19	128.03	117.8		131.7		156.6			83.7
Aug.		9.75	8.22	126.54	120.2							83.7
Sept.		9.74		125.03	117.2							83.7
Oct.		9.71		117.70								

[1] After January, 1928, only gold mortgage bonds of the mortgage banks.

INDEX

A

Aftalion, A., 5
Agriculture, cyclical-fluctuation relationship between agriculture and industry, 167
cyclical fluctuations, prewar, 168
Agriculture's demand, industrial products, 169
Agriculture's takings, expenditure stages, 170

B

Babson chart, 123
Babson statistical organization, 7
Balance of payments, 196
Banks, trade cycle and, 188
Barometers, general economic, 121
survey of, 146
Benini, R., "Il totalizzatore applicato agli indici del movimento economico," 127
Beveridge, W. H., 6
Bouniatian, M., 5
"Studien zur Theorie und Geschichte der Wirtschaftskrisen," 87, 94
Bramstedt, P., municipal-expenditure investigations, 243
Brookmire barometers, commodity prices, 136
three-market, 128
Brookmire Economic Service, 7
Business barometer, 153
Business cycle, origin, 86

C

Cassel, Gustav, 89, 111
business-cycle theory classified, 253

Census, Germany, occupational and industrial, 1925, 37, 270–271
Commodity-market barometer, Institut für Konjunkturforschung, 158
Commodity-prices barometer, Institut für Konjunkturforschung, 159
Conjuncture, meaning of, 50
Consumers' goods, industries producing, 38
Correlation, 105, 109
Cost survey, Ruhberg, 164
Countervariation (scissors movement), 114
Credit, long and short vs. long term and short term, 195
scissors movement, 115
short term, 196
Credit barometer, 155
Credit cycles (see Cyclical fluctuations).
Crises, prewar, 85
Cyclical fluctuations, agriculture, prewar, 168
agriculture and industry, relationship, 167
balance of payments and, 197
barometers, 121
credit cycles, 185
employment index and, 222
imports and exports, 1881–1913, Soltau, 177
industry, prewar, 168
limits within which they move, 224
long-wave movement vs. trend, 77
physical volume, price and, 202
price movements and, 199
seasonal vs., 58
situations and tensions, 160
symptomatology, 211
tensions and situations, 160

Cyclical fluctations, trade cycle, banks and, 188
foreign capital and, 195
prices in, 207
types of, 179
Cyclical positions, 98
Cyclical tensions, 98

D

Dawes loan, 196, 197
De Wolff, "Lebendige Marxismus," 77, 84
Demand, agriculture for industrial products, 169
predominance of, in case of industrial products, 206
Diehl, Karl, ed., "Wissenschaftliche Gutachten über Konjunkturforschung und Konjunkturtheorie," 14
Durable goods, 204

E

Employment, output and, 227
wage income and, 225
Employment index, Institut für Konjunkturforschung, construction, 149
Employment statistics, 222
Engineering industry, trade-cycle parallelism, 180
Ephemeral goods, 204
Esslen, J. S., 6
Eulenburg, Dr., 6
Exports of finished goods, Institut für Konjunkturforschung, construction, 150

F

Federal Reserve System, United States, credit policy of Federal Reserve Board, 238
Open-market Investigating Committee of Federal Reserve Board, 240
Feiler, A., 6
Finance capital, flow of, 48

Fluctuations (*see also* Cyclical fluctuations; Seasonal fluctuations; Retail-trade fluctuations).
classification, 51
Forecasting cyclical conditions, 211
Foville, A. de, 6
barometer, 126
"Essai de météorologie économique et sociale," 125
Franklin Statistical Service, barometer, 137

G

Germany, agriculture, receipts of, 1924–1925 to 1926–1927, Paetzmann, 170
business cycles, 1848–1914, duration, 93
commodity-price index, 201
credit policy, 195
employment and output, 227
labor-market statistics, 222
national income, 1913, 35
unemployment, 1906–1914, 224
unemployment insurance, 242
Goethe, Panama Canal prophecy, 214
Grünbaum, Heinz, "Umsatzschwankungen des Einzelhandels als Problem der Betriebspolitik," 60

H

Hahn, A., business-cycle theory classified, 253
"Zur Frage des Volkswirtschaftlichen Erkenntnisinhalts der Bankbilanzen," 187
Hanau, Dr. A., Prognose der Schweinepreise, 141
Haney, Lewis H., Franklin Statistical Service barometer, 137
Harvard barometer, 128, 130
Harvard University Committee of Economic Research, 8
business-cycle classification, 73
fluctuations, classification of, 51
Hawtrey, R. G., business-cycle theory classified, 253

LIBRARY OF
Southern Methodist University
DALLAS, TEXAS